with
love
Carissa

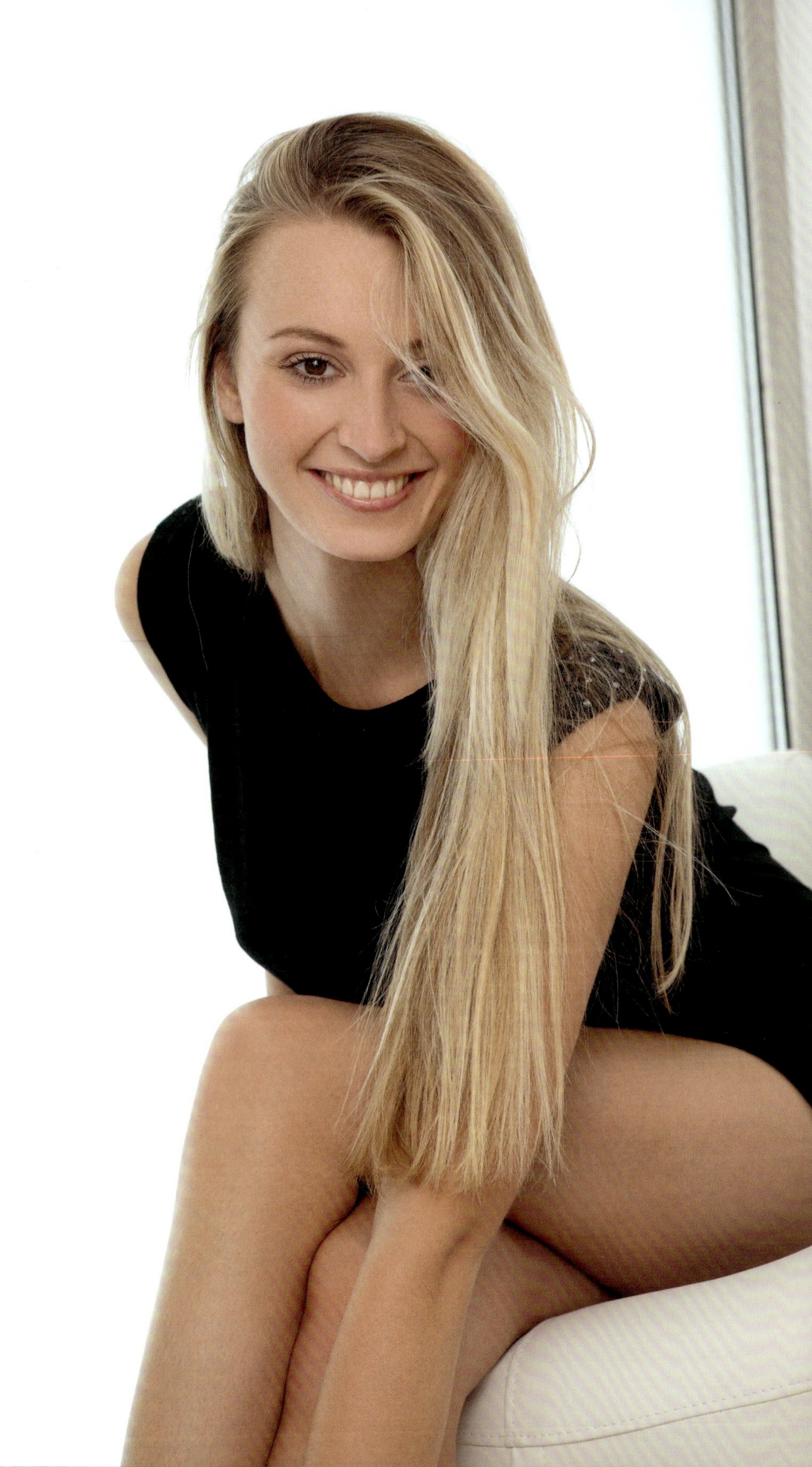

STEFAN SOELL
CARISHA

EDITION Skylight

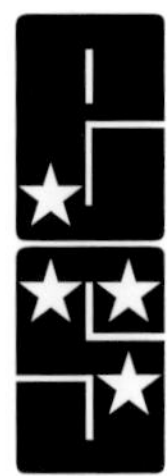

3rd Edition in Paperback, revised and enlarged 2024
Copyright© 2013 by Edition Skylight

EDITION SKYLIGHT
Rosengartenstrasse 13B
CH-8608 Bubikon/Zürich
Switzerland

Mail: info@edition-skylight.com
Web: www.edition-skylight.com

ISBN 978-3-03766-685-2

Bibliographic information published by Die Deutsche Bibliothek
Die Deutsche Bibliothek lists this publication in the
Deutsche Nationalbibliografie; detailed bibliographic data
are available in the Internet at http://dnb.ddb.de.

www.stefansoell.de
Design: Weiß-Freiburg GmbH — Graphik & Buchgestaltung

Printed in Slovenia

CARISHA

Hi! Please introduce yourself. — My name is Carisha and I come from Slovakia, a charming country in Eastern Europe. I was born there and that's where I have spent most of my 21 years.

What are your hobbies? — As you may have noticed, I am a sporty person. I love all kinds of sports, but my favourites are roller-blading and tennis. In addition to sports, I enjoy exploring other countries, people, cultures, and also learning new languages. I always say "Speaking another language is to possess another soul".

How do you spend your spare time? — I usually just try to relax, but my idea of relaxation is slightly different from other people's: I go out and spend some time in nature with my friends, or I just fly to a different country and explore everything there.

Do you like reading? What type of books do you prefer? — I like reading, but I unfortunately don't have enough time to read that many books. I love Paolo Coelho, a very famous Brazilian author. His novels are very real, and I can relate to his stories.

Do you like going to the movies? What are your favourite ones? — I do enjoy going to the movies more than watching them at home. I just love the atmosphere there. I like movies dealing with the Second World War. I also like movies with Will Smith, as I am a very big fan of his.

Do you like travelling? What are the countries that you'd like to visit? — I am addicted to travelling. Any money that I earn can't stay in my bank account for too long, as I always find a tour package that is too tempting and off it goes. I would love to explore South Africa and Latin America next.

Could you please describe your personality? — It is always hard for anyone to describe themselves, but I will try to do my best. If I am to look for some words that describe my personality well, then sensitive and vulnerable are the ones that come to mind, but I also have a very vivid personality. I am always looking for adventure.

What are your own personal qualities that you value the most? — Honesty and dedication are the ones that I appreciate the most about myself, and I think that the world would be a much better place if there were more people with these qualities.

What is the best compliment that you ever received? — "You are unbelievable!" (meant in a good way, of course!)

Do you consider yourself a shy type of person? — I am in a way. Some people may think that nude models can't be shy, considering the stereotype that nude models need to be comfortable being nude with strangers around. However, you can still be shy and be a nude model. Nude modelling is all about art and female beauty. A good photographer can even capture that shyness in his pictures.

Why did you decide to become a nude model? — Stefan's professional pictures led me into this beautiful world of artistic nude photography. I am happy to be one of his models because he does such a great job.

Which do you prefer to be around more, men or women? What are the qualities that you appreciate in your friends? — I can't say that I prefer men to women or vice versa, it depends on the character of the person that I spend time with. The group of my closest friends consists of both boys and girls. Their characters are very similar to mine, but every one of them is different in a way, and that brings a healthy variety into our friendship.

What are your plans for the future? — I am pursuing a Major that will give me the opportunity to work in pretty much any field. I still haven't decided what I exactly want to do. But I would definitely like to have a job that would allow me to travel all over the world.

Thank you for your time, and for allowing us to have this interview with you!

Hallo! Bitte stellen Sie sich kurz vor. — Ich heiße Carisha und komme aus der Slowakei, einem bezaubernden Land im Osten Europas. Ich bin dort geboren und habe den größten Teil meiner 21 Lebensjahre dort verbracht.

Was für Hobbies haben Sie? — Wie Sie vielleicht schon bemerkt haben, bin ich ein sportlicher Typ. Ich liebe Sport aller Art, aber am meisten Spaß machen mir Inlineskaten und Tennis. Außerdem erkunde ich gerne fremde Länder, Leute und Kulturen und lerne gerne neue Sprachen. Ich sage immer: «Eine andere Sprache zu sprechen ist, als besäße man eine andere Seele.»

Wie verbringen Sie Ihre Freizeit? — Normalerweise versuche ich einfach zu entspannen, aber meine Vorstellung von Entspannung weicht wohl etwas von dem ab, was sich andere Leute darunter vorstellen: Ich gehe nach draußen, in die Natur, und verbringe dort Zeit mit meinen Freunden. Oder ich fliege in ein anderes Land und schaue mir alles dort an.

Lesen Sie gerne? Was lesen Sie am liebsten? — Ich lese wirklich gerne, aber leider fehlt mir die Zeit, viele Bücher zu lesen. Ich mag Paolo Coelho, einen bekannten brasilianischen Autor. Seine Geschichten sind sehr real, da finde ich immer Anknüpfungspunkte.

Gehen Sie gern ins Kino? Was sind Ihre Lieblingsfilme? — Ich gehe viel lieber ins Kino als mir zuhause Filme anzuschauen. Ich liebe einfach die Atmosphäre im Kino. Mir gefallen Filme, in denen es um den Zweiten Weltkrieg geht. Und ich mag Filme mit Will Smith, ich bin ein großer Fan von ihm.

Sie haben ja schon gesagt, dass Sie gerne verreisen. In welche Länder zieht es Sie? — Ich bin regelrecht reisesüchtig. Alles Geld, das ich verdiene, bleibt nicht lange auf meinem Konto, ich finde immer ein Reiseangebot, dem ich nicht widerstehen kann, und los geht's. Ich würde gerne Südafrika kennenlernen und danach Lateinamerika.

Wie würden Sie Ihre Persönlichkeit beschreiben? — Es ist immer schwierig, sich selbst zu beschreiben, aber ich will es versuchen. Wenn ich Worte finden soll, die meine Persönlichkeit beschreiben, dann fallen mir zuerst Empfindsamkeit und Verletzlichkeit ein. Aber ich bin auch ein sehr lebendiger Typ, immer auf der Suche nach Abenteuern.

Welche Ihrer persönlichen Eigenschaften schätzen Sie am meisten? — Ich bin ehrlich und engagiert, kann mich einer Sache ganz hingeben, das mag ich an mir. Ich glaube, die Welt wäre ein besserer Ort, wenn es mehr Leute mit diesen Eigenschaften gäbe.

Was war das schönste Kompliment, das Ihnen je gemacht wurde? — «Du bist unglaublich!» (im positiven Sinne natürlich!)

Würden Sie sich selbst als schüchtern bezeichnen? — Irgendwie schon. Manche Leute denken vielleicht, Aktmodelle können überhaupt nicht schüchtern sein, gemäß dem Klischee, dass Fotomodelle sich ungezwungen geben müssen, wenn sie nackt und von lauter fremden Leuten umgeben sind. Aber man kann ein Aktmodell sein und trotzdem schüchtern. Bei der Aktfotografie geht es um Kunst und weibliche Schönheit. Ein guter Fotograf kann diese Schüchternheit in seinen Bildern einfangen.

Warum haben Sie sich dazu entschieden, Aktmodell zu werden? — Stefans professionelle Bilder haben mich in diese wundervolle Welt der künstlerischen Aktfotografie geführt. Ich bin froh, dass ich eines seiner Modelle bin, denn er ist einfach großartig in dem, was er macht.

Mit wem umgeben Sie sich lieber, mit Frauen oder mit Männern? Welche Eigenschaften schätzen Sie an Ihren Freunden? — Ich kann nicht sagen, ob ich lieber Männer oder lieber Frauen um mich habe, das kommt ganz auf den Charakter der Person an, mit der ich Zeit verbringe. Mein engster Freundeskreis besteht aus Männern und Frauen. Charakterlich sind wir uns ziemlich ähnlich, aber jeder von ihnen ist auf seine Art verschieden, und das bringt eine gesunde Vielfalt in unsere Freundschaft.

Wie sehen Ihre Zukunftspläne aus? — Ich studiere etwas, das mir später die Möglichkeit gibt, in so gut wie jedem Bereich zu arbeiten. Ich habe mich noch nicht entschieden, was genau ich machen will. Aber ich hätte auf alle Fälle gerne einen Job, der es mir erlaubt, durch die ganze Welt zu reisen.

Vielen Dank, dass Sie Zeit für uns hatten und uns dieses Interview gewährt haben!

Bonjour ! Pourriez-vous vous présenter en quelques mots, s'il vous plaît. — Je m'appelle Carisha et je viens de Slovaquie, un merveilleux pays en Europe de l'Est. Je suis née là-bas il y a 21 ans et j'y ai passé la plus grande partie de ma vie.

Quels sont vos hobbies ? — Comme vous l'avez peut-être déjà remarqué, je suis du genre sportif. J'adore toutes les sortes de sport, mais ce que je préfère c'est faire du roller et jouer au tennis. Et puis j'aime découvrir les autres pays, les gens et les cultures. J'aime aussi apprendre de nouvelles langues. Je dis toujours : « Parler une nouvelle langue, c'est comme posséder une autre âme. »

Comment occupez-vous vos loisirs ? — Normalement, j'essaie simplement de me détendre mais ma conception de la détente diffère apparemment un peu de celle des autres : je sors, dehors, dans la nature, et j'y passe des heures avec mes amis. Ou bien je m'envole vers un autre pays et visite tout ce qu'il y a à voir.

Aimez-vous lire ? Qu'aimez-vous lire le plus ? — J'aime vraiment lire mais je n'ai malheureusement pas le temps de lire beaucoup de livres. J'aime Paolo Coelho, un auteur brésilien célèbre. Ses histoires sont très réelles, j'y retrouve toujours des éléments de réflexion.

Aimez-vous aller au cinéma ? Quels sont vos films préférés ? — Je préfère de beaucoup aller au cinéma plutôt que regarder des films à la maison. J'aime tout simplement l'atmosphère au cinéma. Les films qui parlent de la seconde Guerre Mondiale me plaisent. Et j'aime les films avec Will Smith, dont je suis une grande fan.

Vous avez déjà dit que vous aimiez voyager. Quels pays vous attirent ? — Je suis accro du voyage. Tout l'argent que je gagne ne reste pas longtemps sur mon compte, je trouve toujours une offre de voyage à laquelle je ne peux pas résister. Alors, je repars. J'aimerais découvrir l'Afrique du Sud et puis ensuite l'Amérique latine.

Comment décririez-vous votre personnalité ? — C'est toujours difficile de se décrire soi-même, mais je vais essayer. Si je devais trouver des mots qui dépeignent ma personnalité, et bien je penserais tout de suite à « sensibilité » et « vulnérabilité ». Mais je suis aussi quelqu'un de très vivant, toujours à la recherche de l'aventure.

Quelles qualités personnelles préférez-vous le plus chez vous ? — Je suis honnête et engagée ; je peux me consacrer entièrement à une chose, c'est ce que j'aime en moi. Je crois que le monde serait meilleur si davantage de monde possédait cette qualité.

Quel est le plus beau compliment que l'on vous ait fait ? — « Tu es incroyable ! » (Dans le sens positif du terme, évidemment !)

Vous décririez-vous vous-même comme timide ? — D'une certaine manière, oui. Certains pensent peut-être que les modèles qui posent nu ne peuvent pas du tout être timides. Conformément au cliché comme quoi ces mannequins doivent être décontractées si elles sont nues et entourées d'une foule d'étrangers. Mais on peut être à la fois une mannequin qui pose nu et timide. Dans la photographie de nu, il s'agit d'art et de beauté féminine. Un bon photographe sait saisir cette timidité dans ses photos.

Pourquoi avez-vous décidé de devenir un modèle de nu ? — Les photos professionnelles de Stefan m'ont guidée vers ce monde extraordinaire de la photographie artistique de nu. Je suis heureuse d'être l'un de ses modèles car il est tout simplement génial dans ce qu'il fait.

De qui préférez-vous vous entourer, de femmes ou d'hommes ? Quelles sont les qualités que vous aimez chez vos amis ? — Je ne peux pas dire si je préfère avoir des hommes ou des femmes autour de moi, cela dépend vraiment du caractère de la personne avec qui je passe mon temps. Mon cercle d'amis proches compte aussi bien des hommes que des femmes. Du point de vue caractère, nous sommes assez semblables, mais chacun d'entre nous est différent à sa manière et cela apporte une diversité saine dans notre amitié.

Comment voyez-vous votre avenir ? — Étudier quelque chose qui me donnera la possibilité de travailler partout, dans le plus de domaines imaginables. Je ne me suis pas encore décidée, je ne sais pas encore exactement ce que je veux. Mais j'aimerais en tout cas avoir un travail qui me permette de voyager dans le monde entier.

Merci beaucoup de nous avoir consacré un peu de votre temps pour cet entretien !

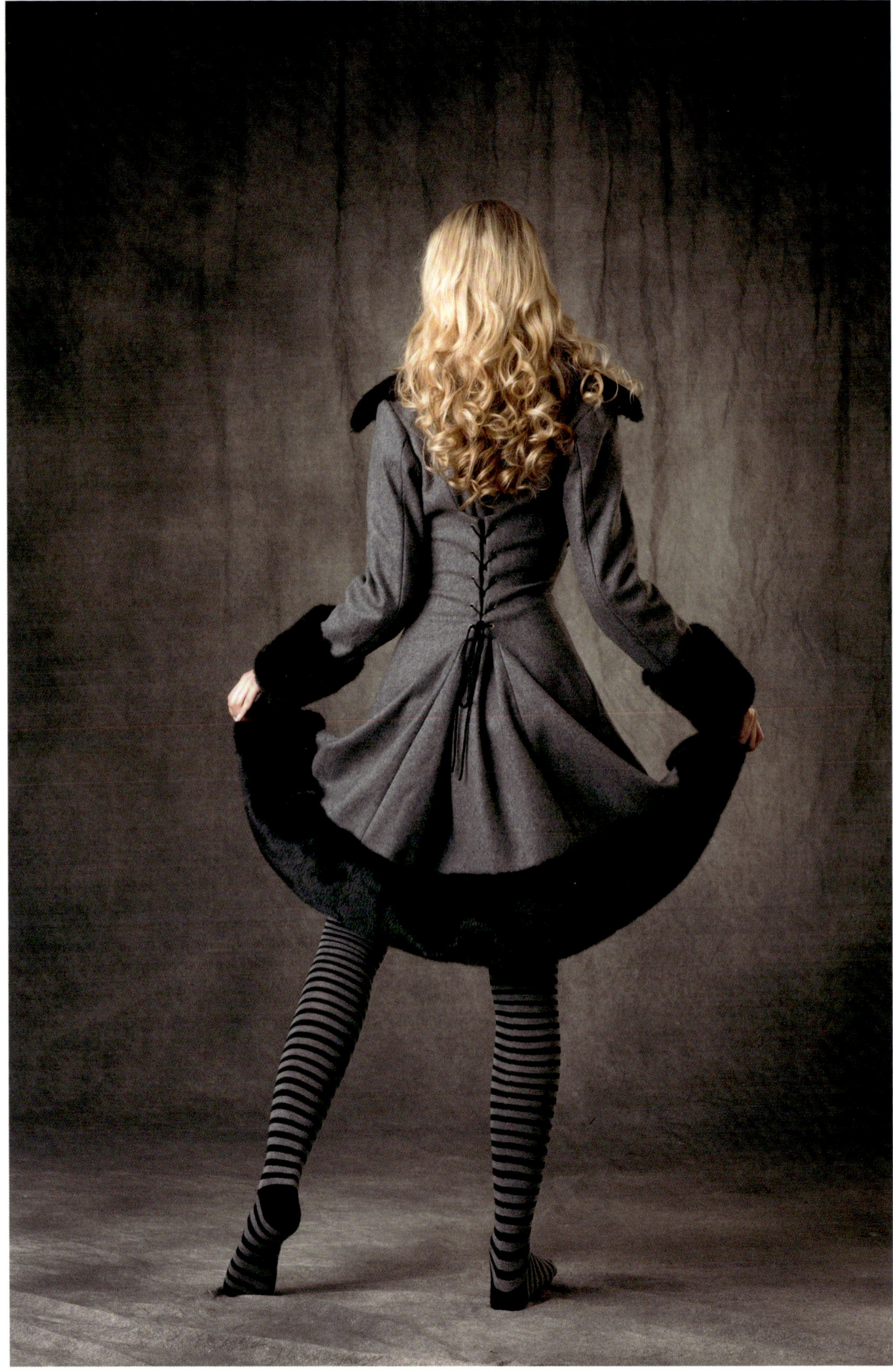

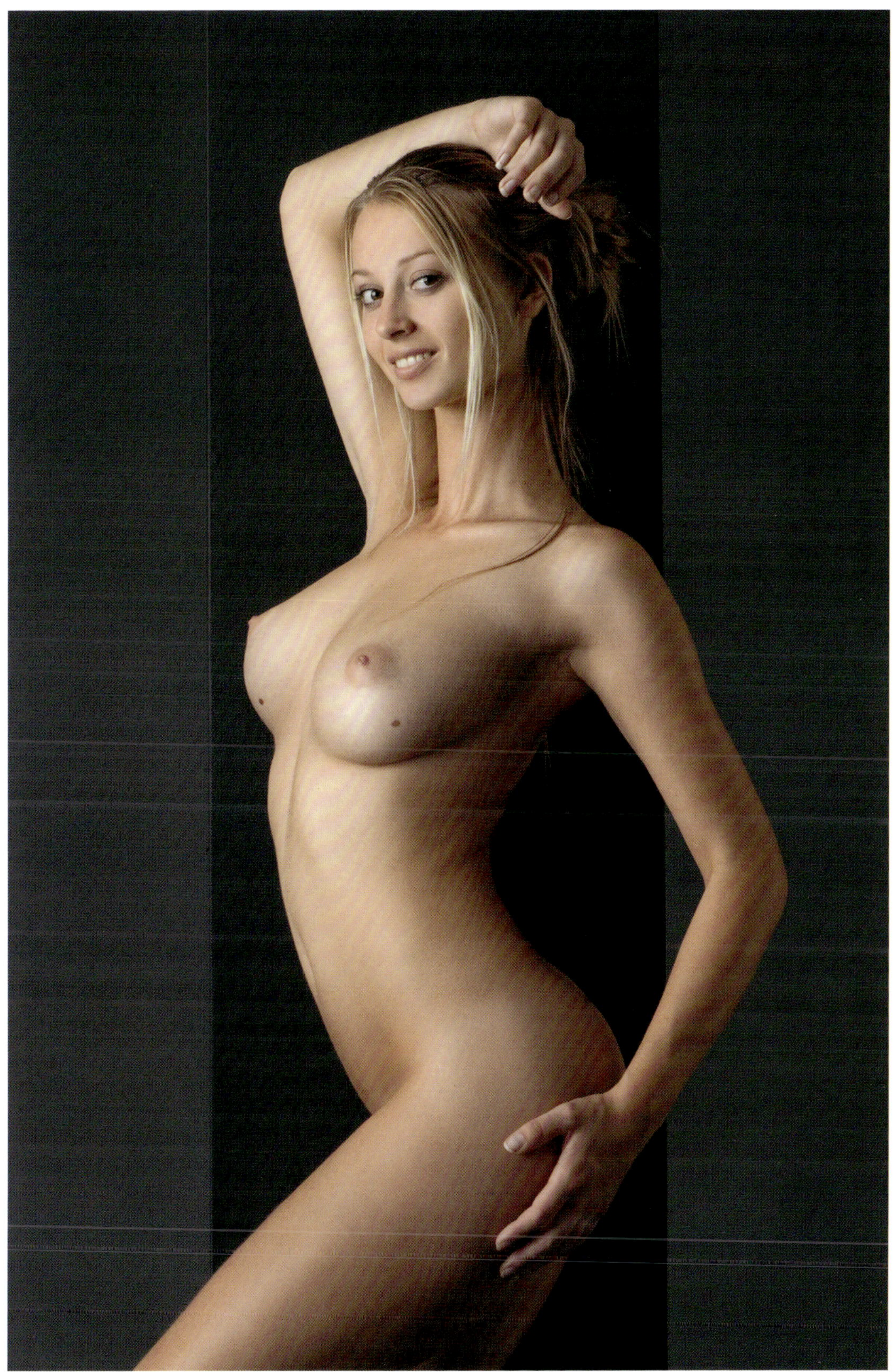

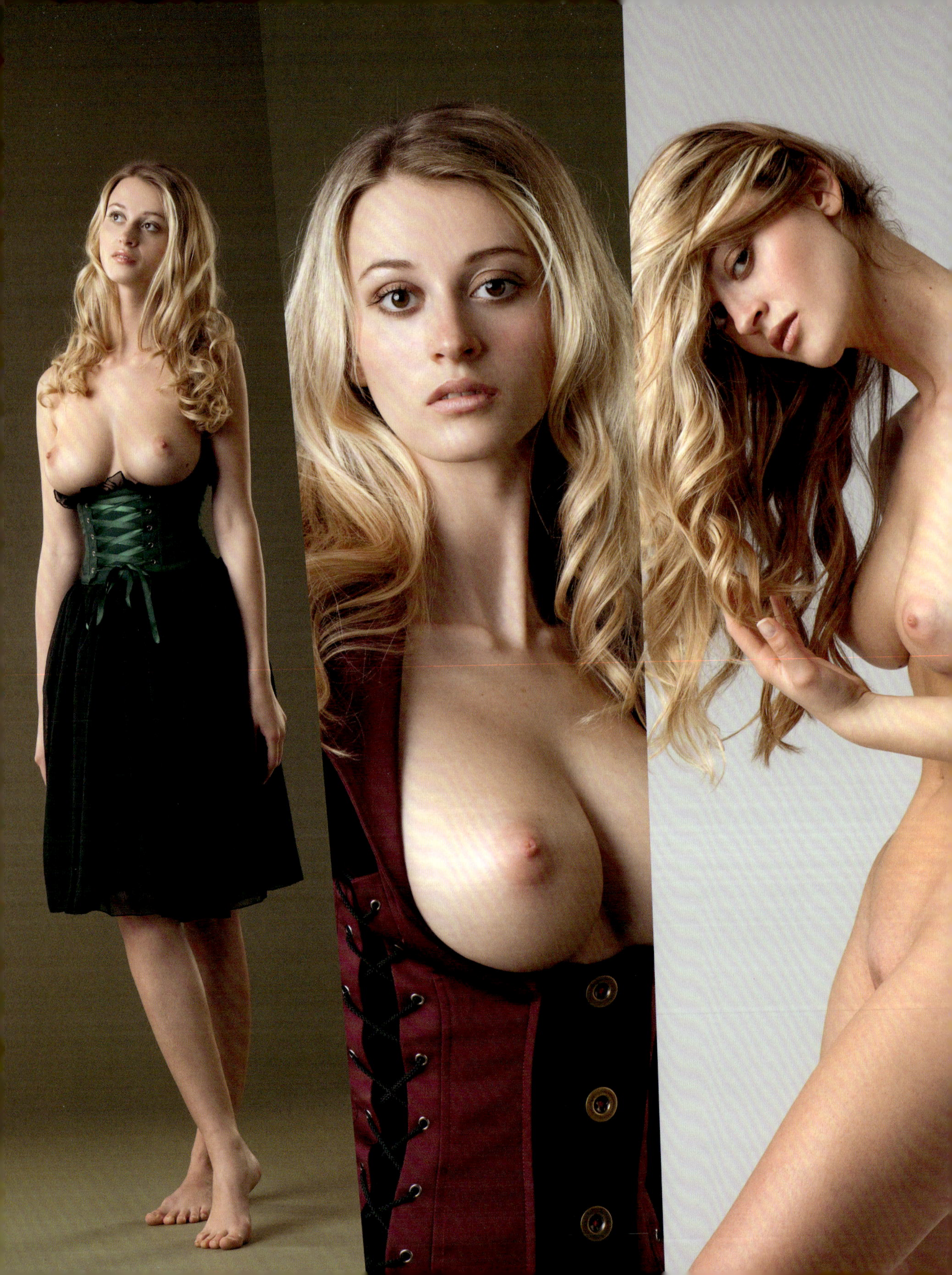

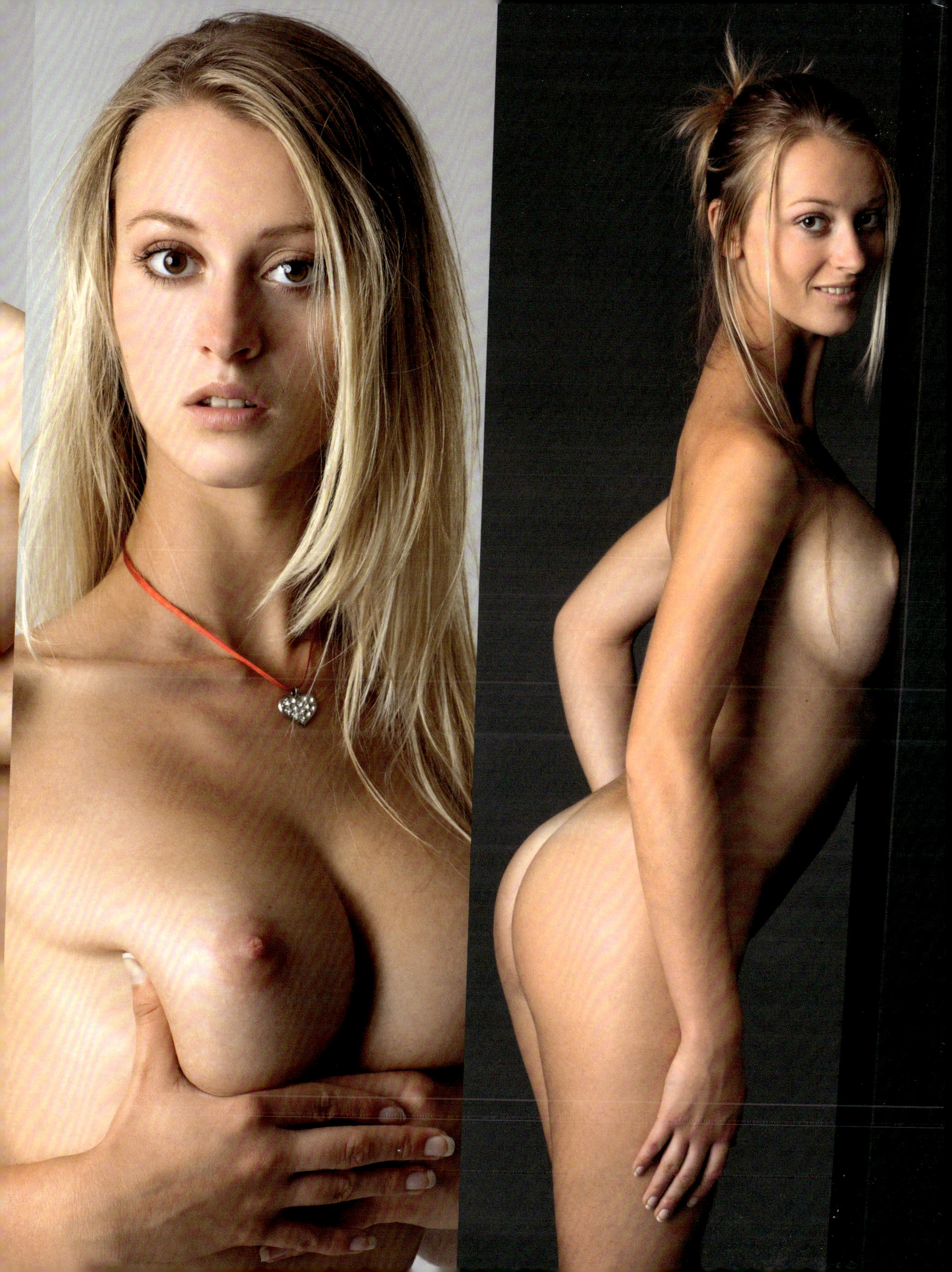

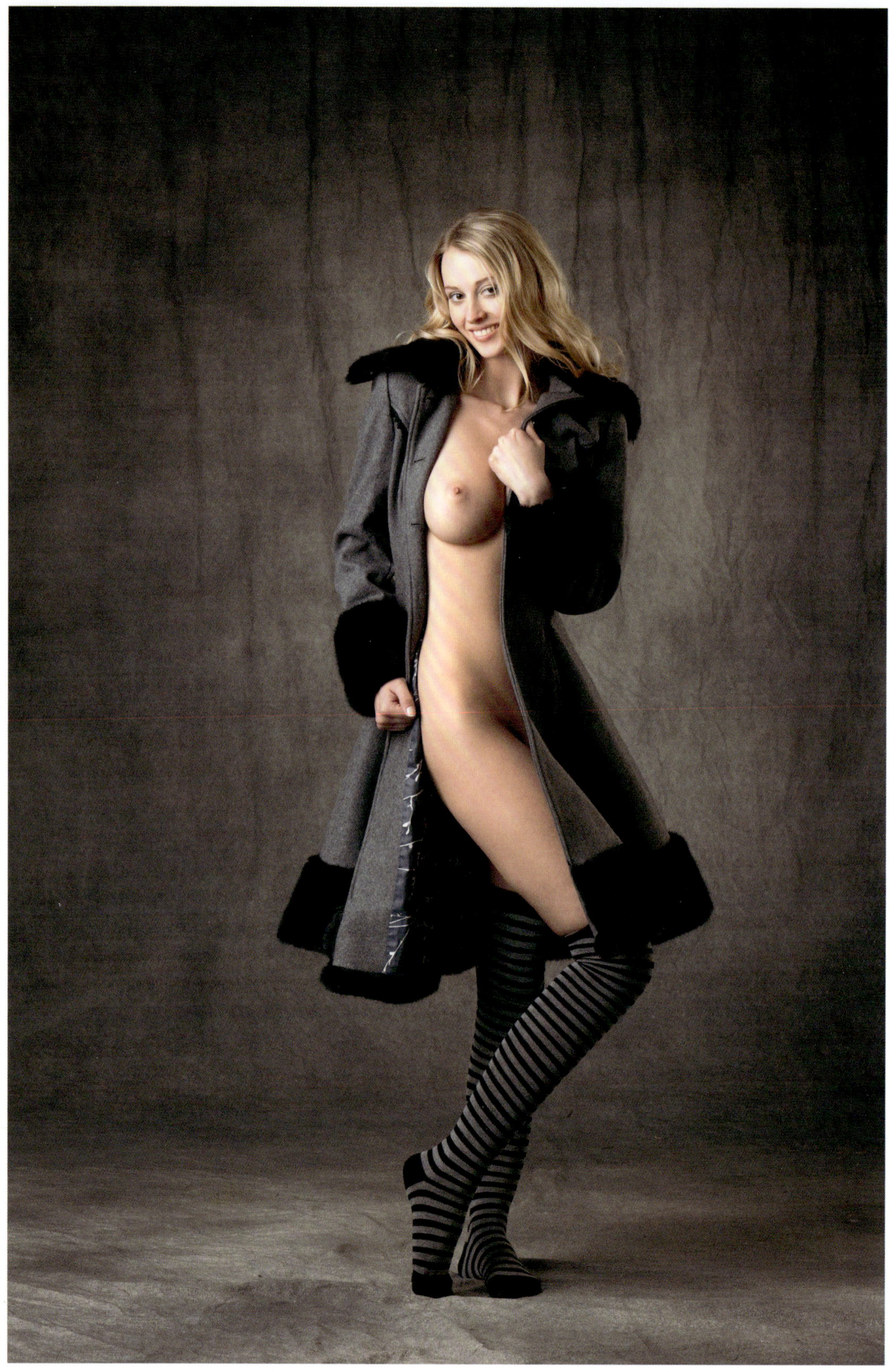

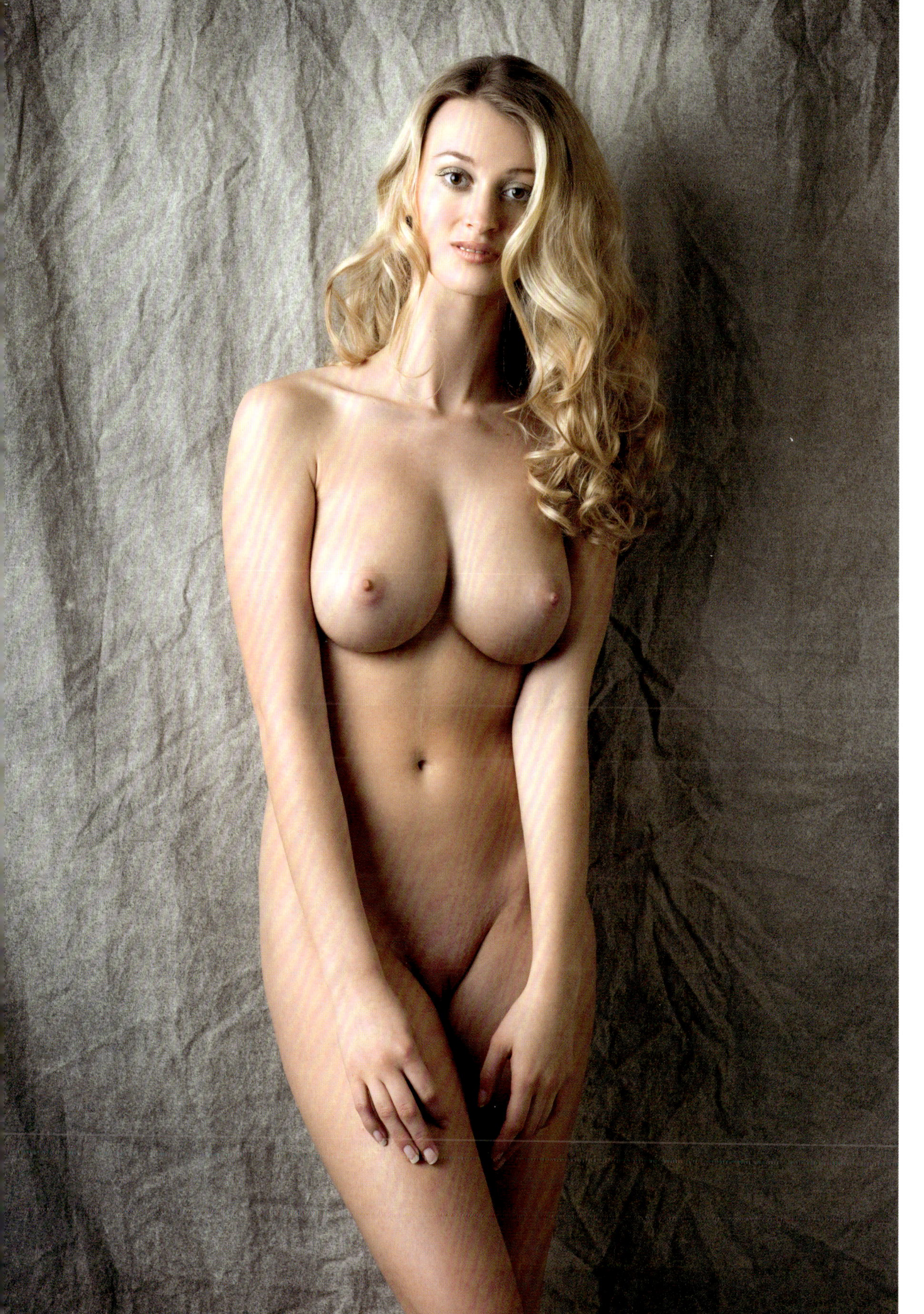

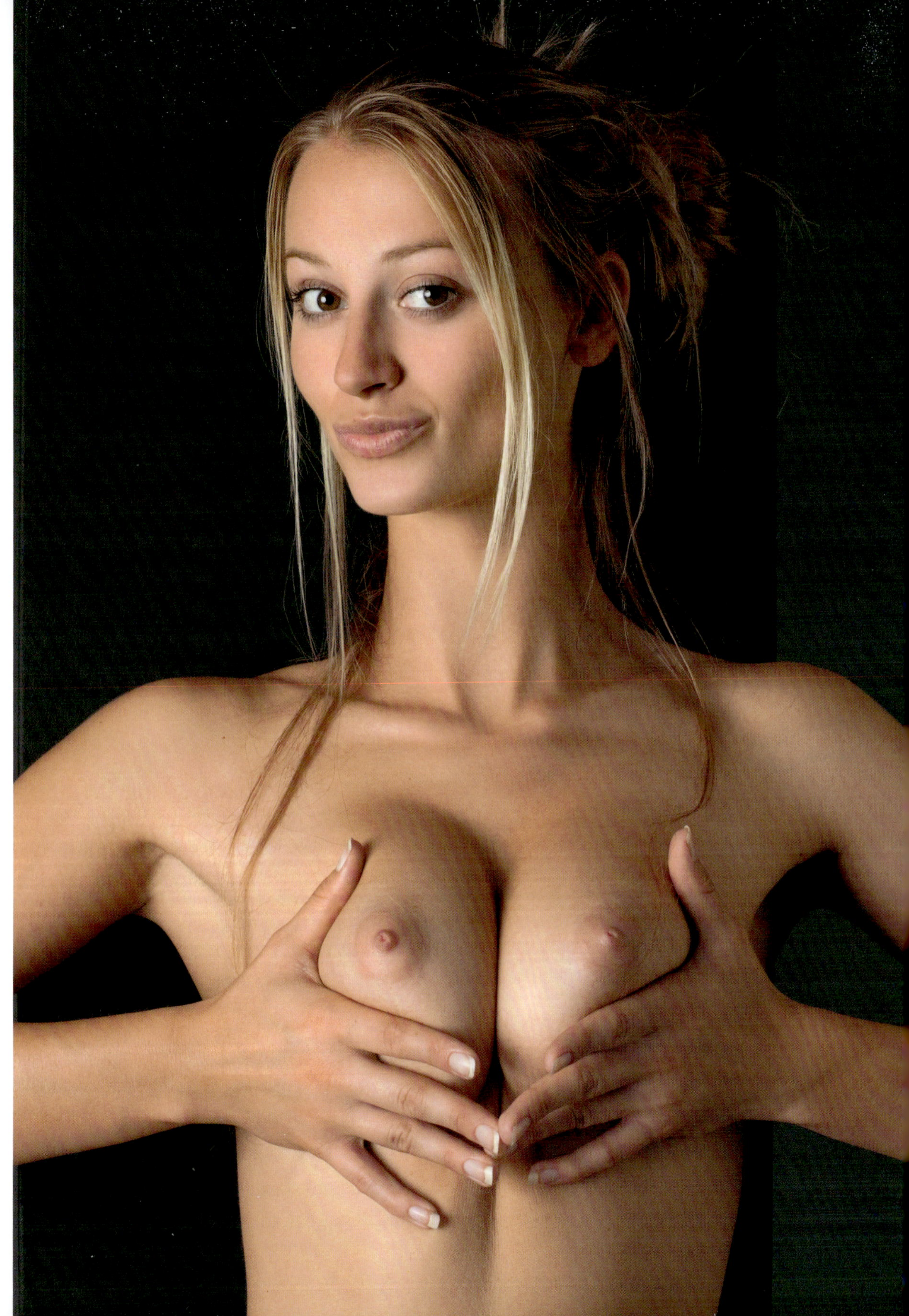

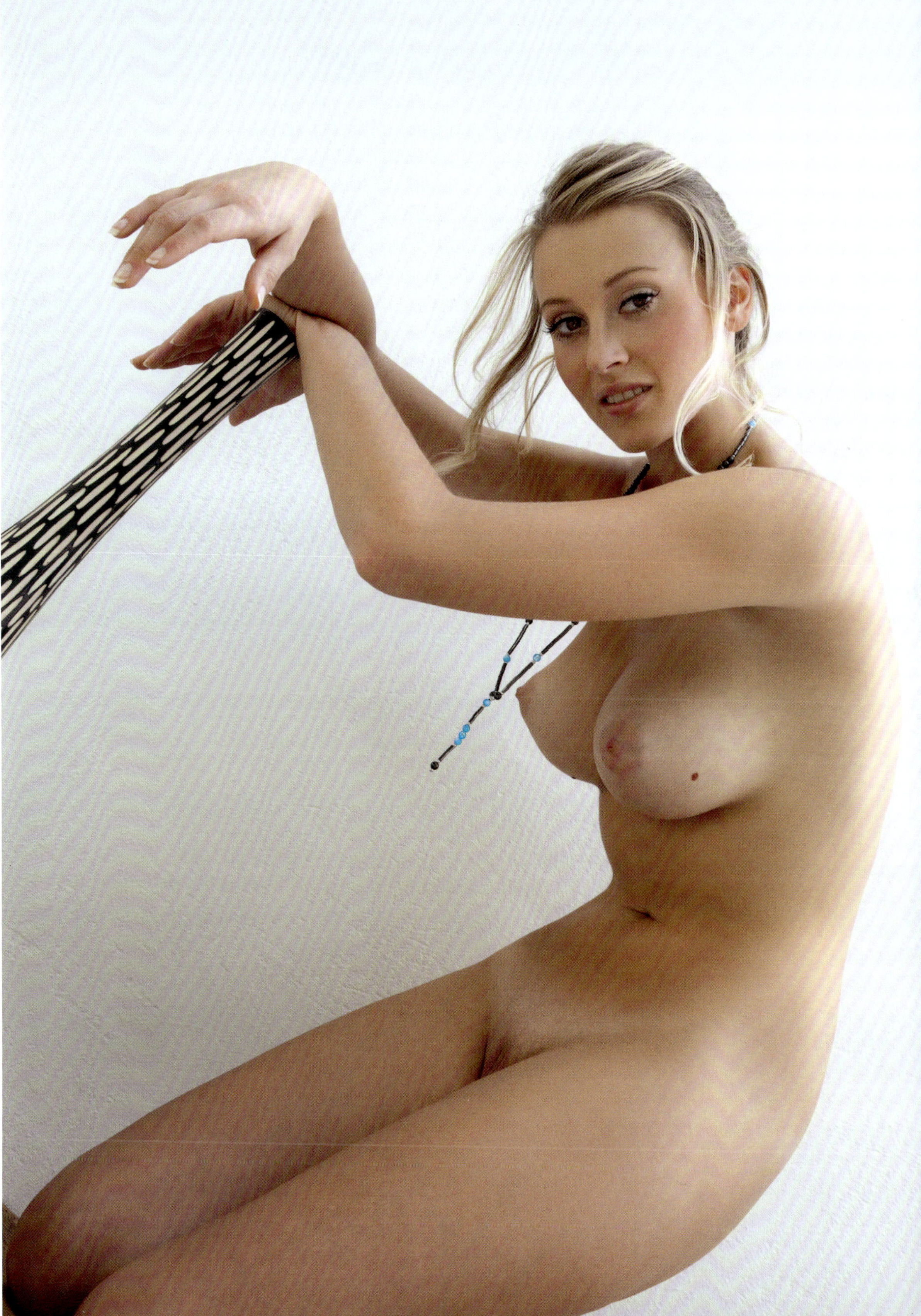

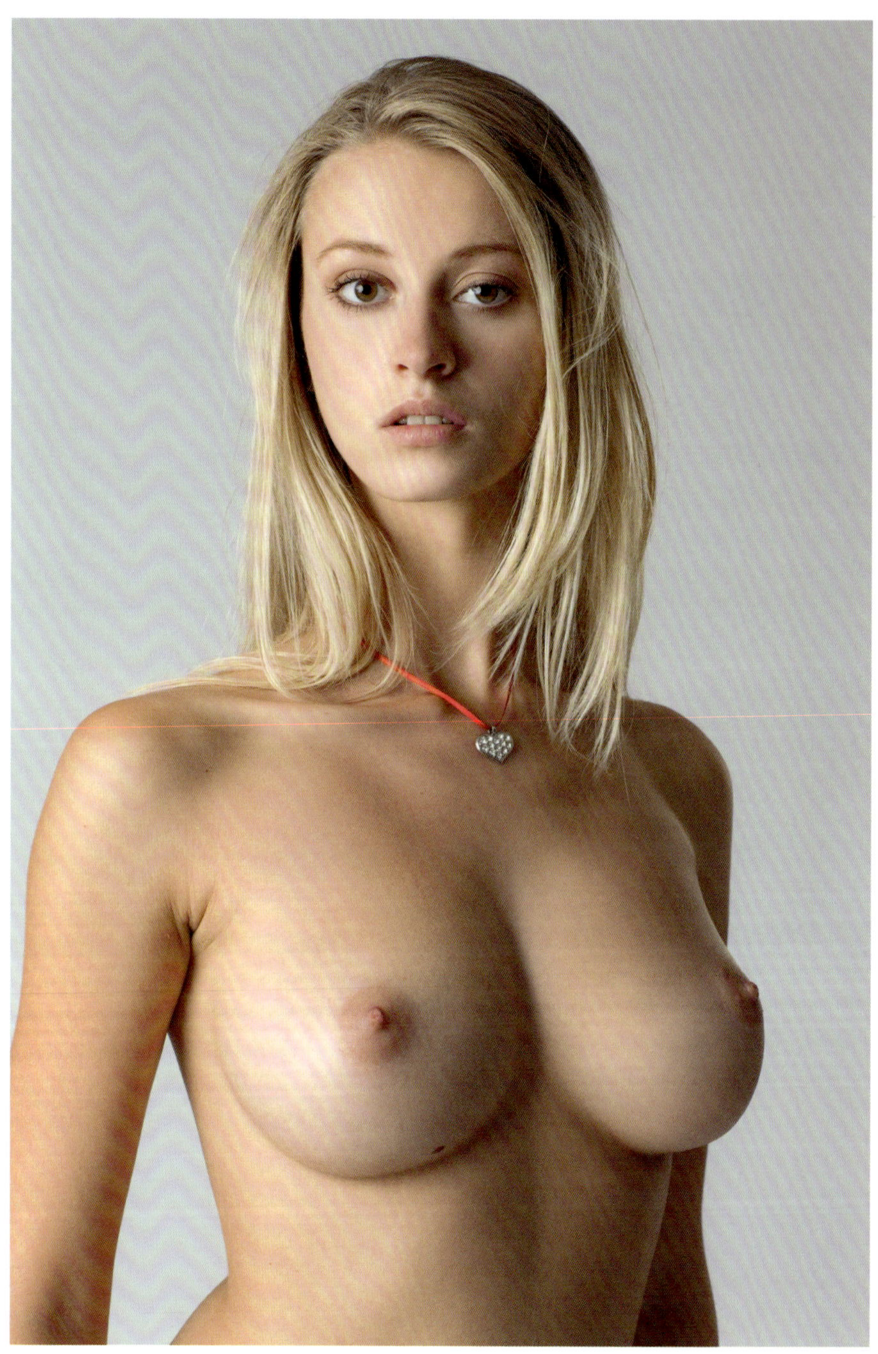

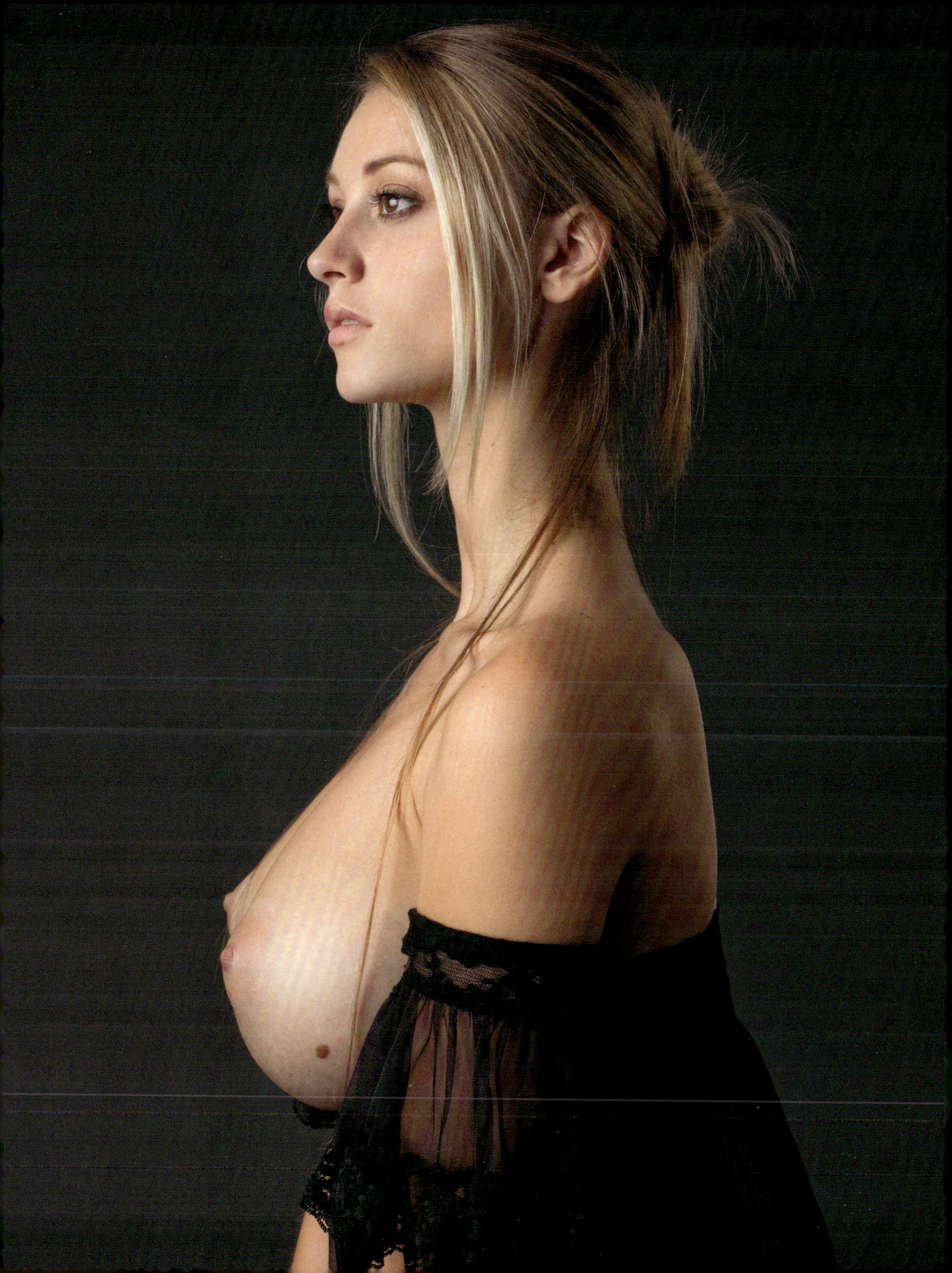

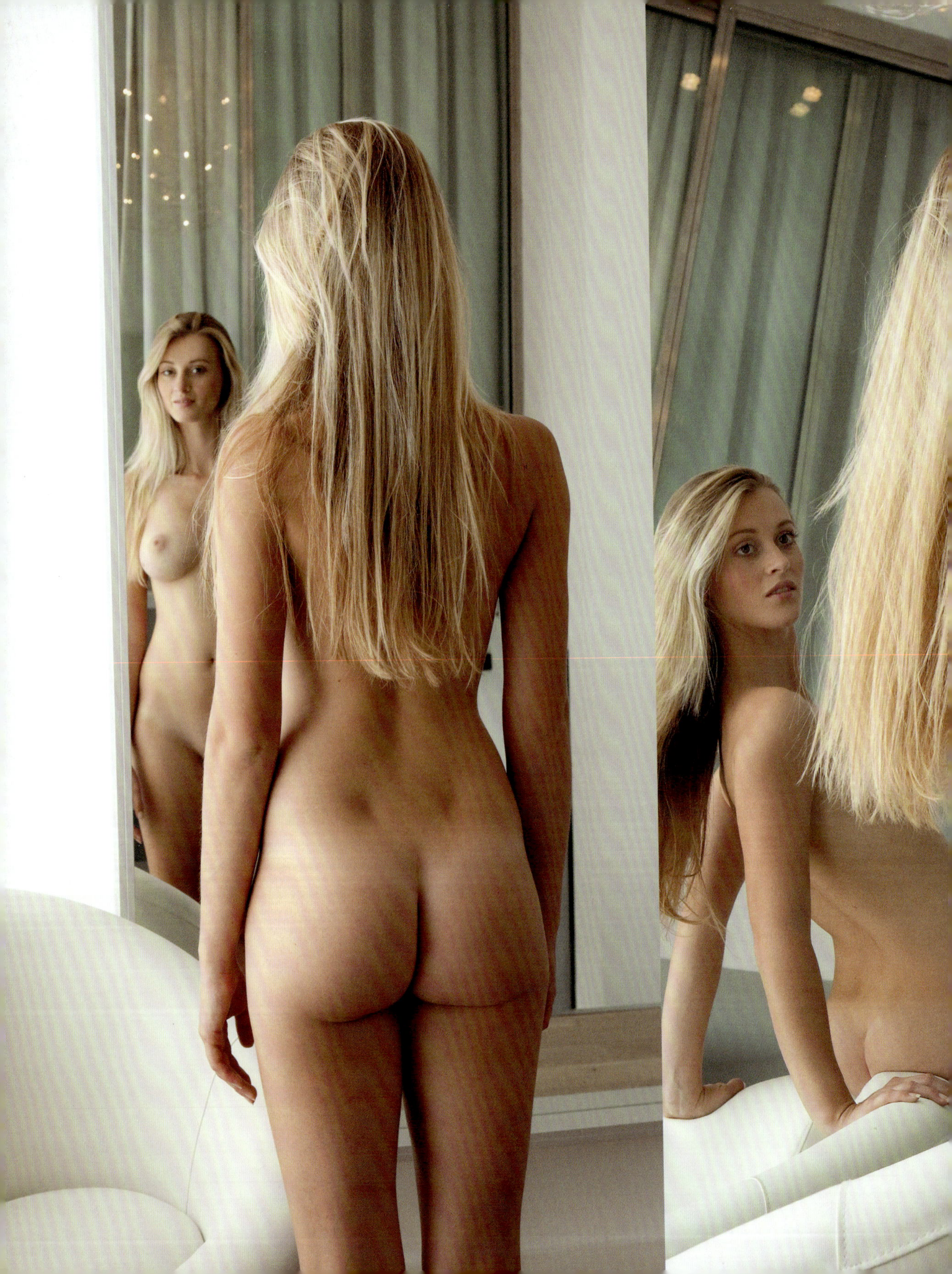

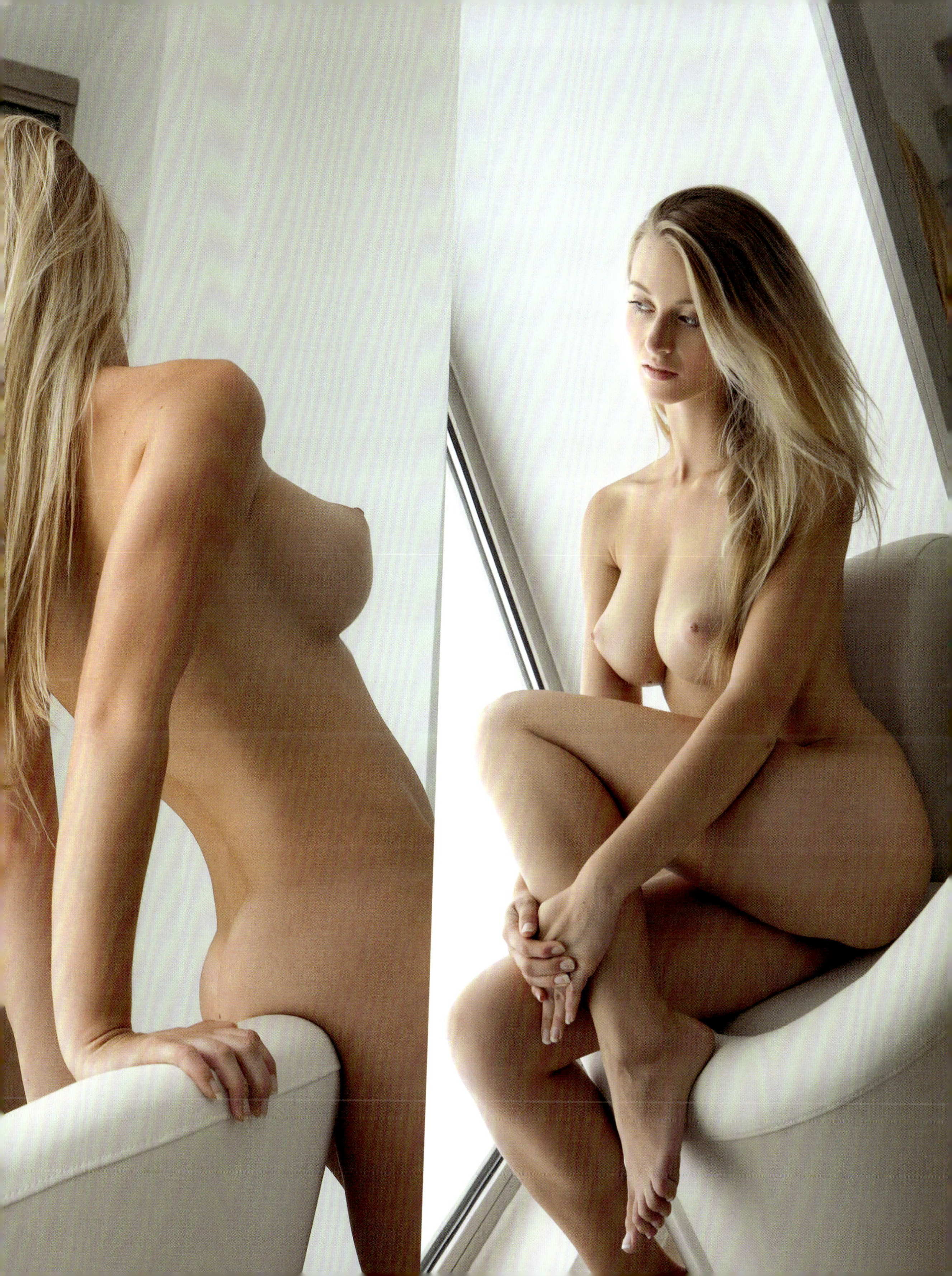

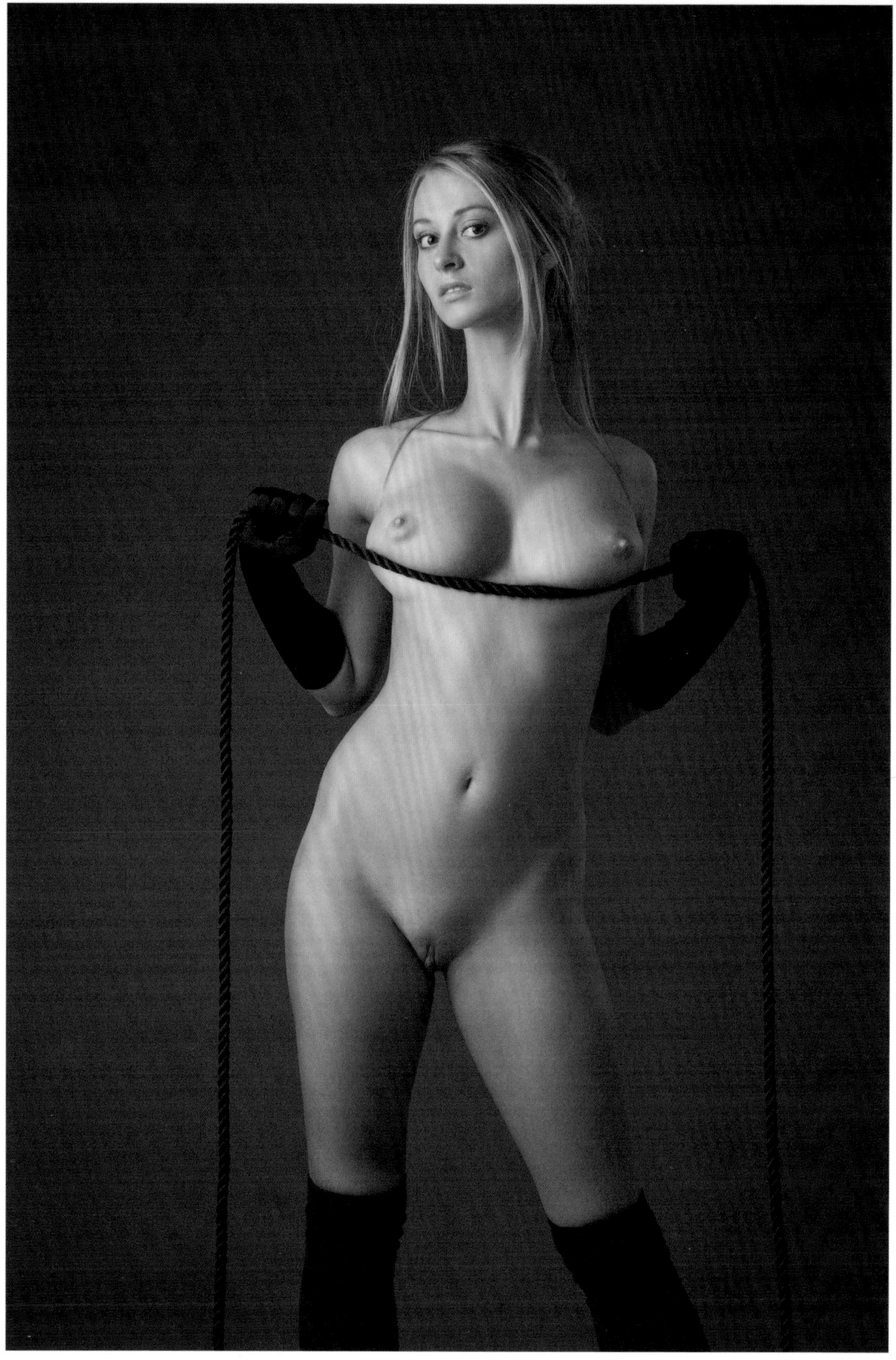

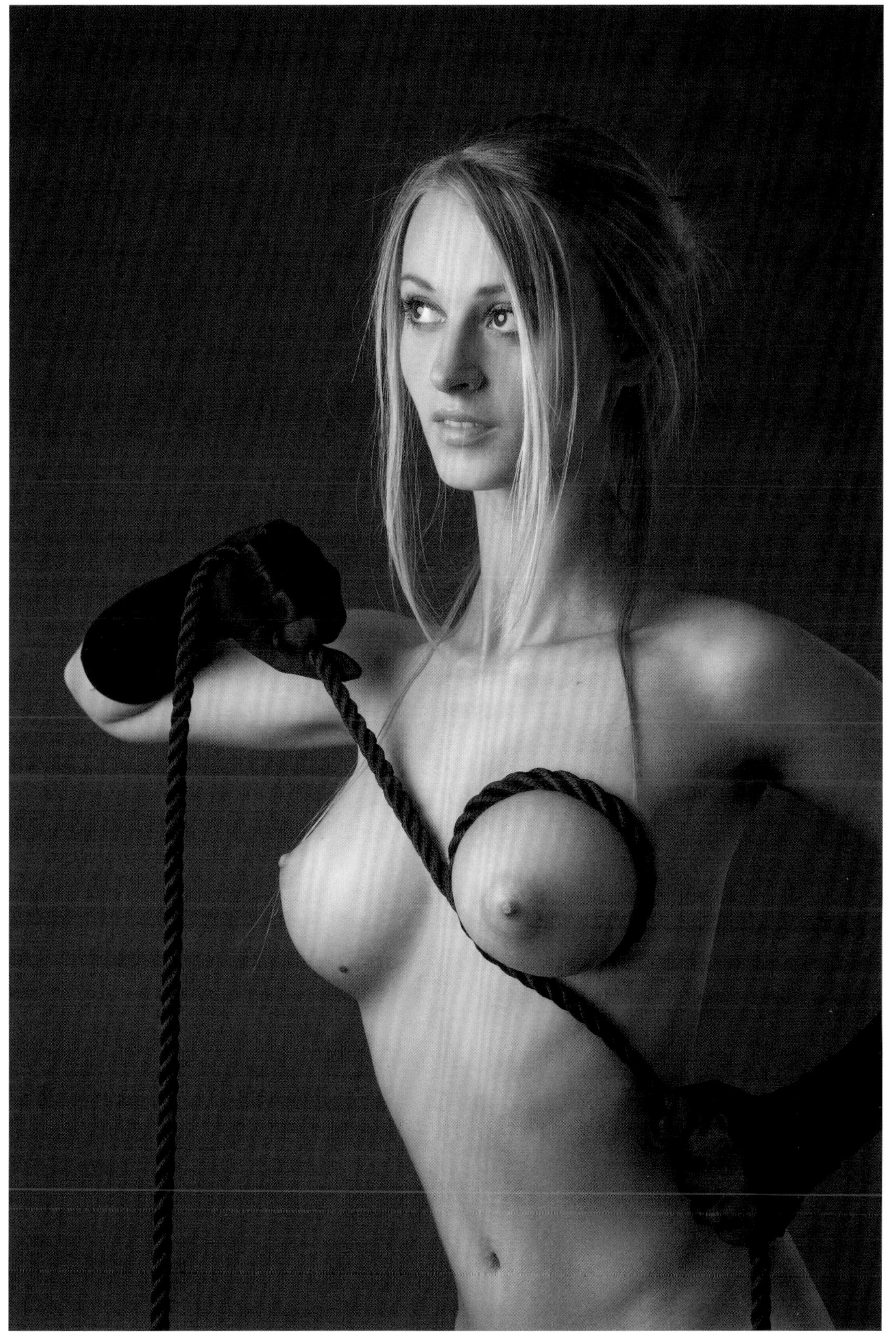

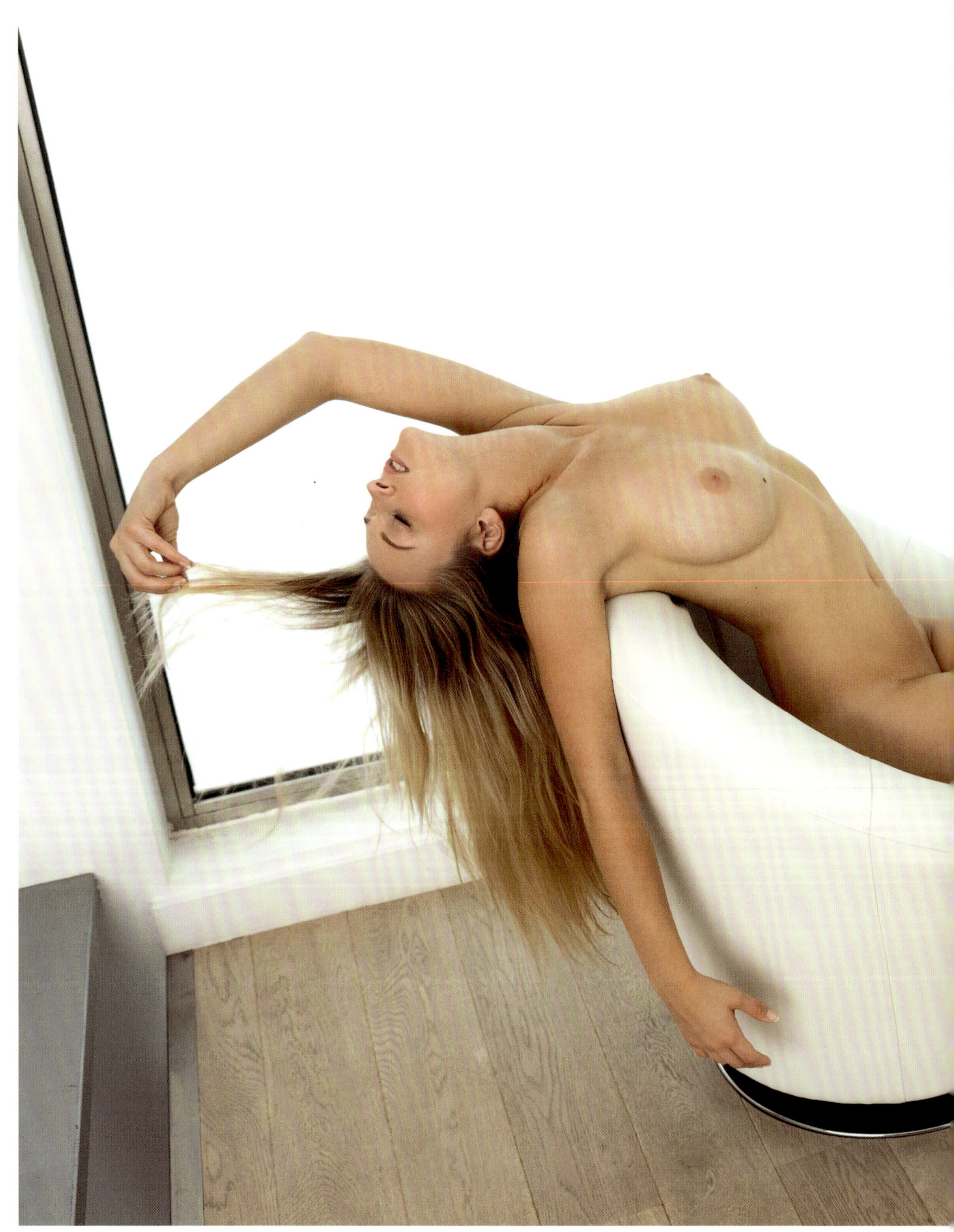

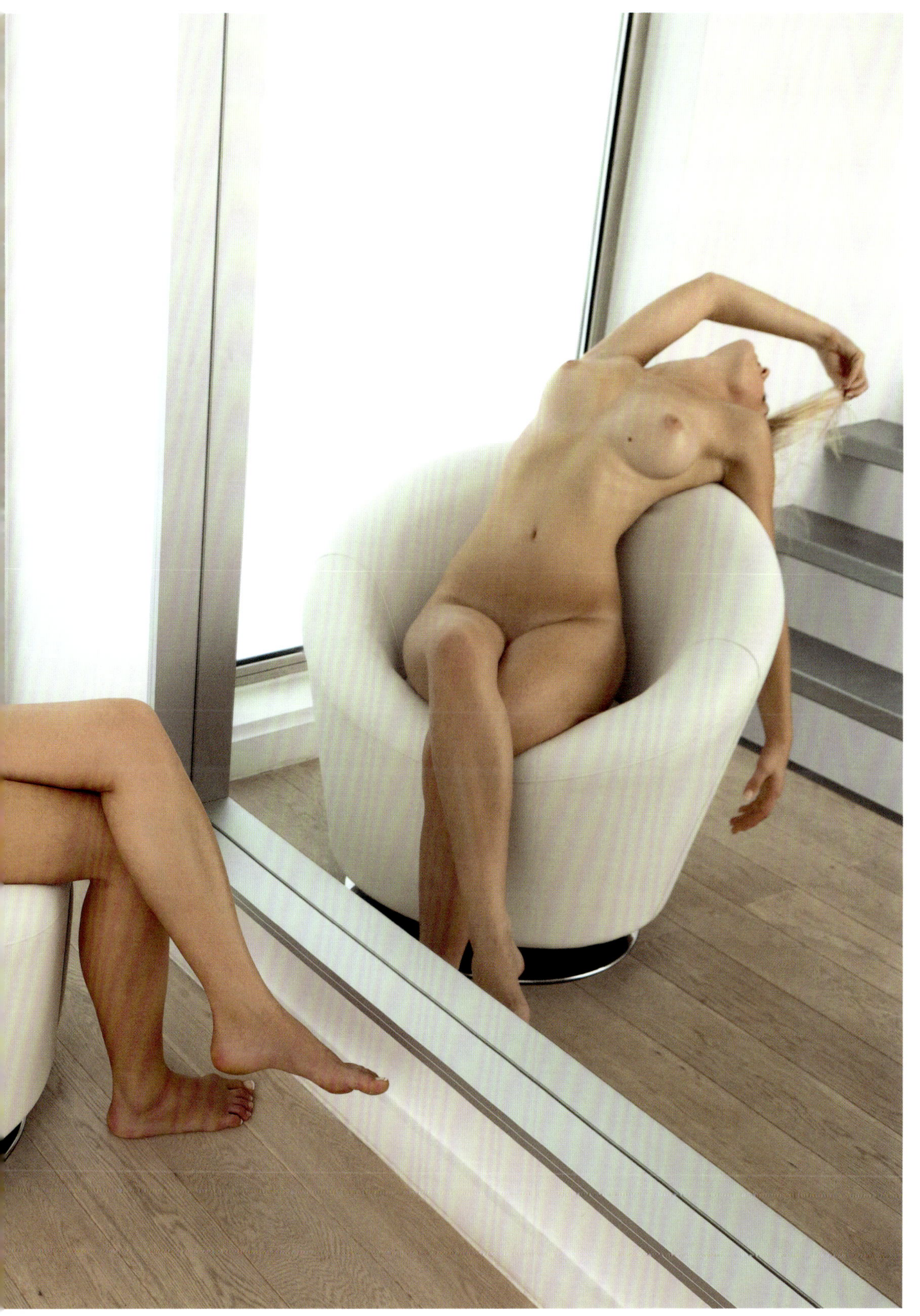

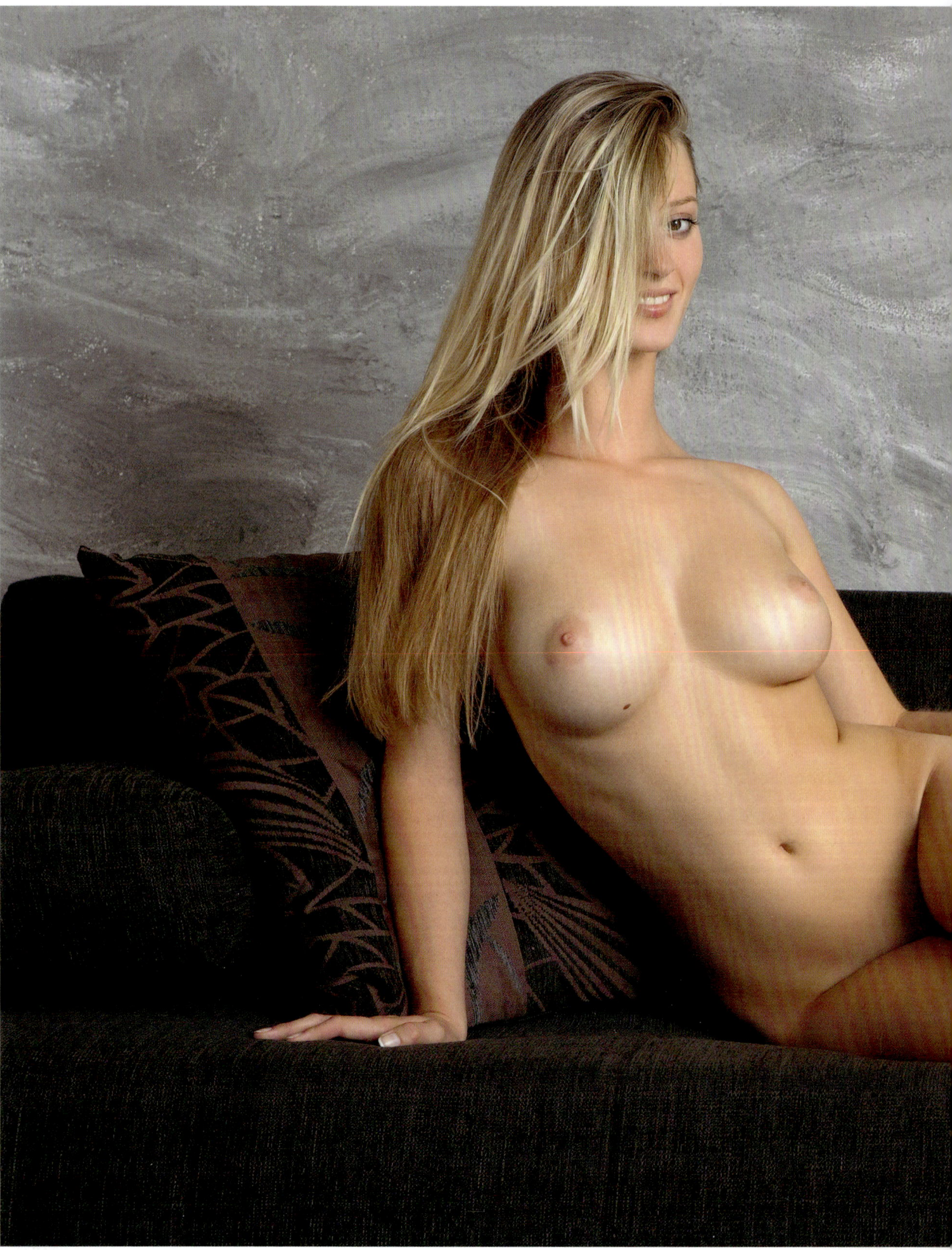

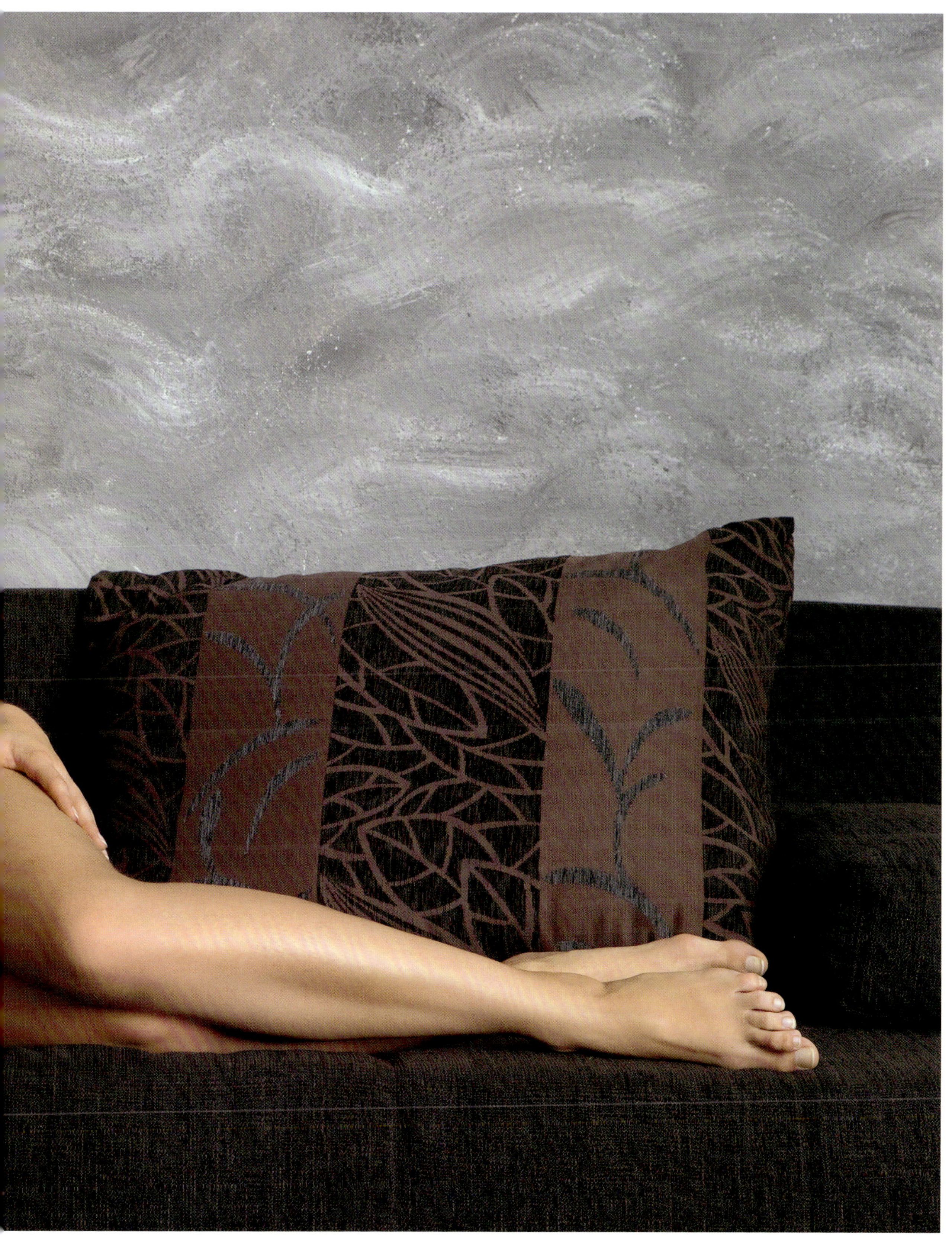

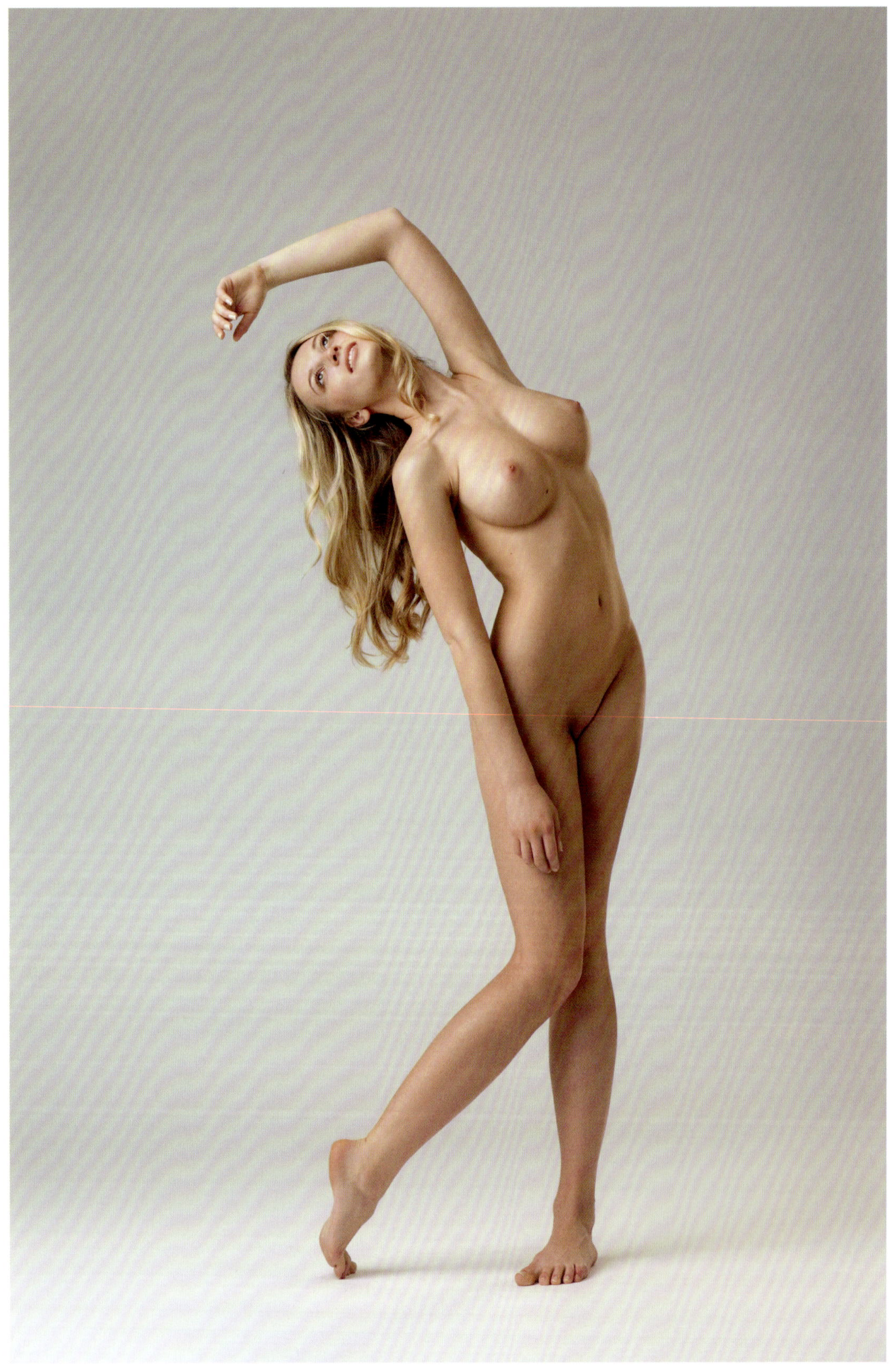

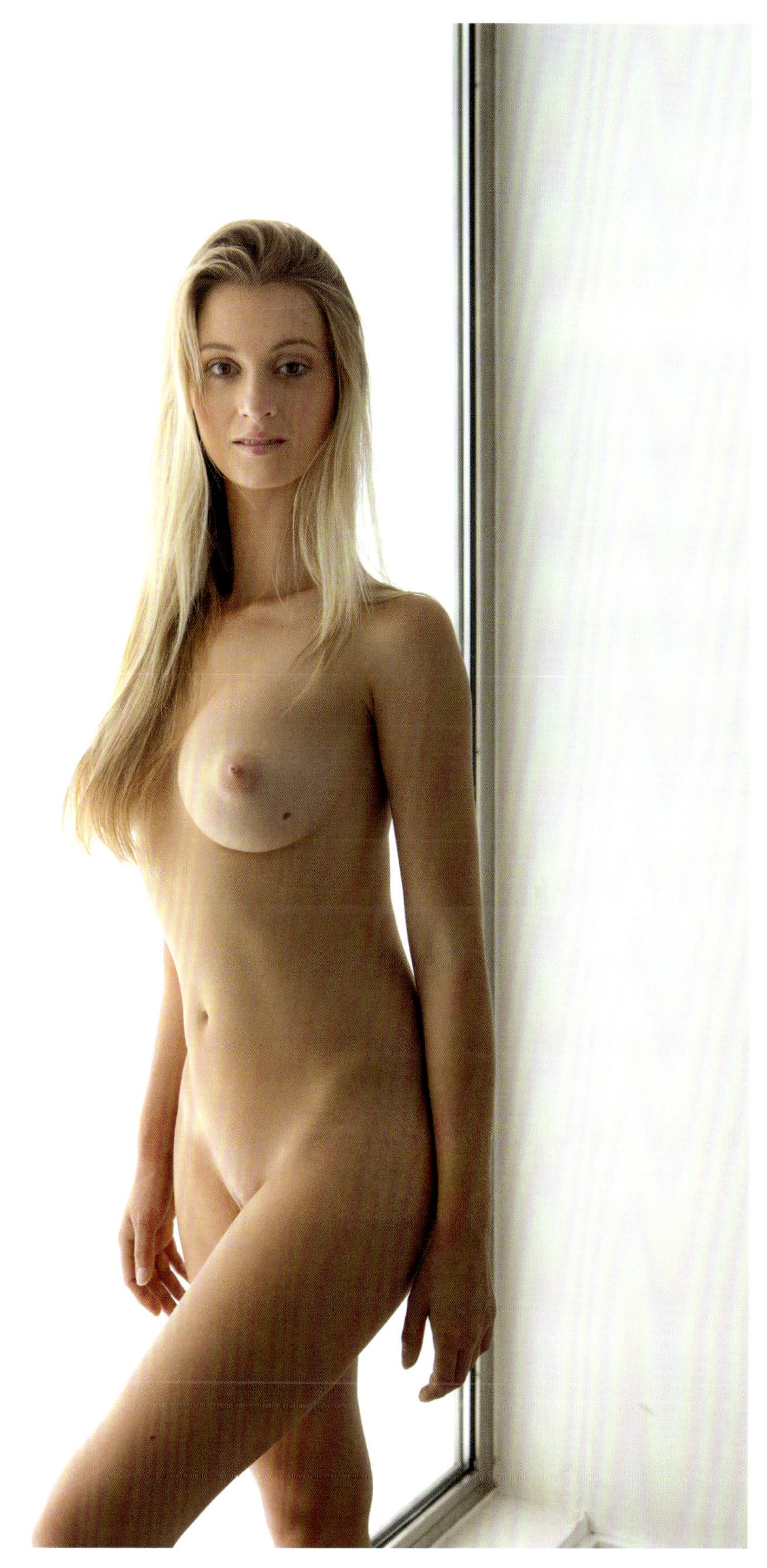

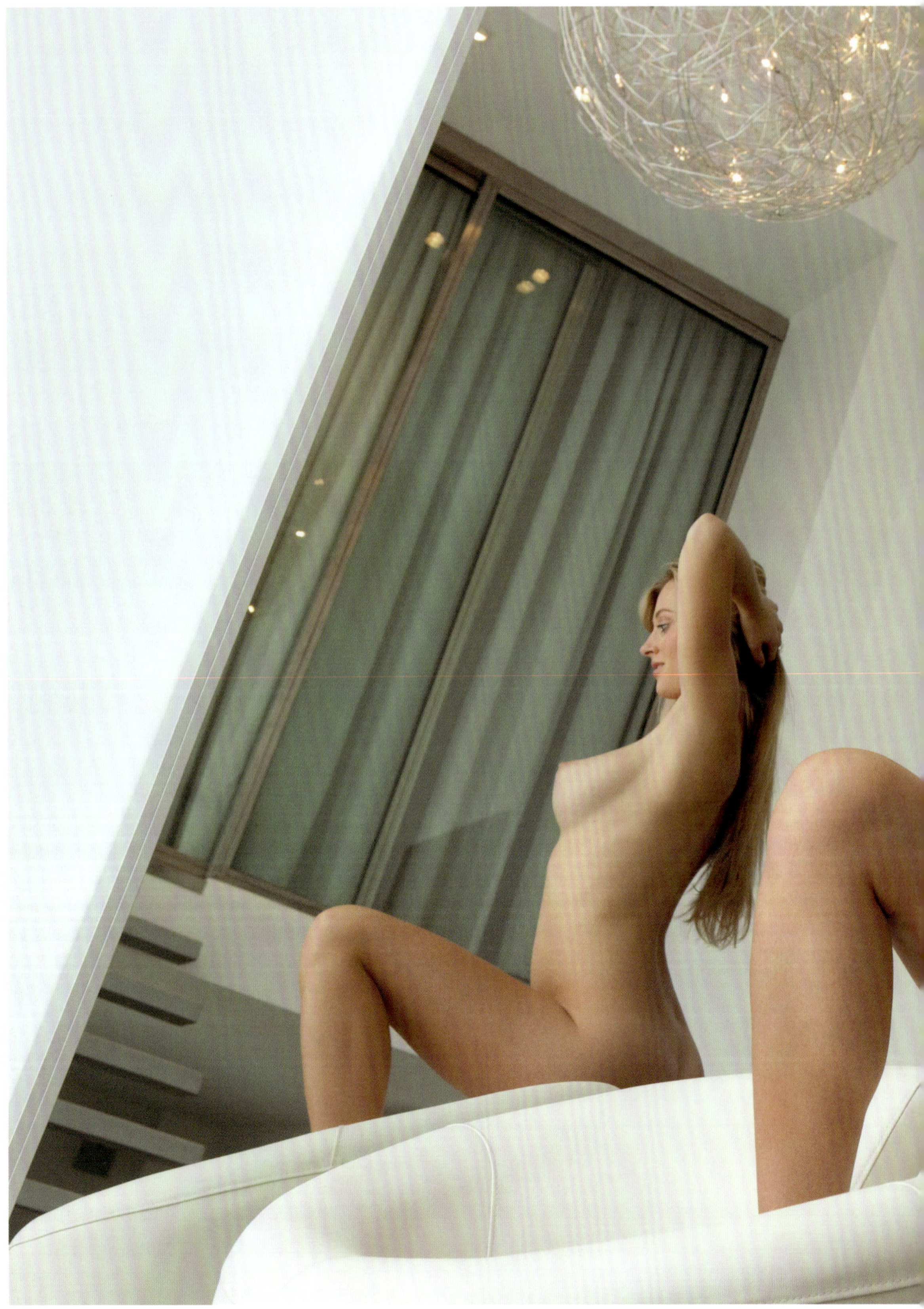

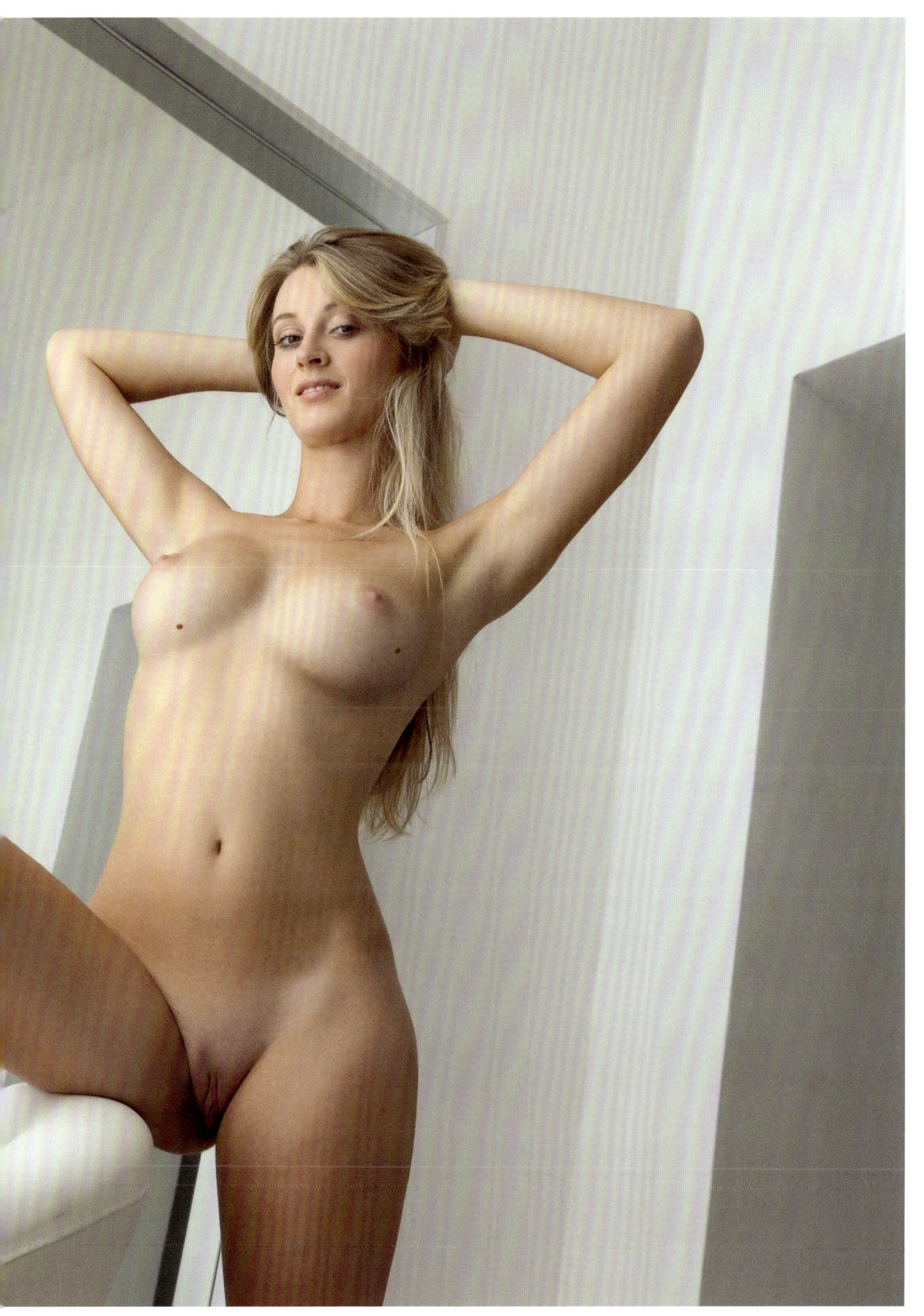

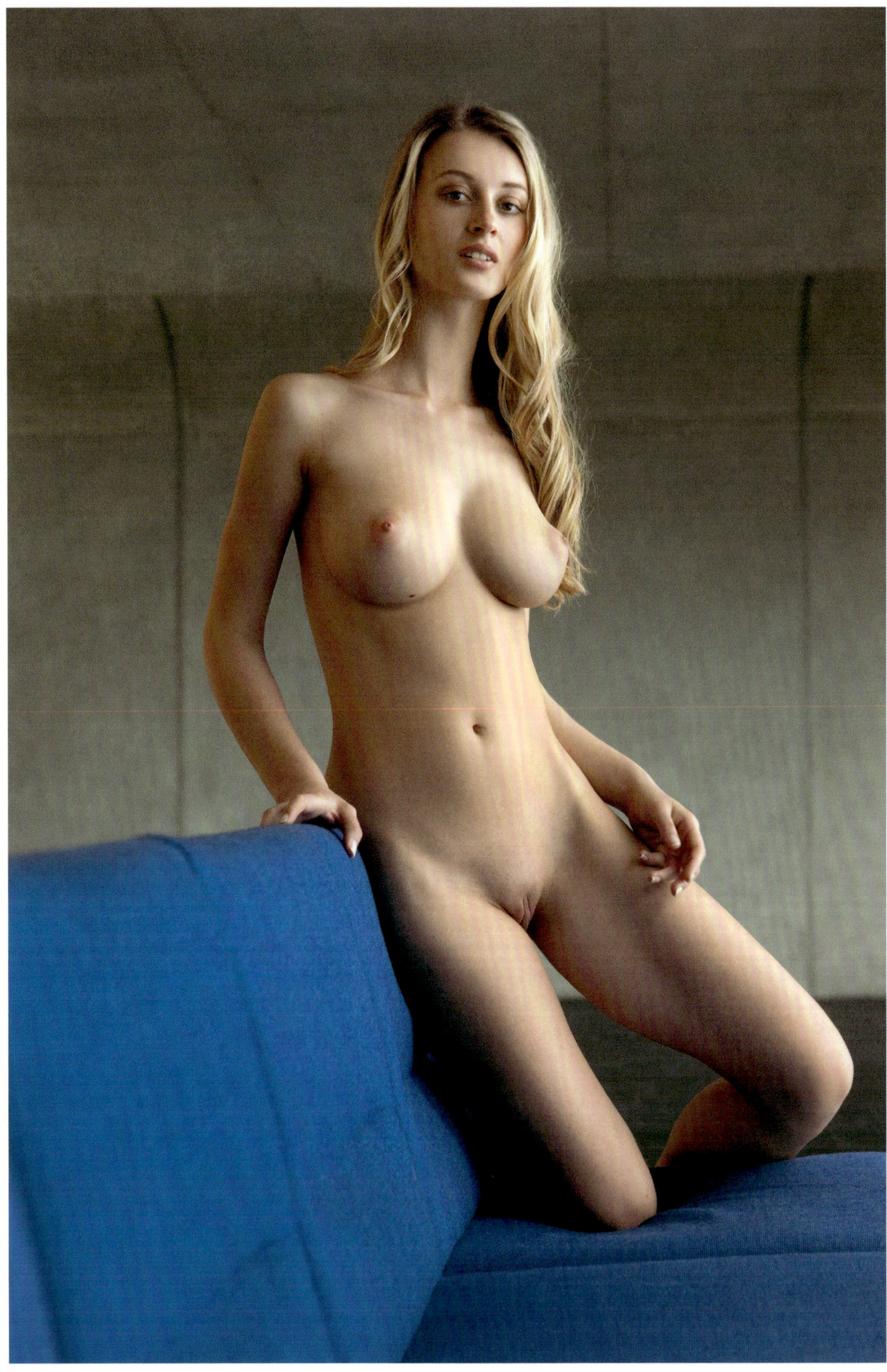

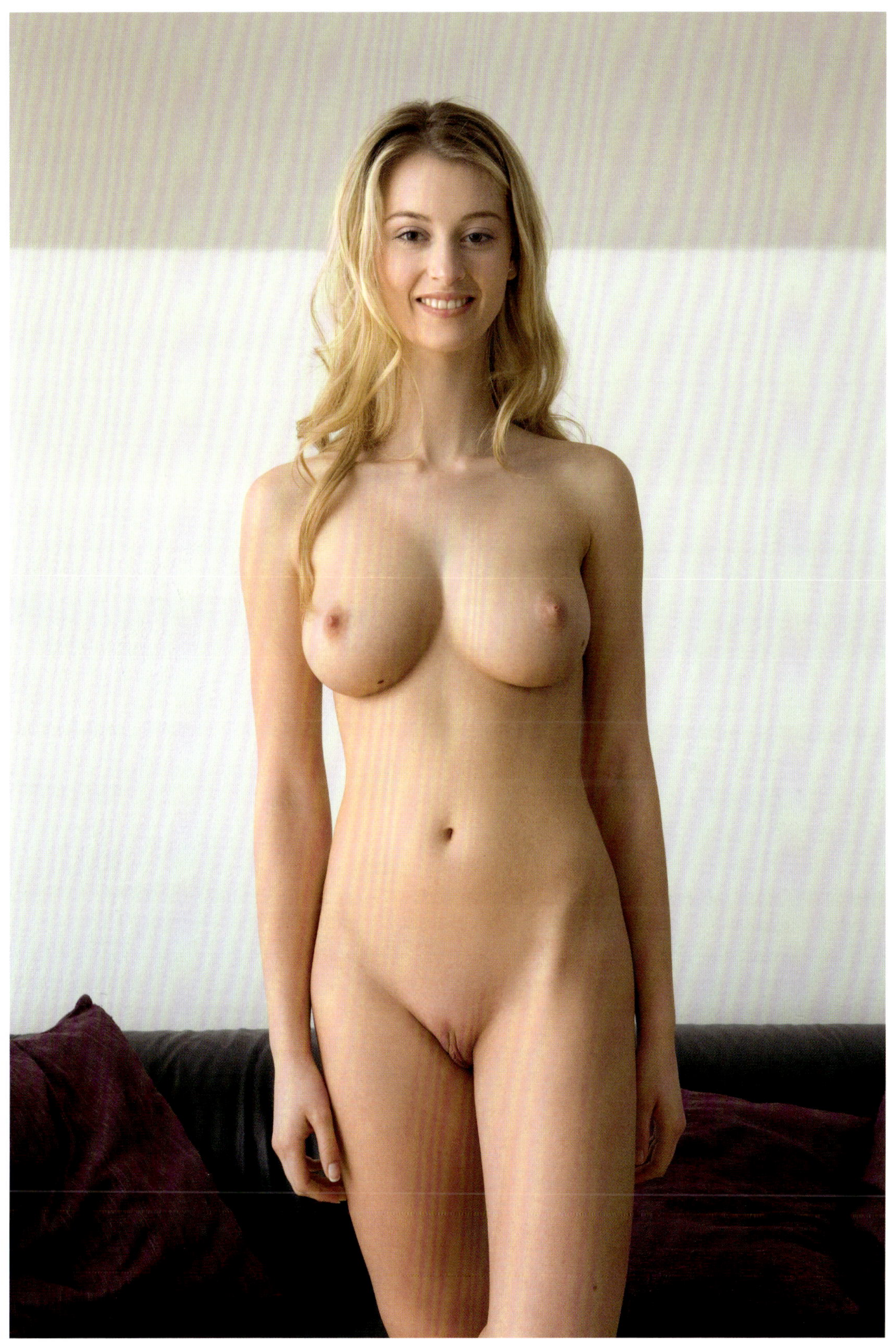

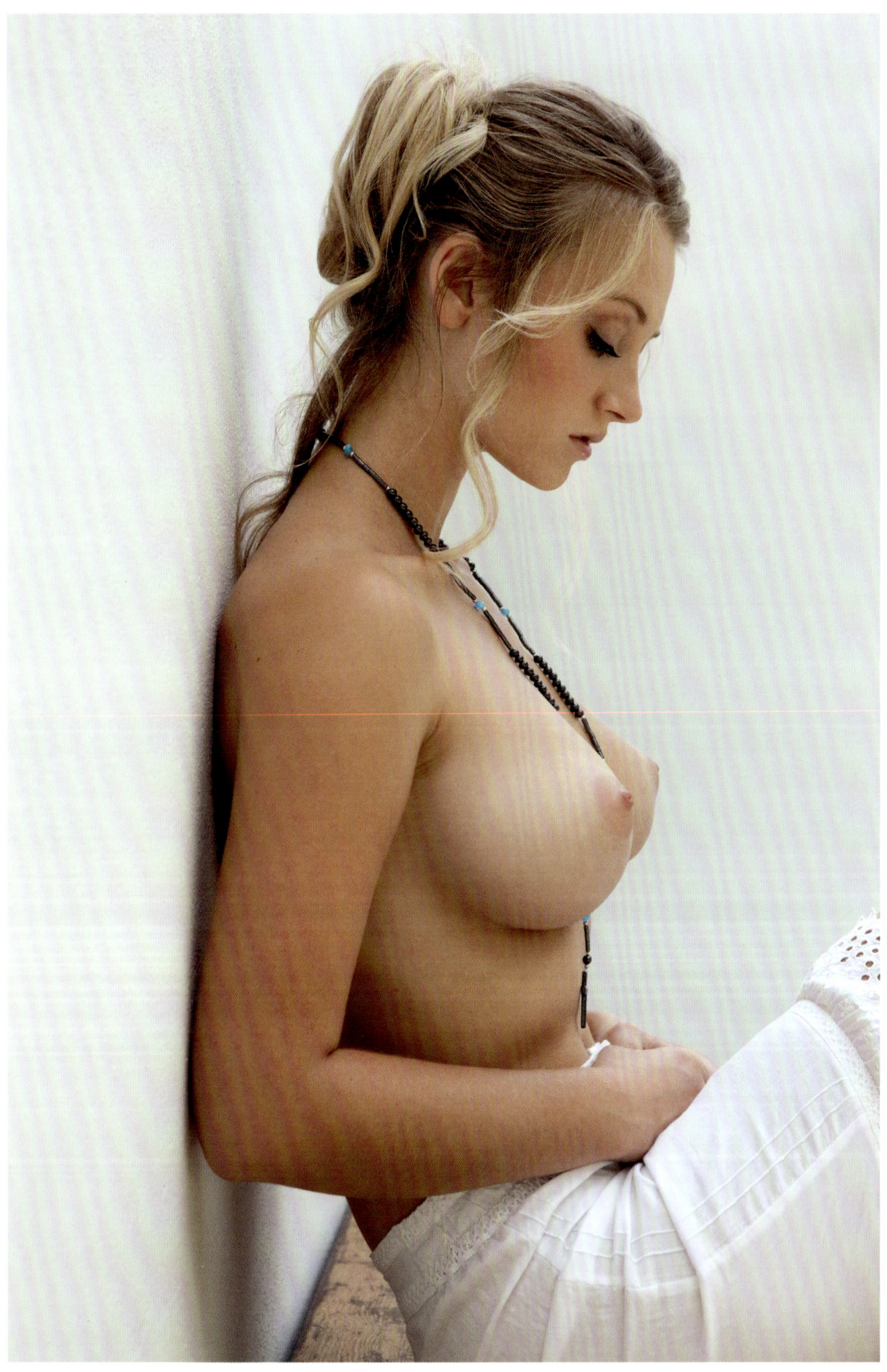

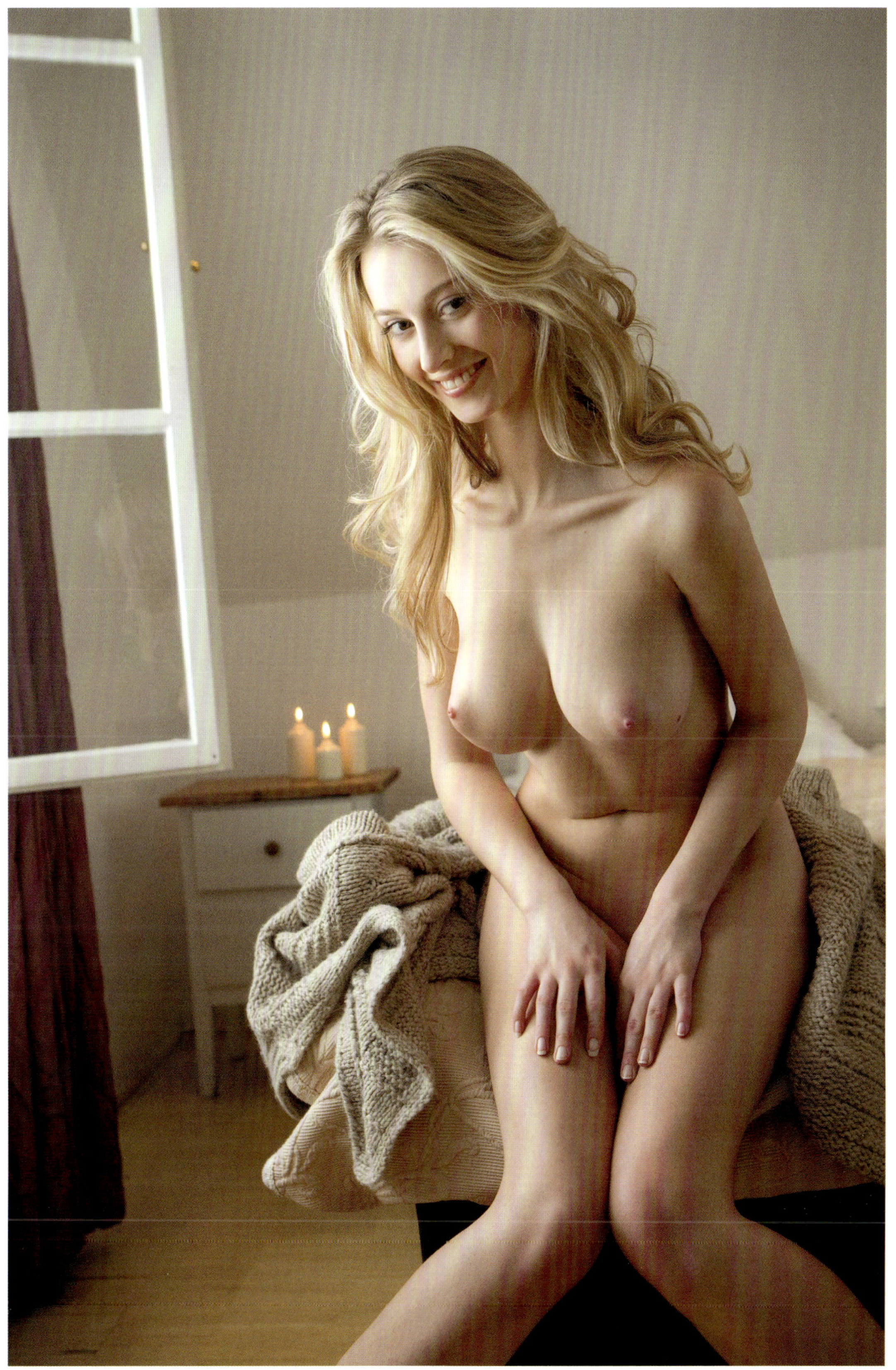

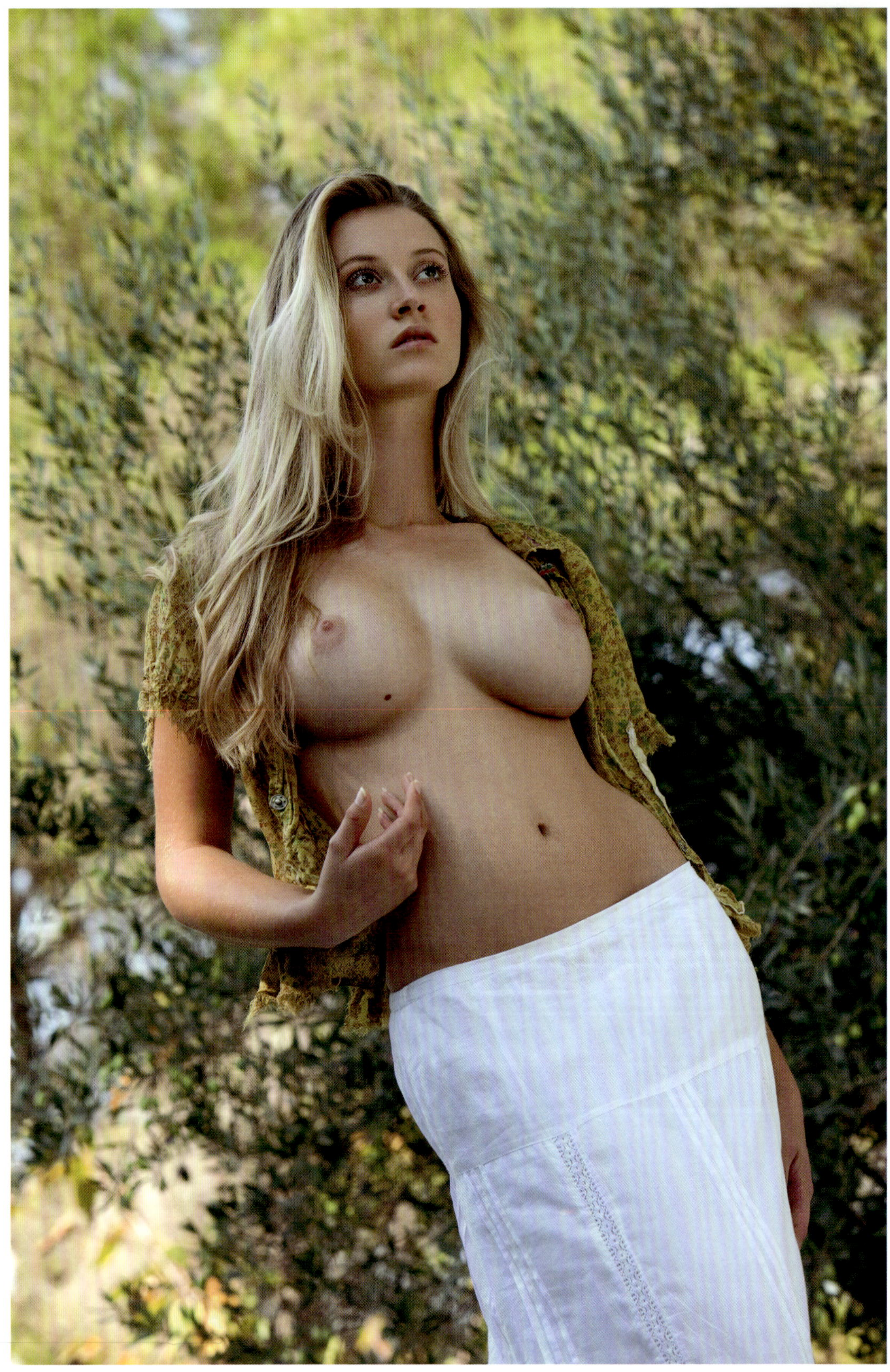

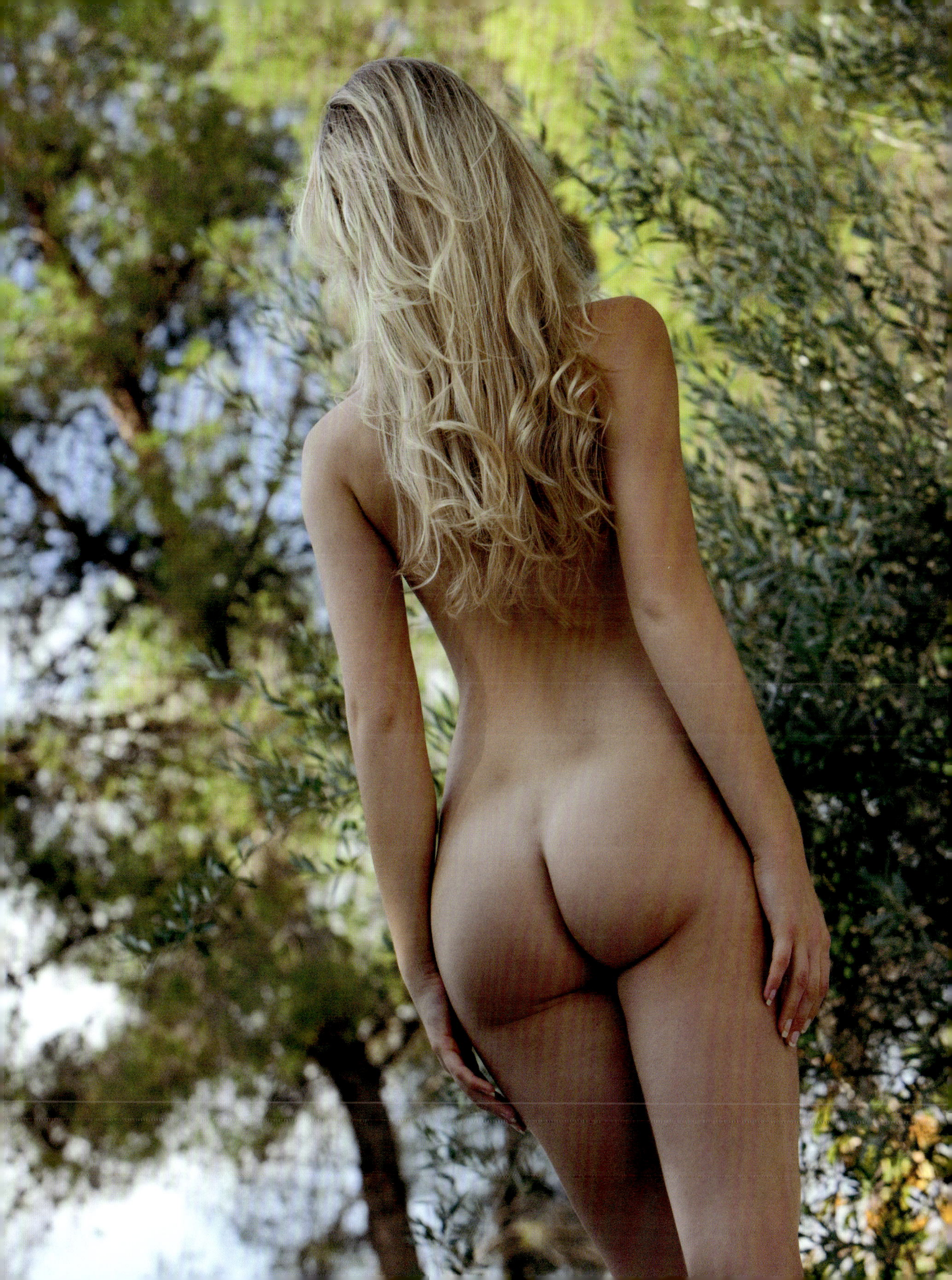

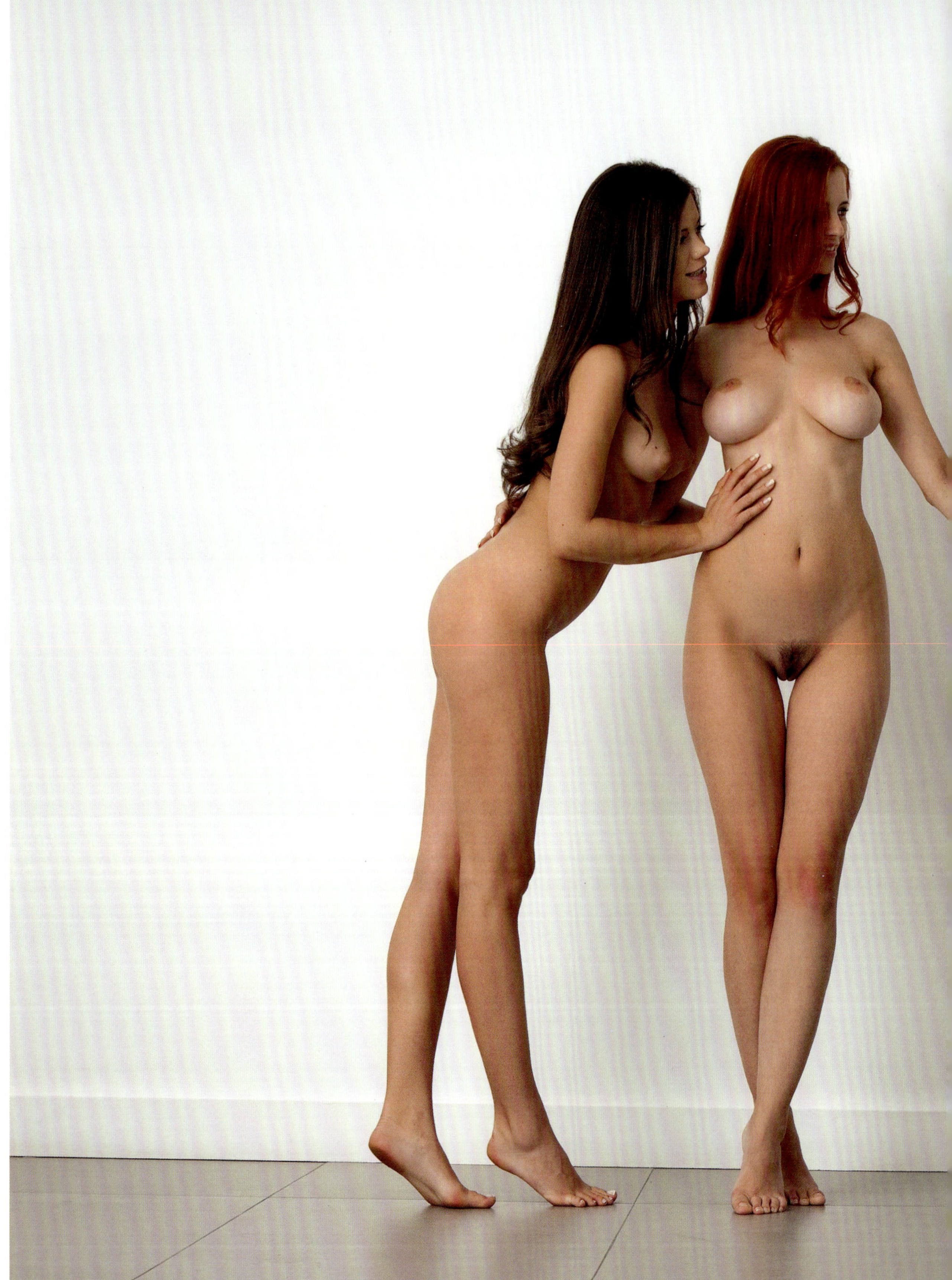

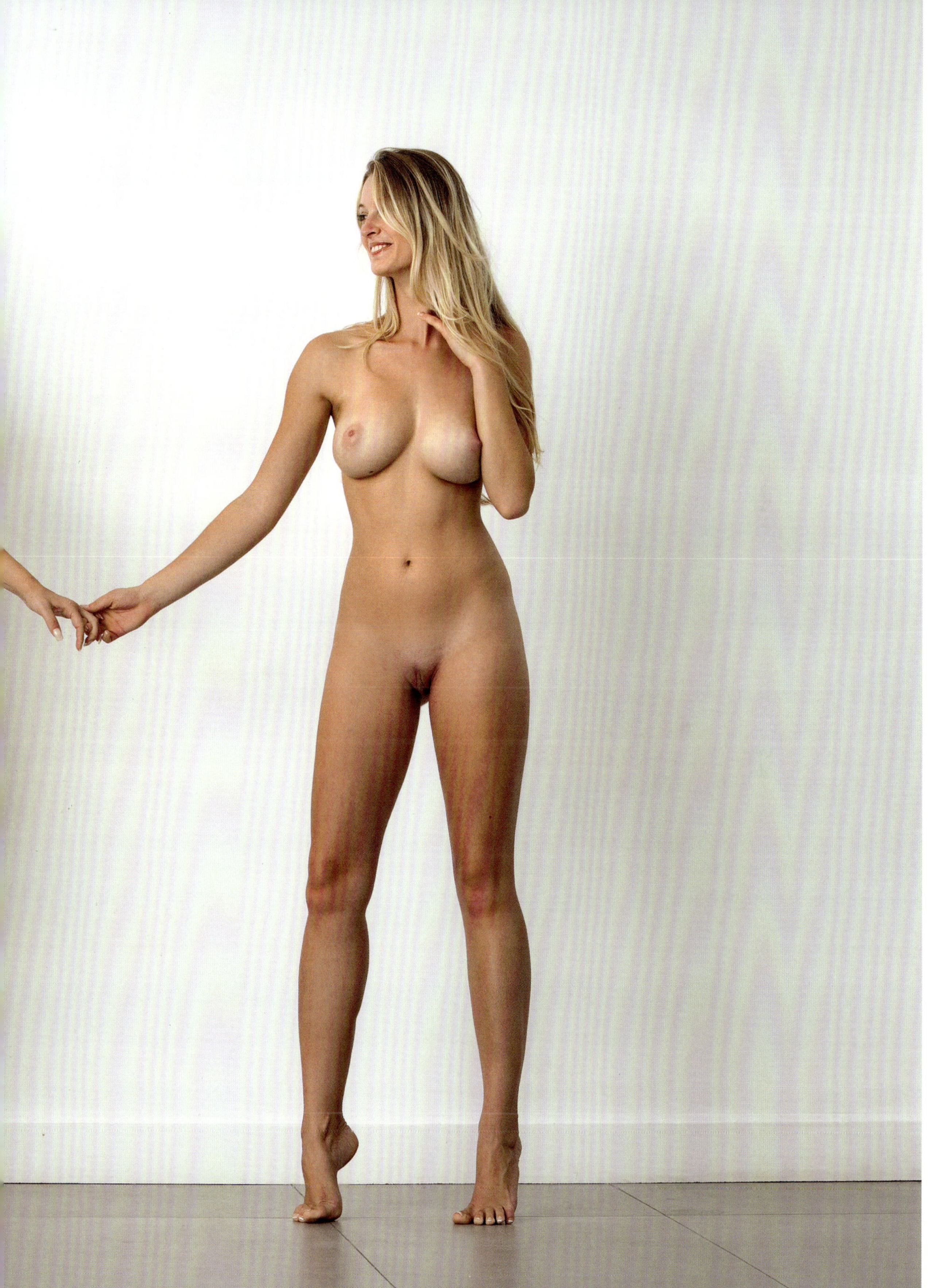

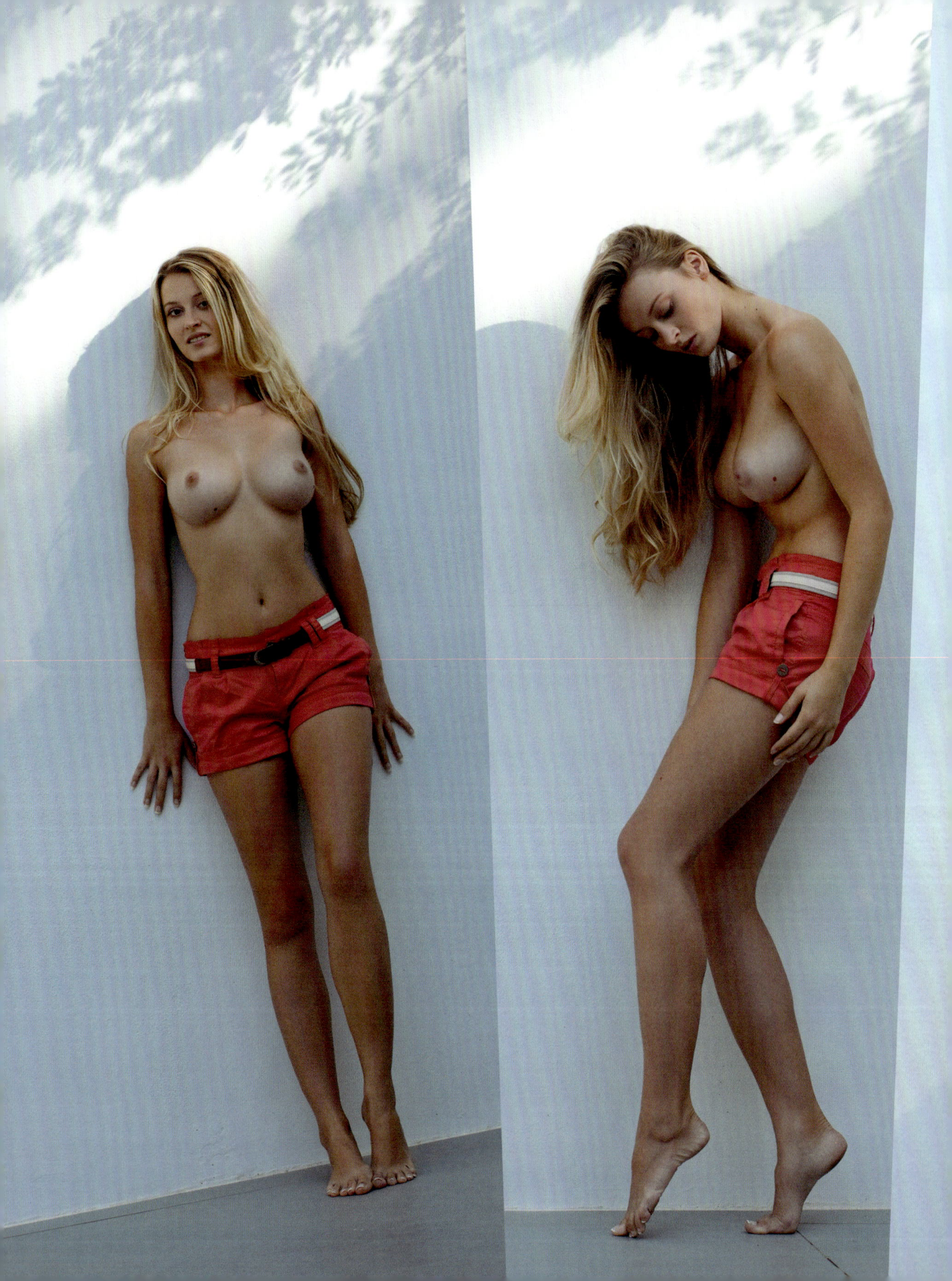

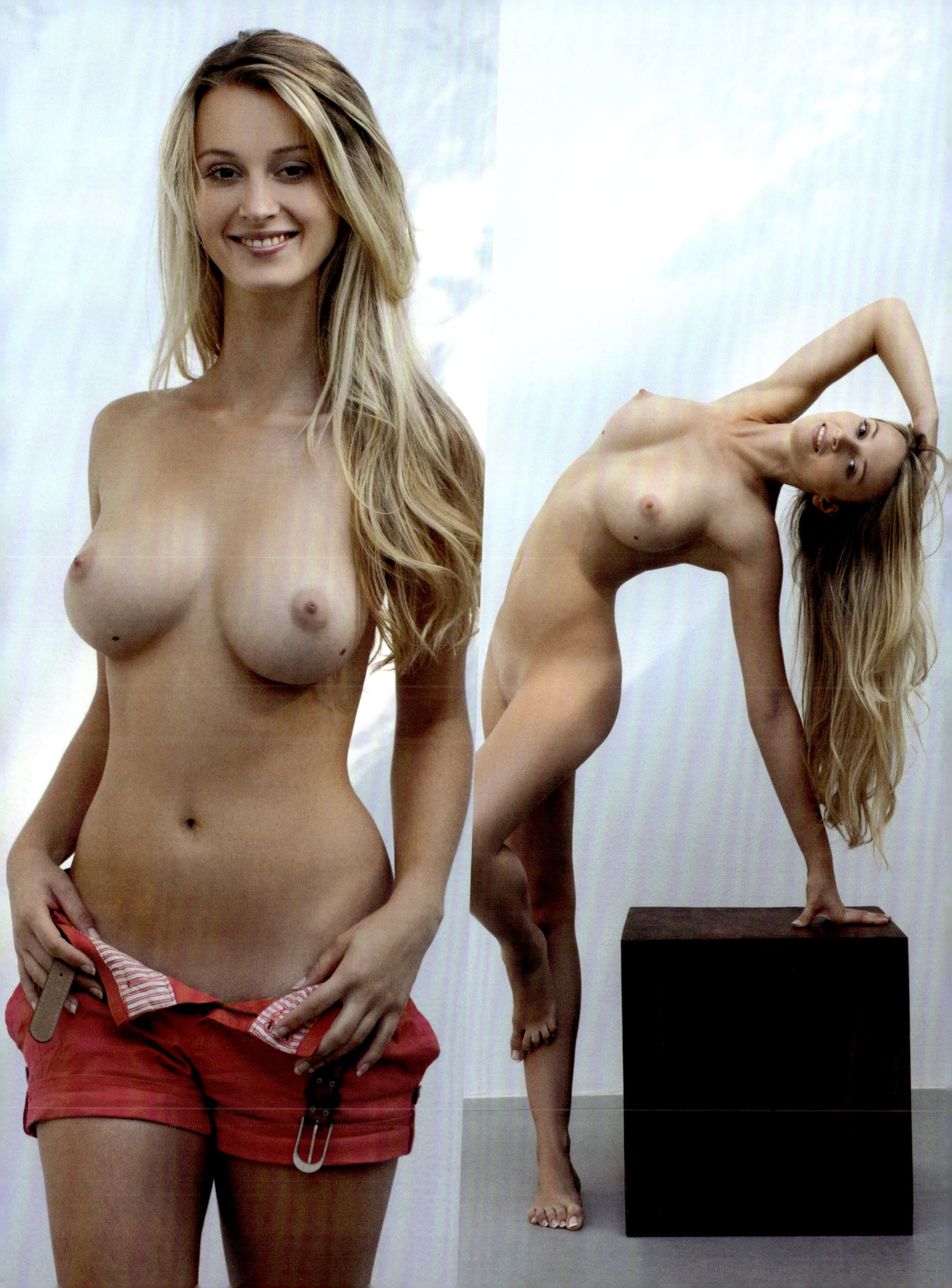

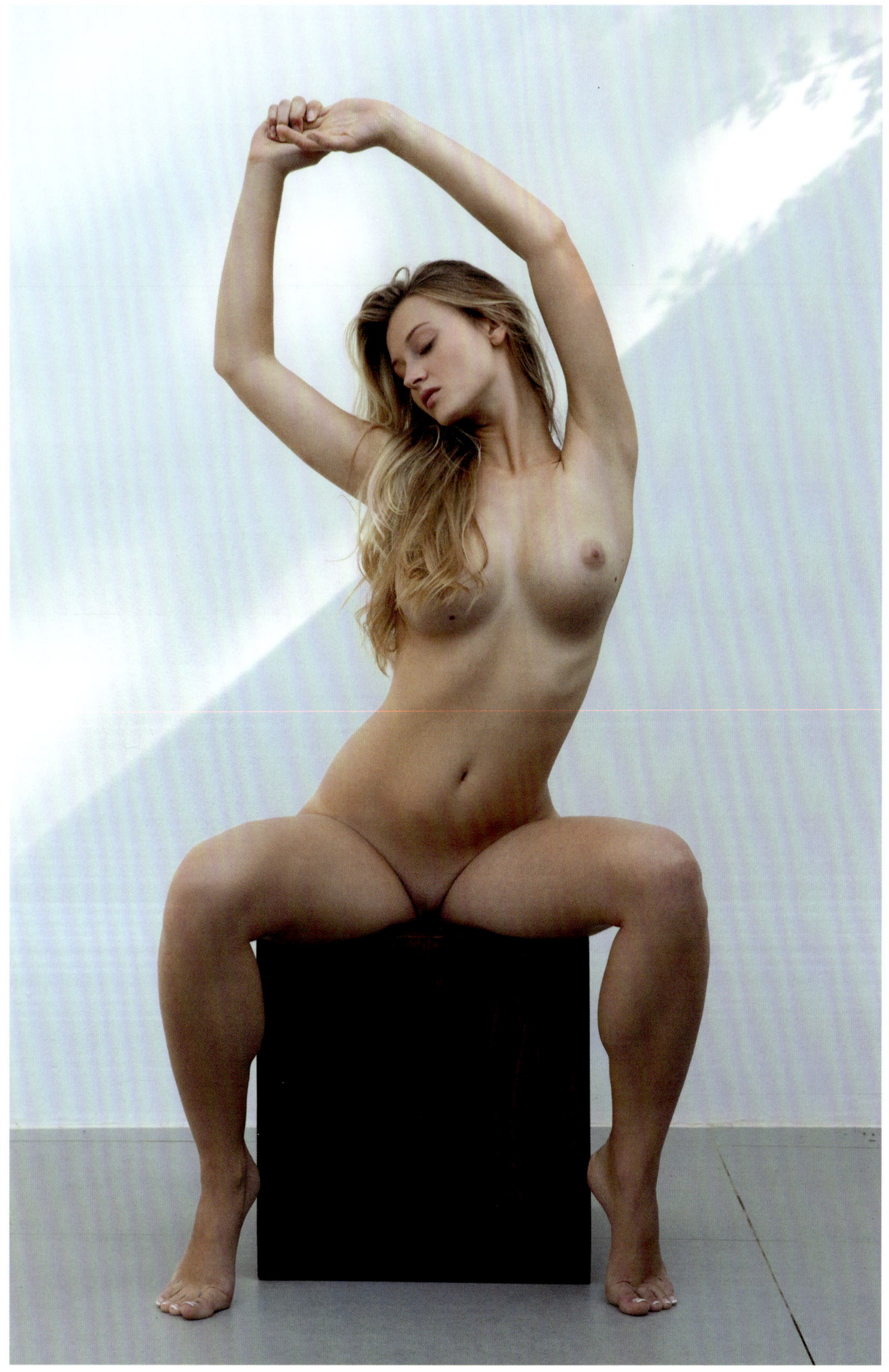

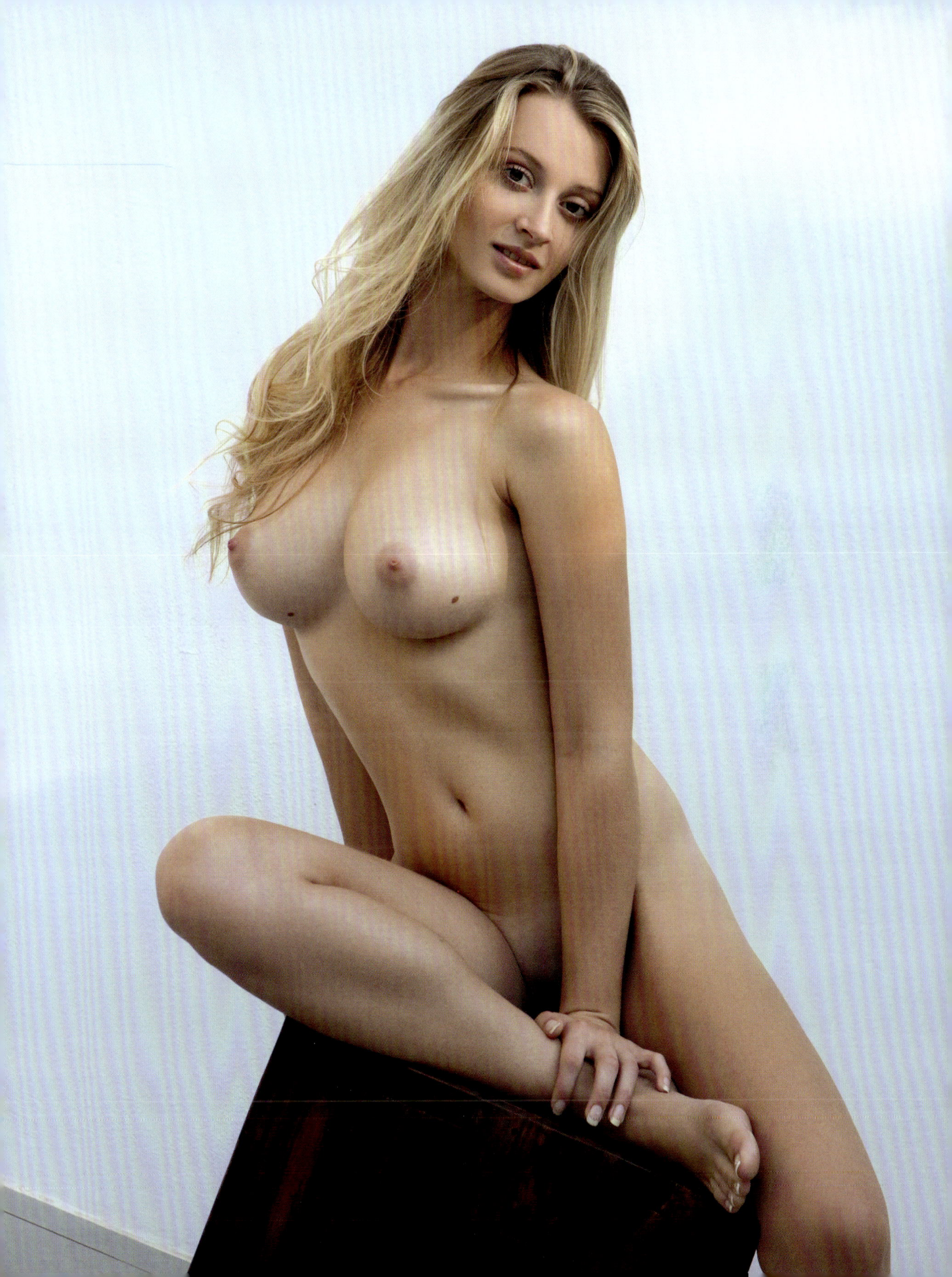

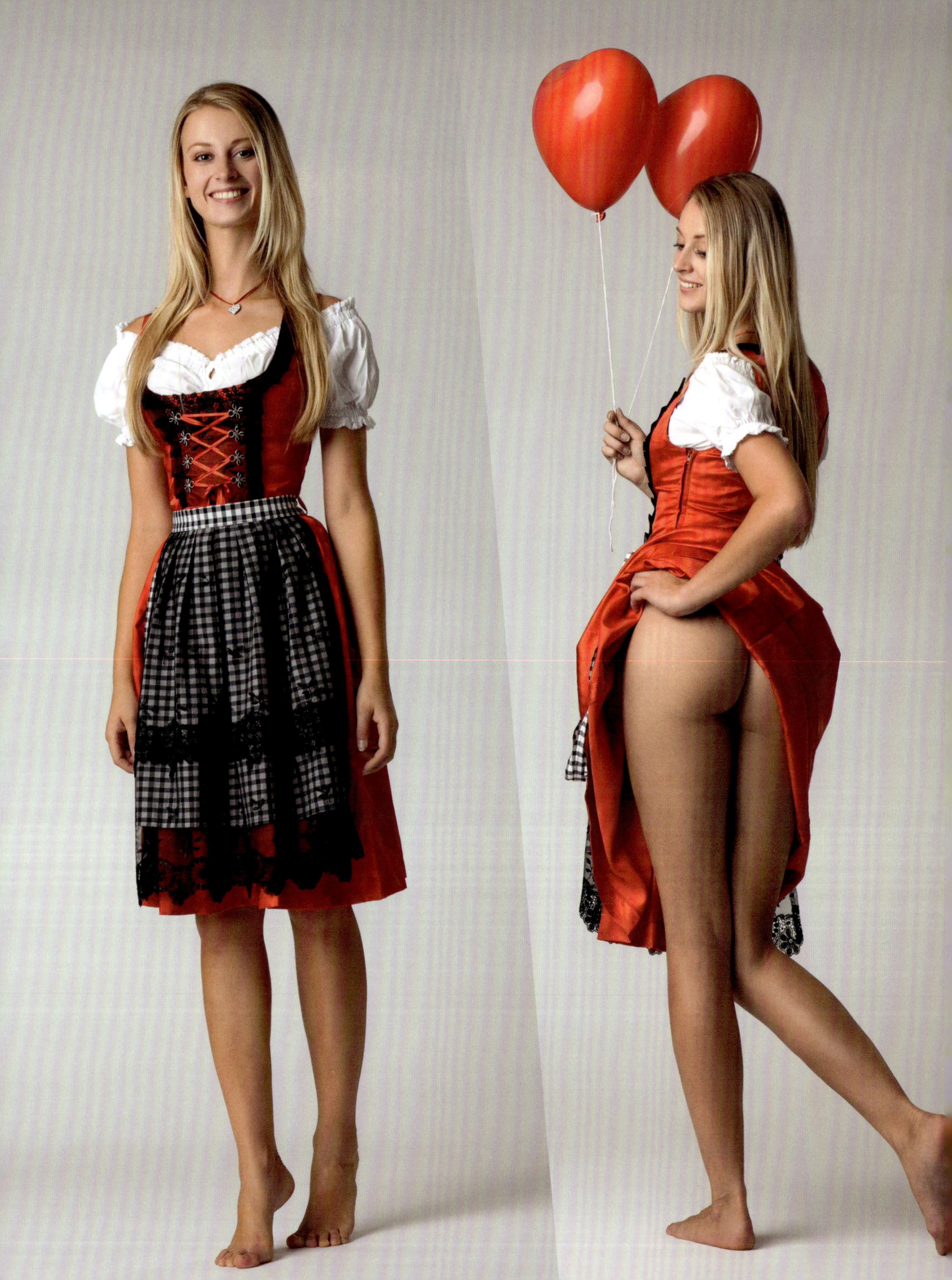

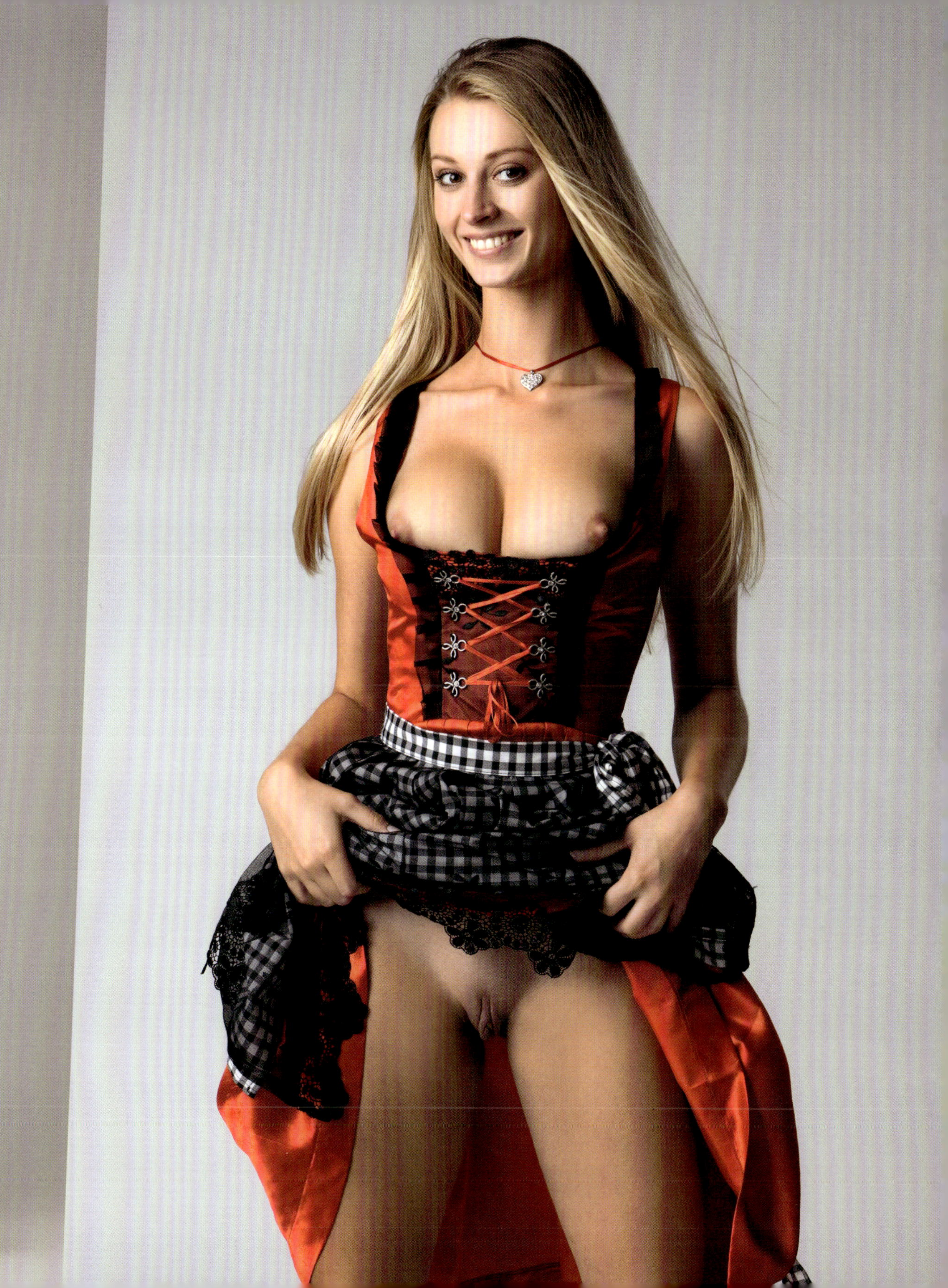

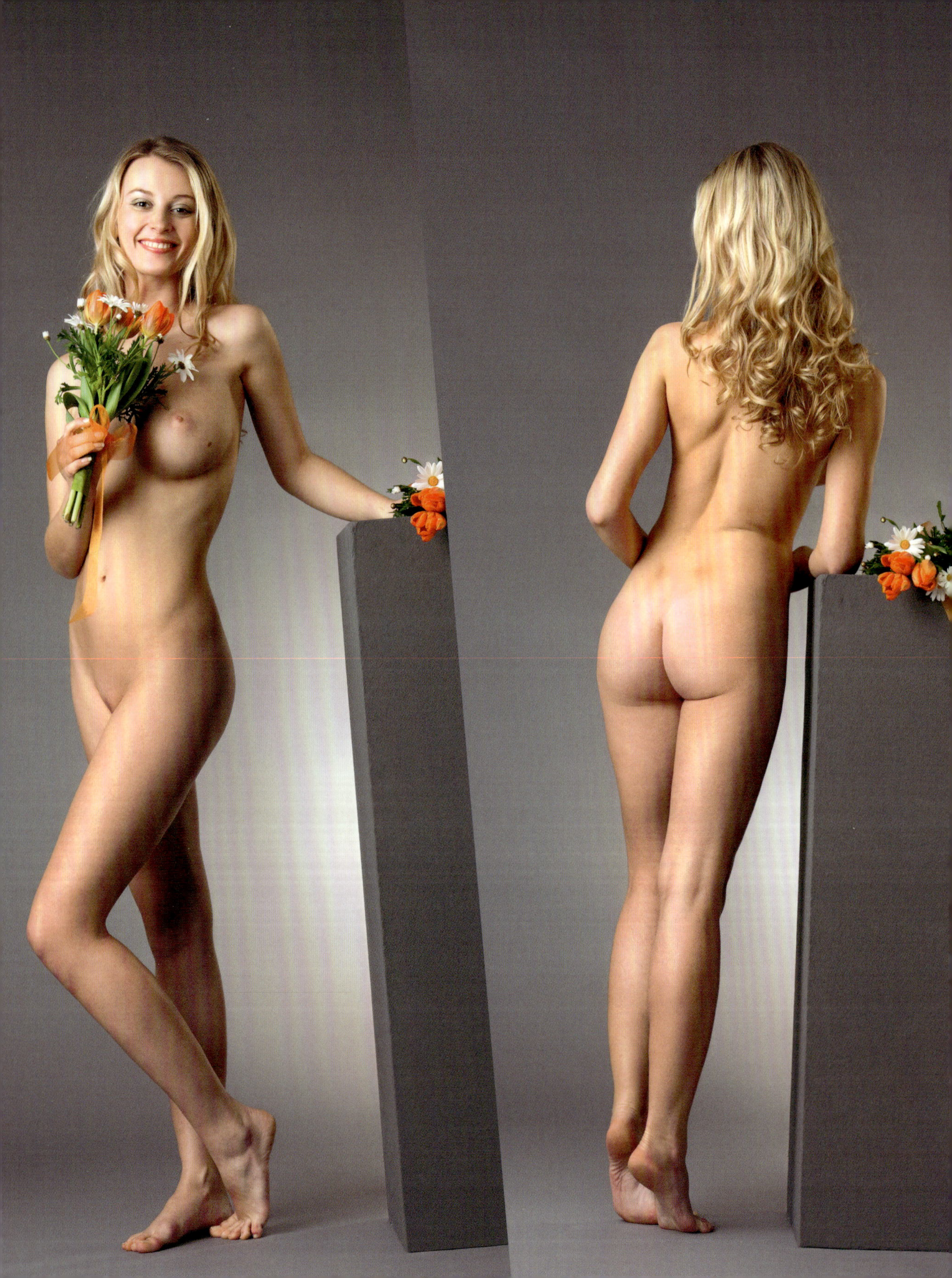

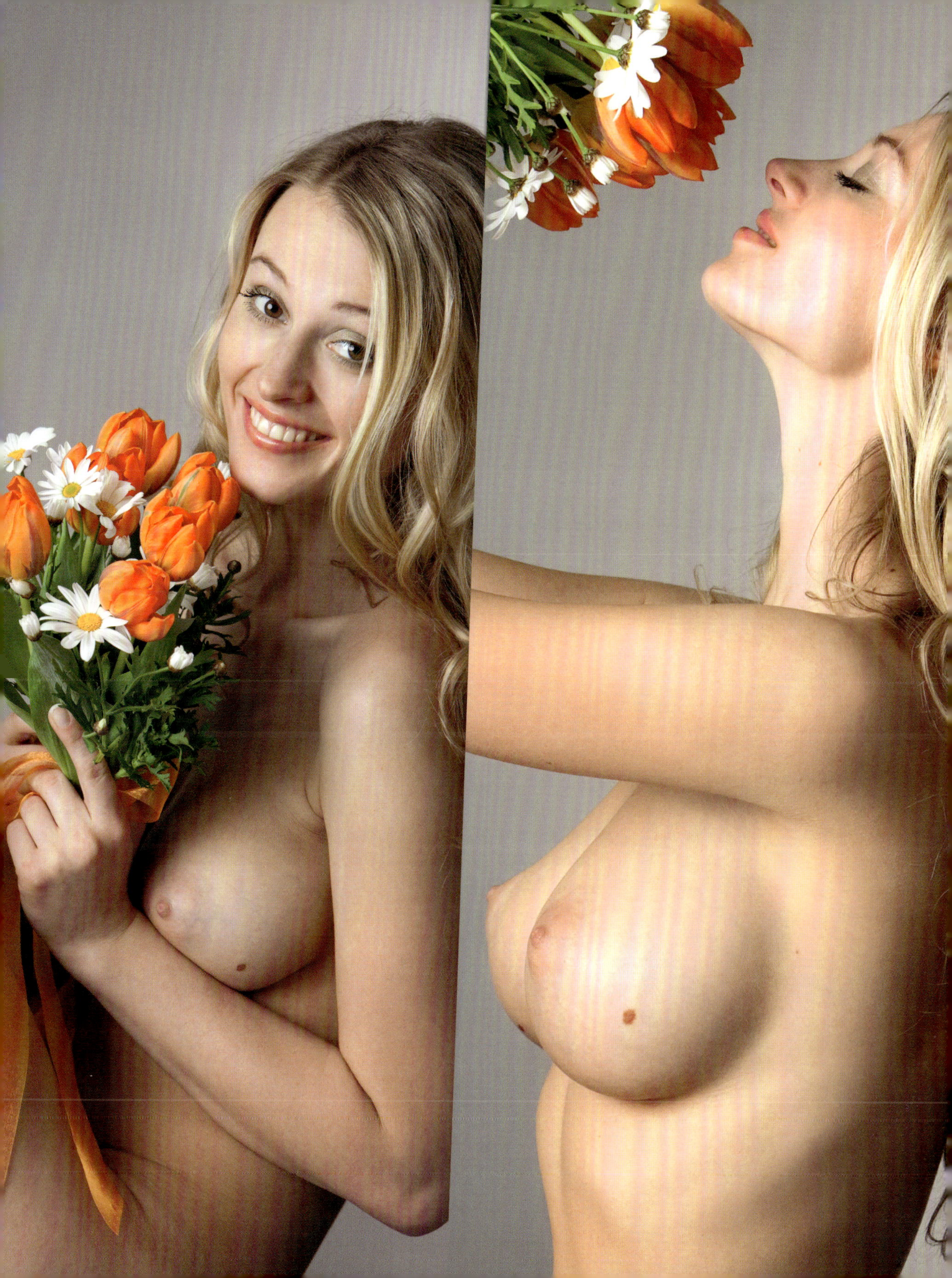

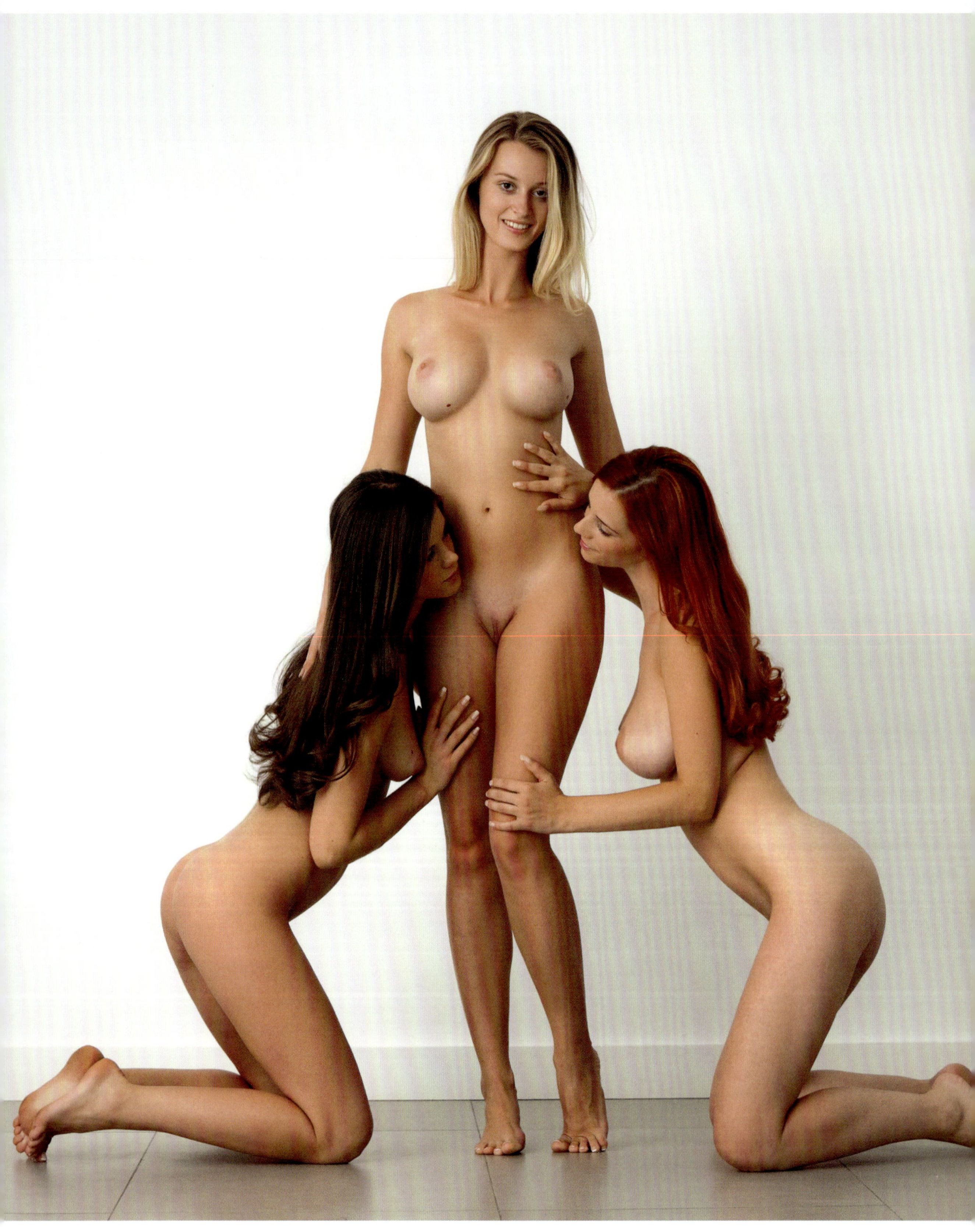

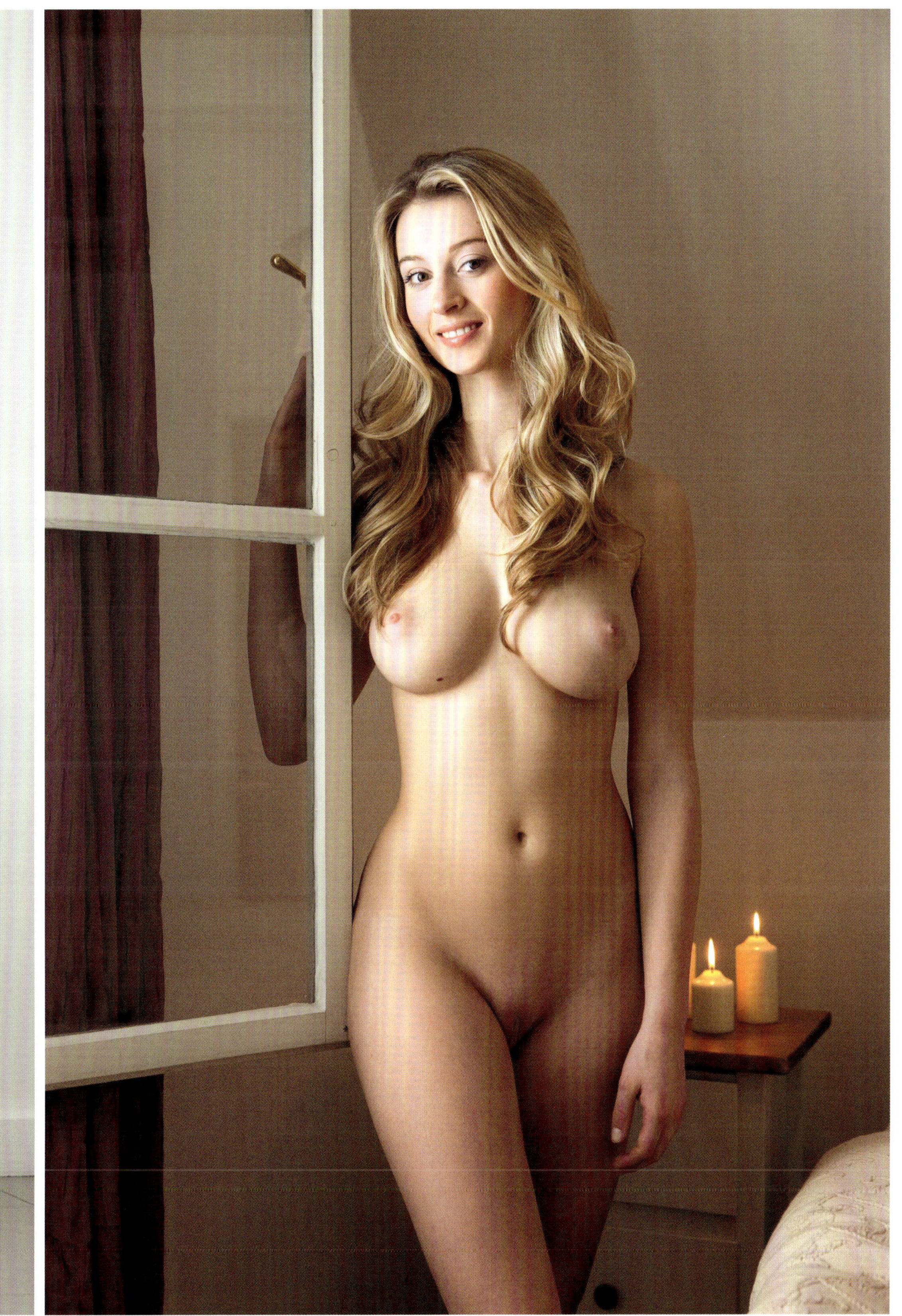

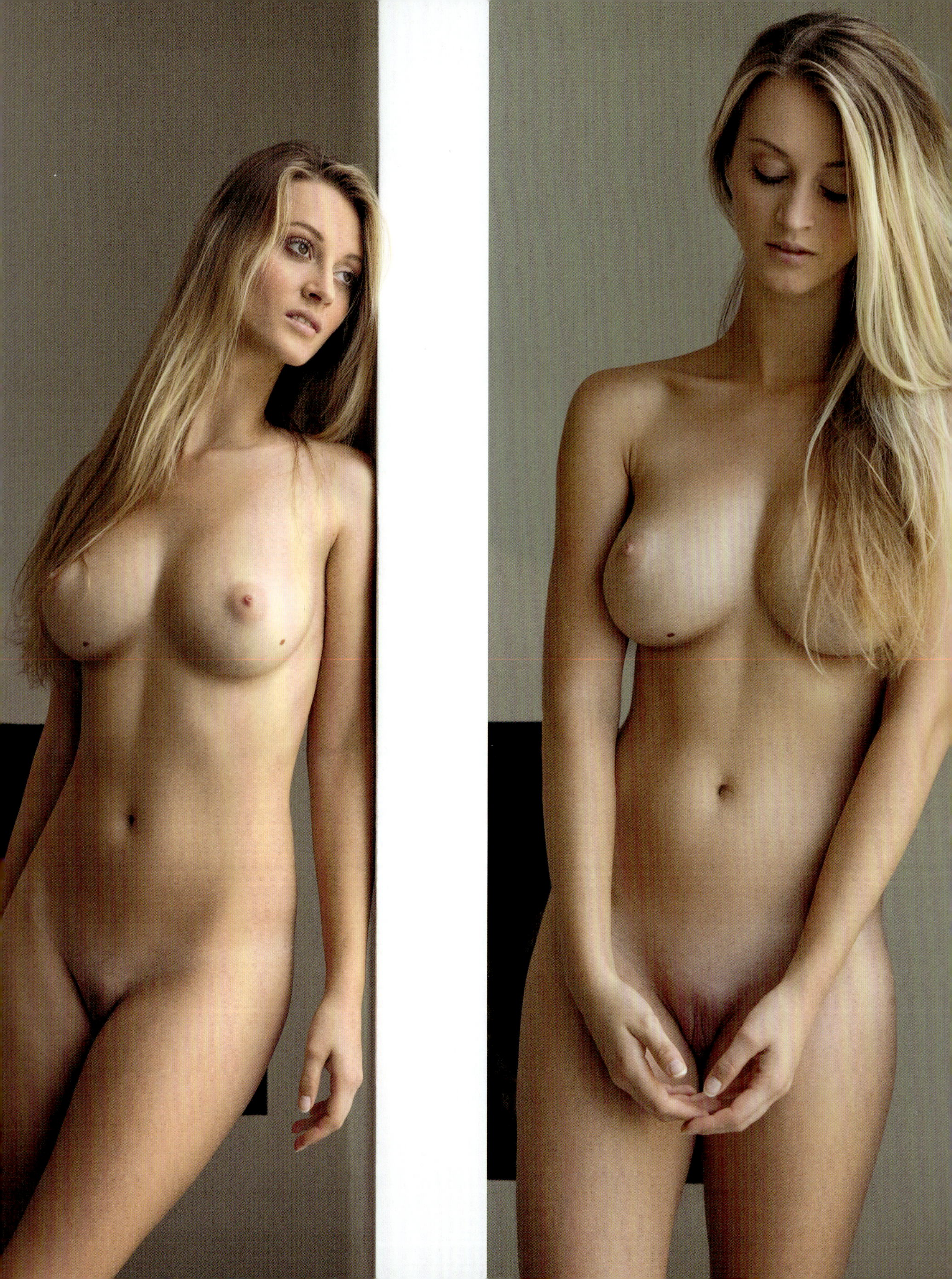

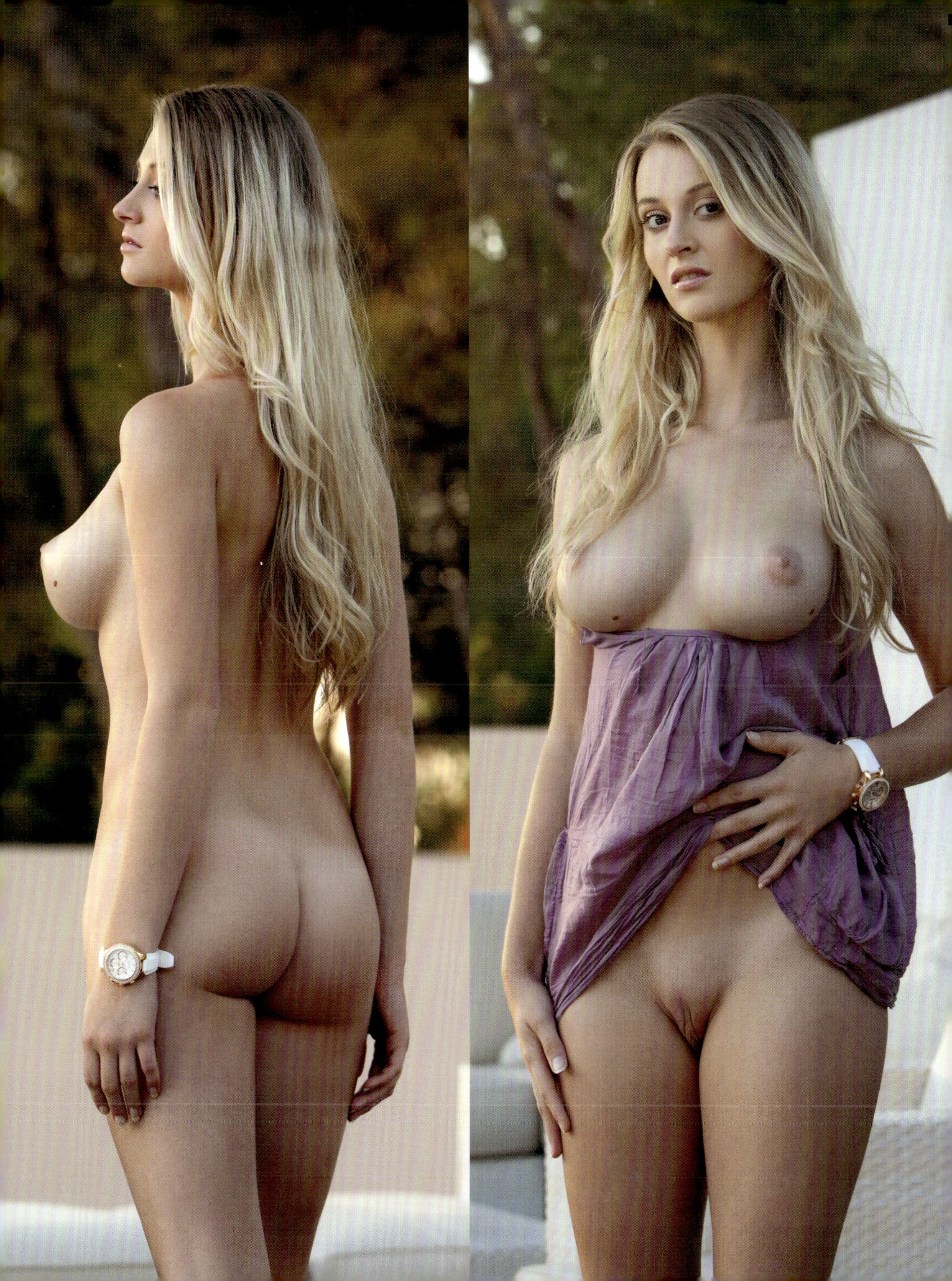

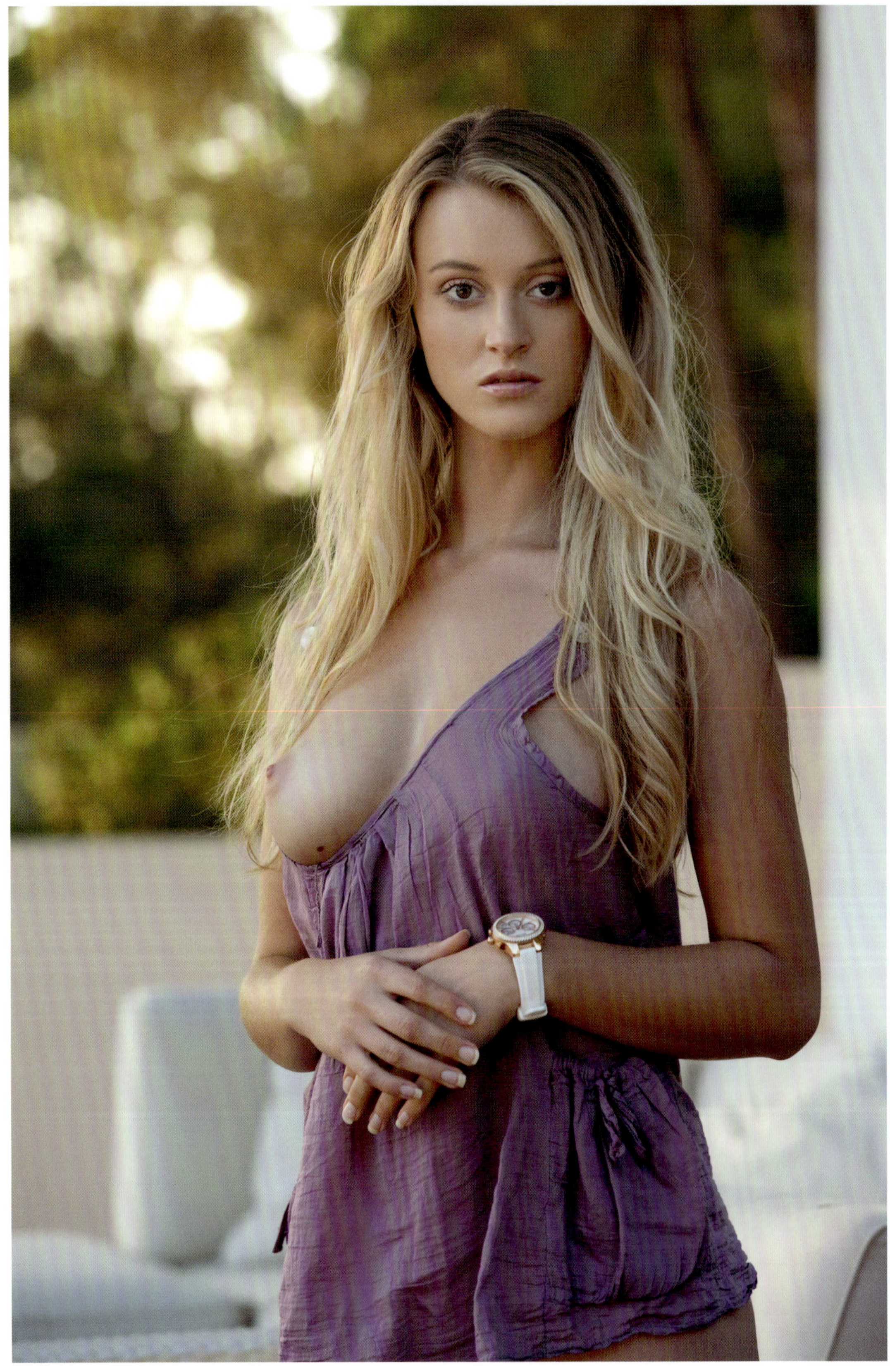

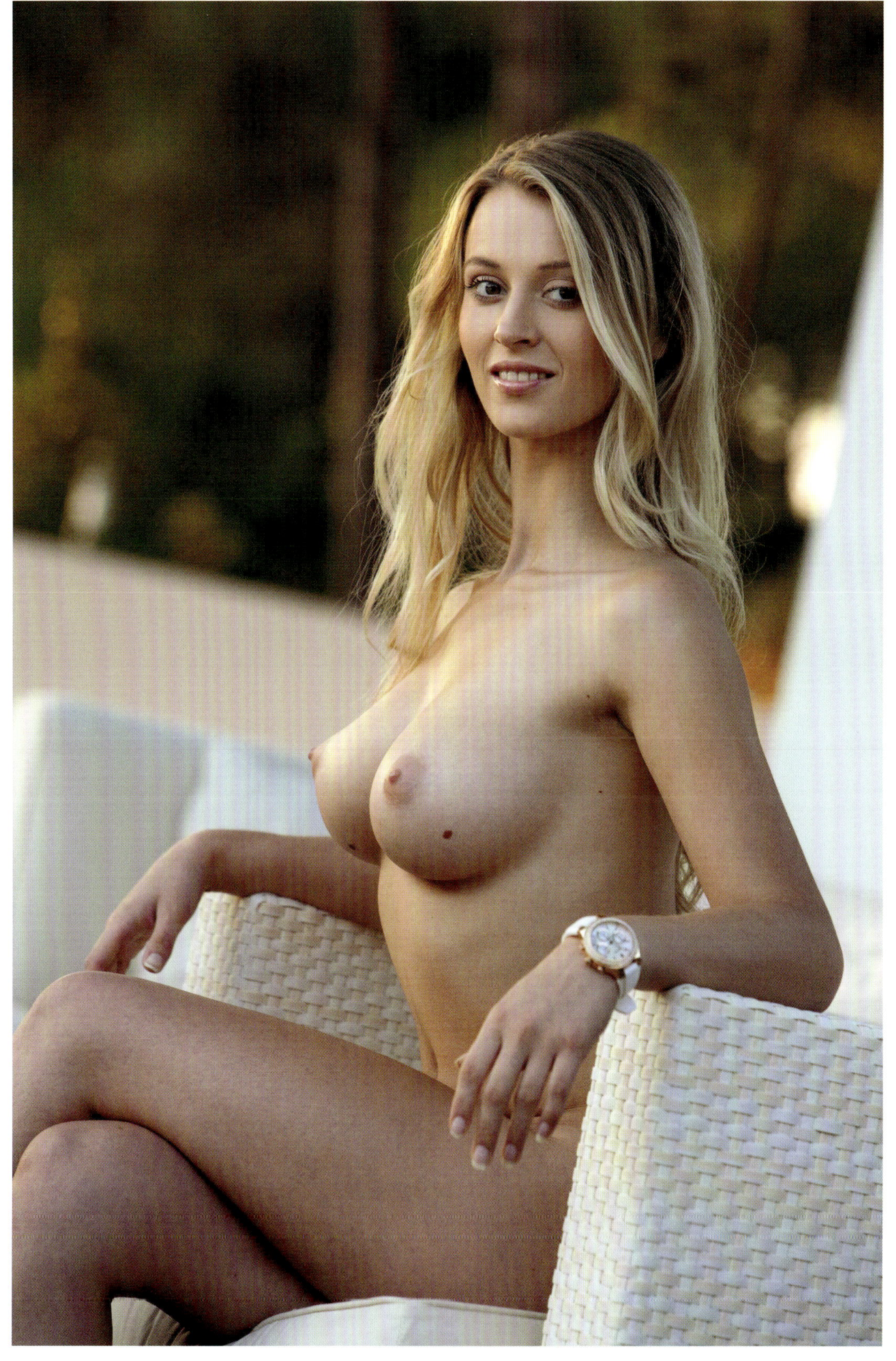

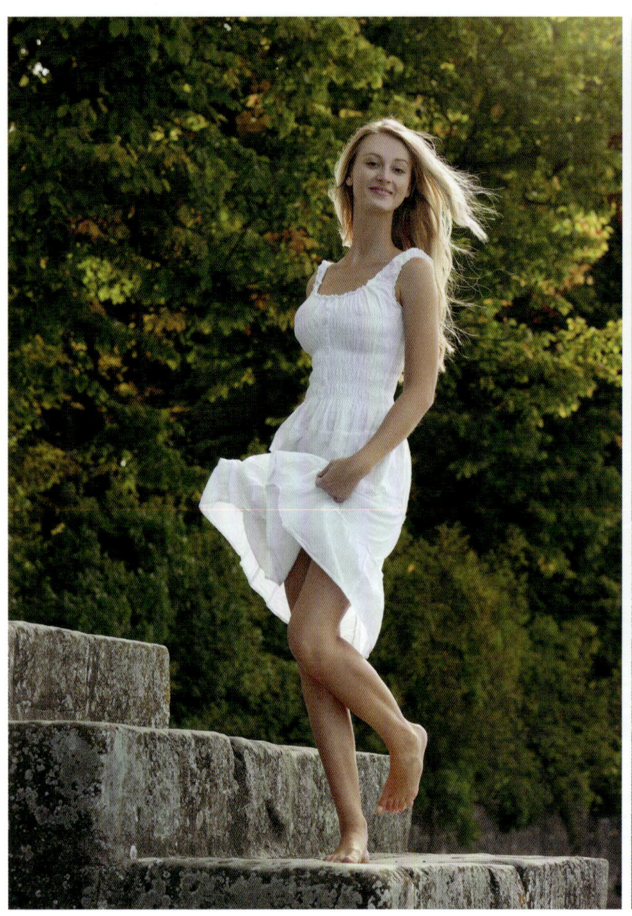
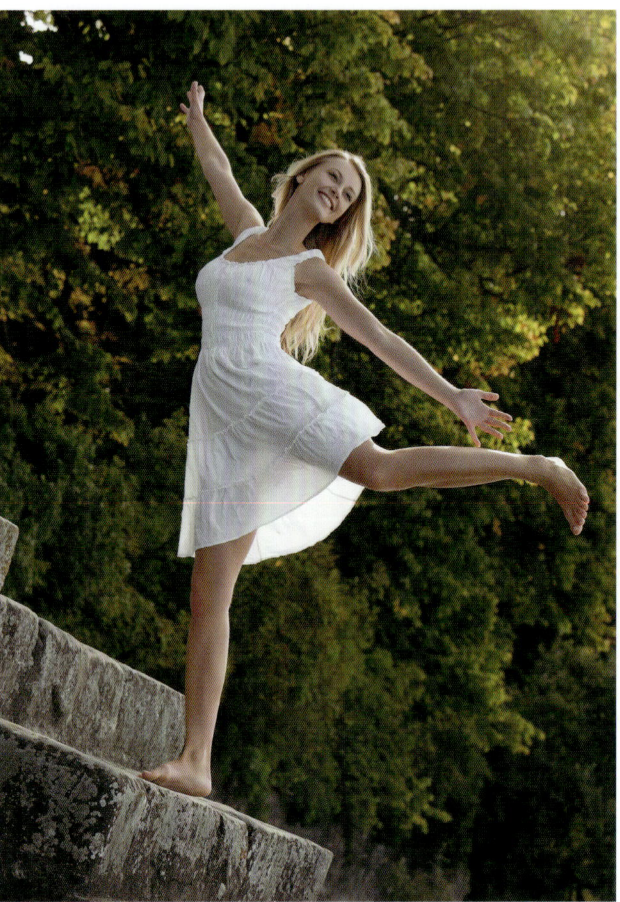

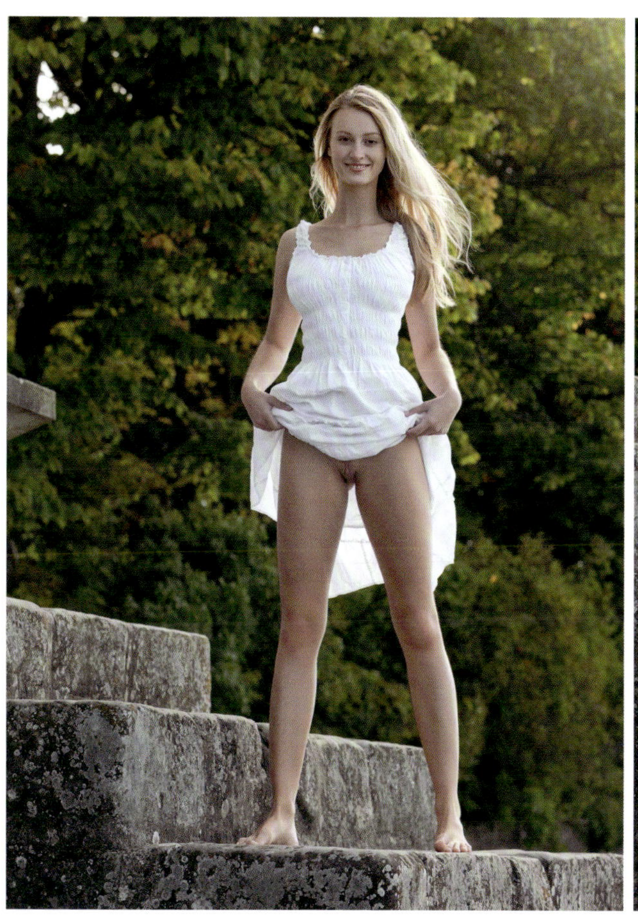 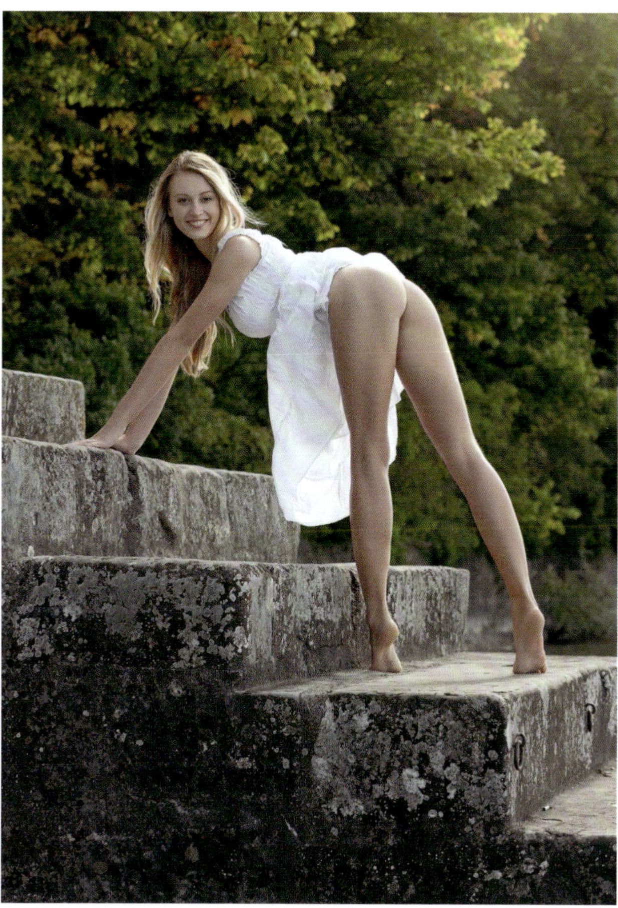

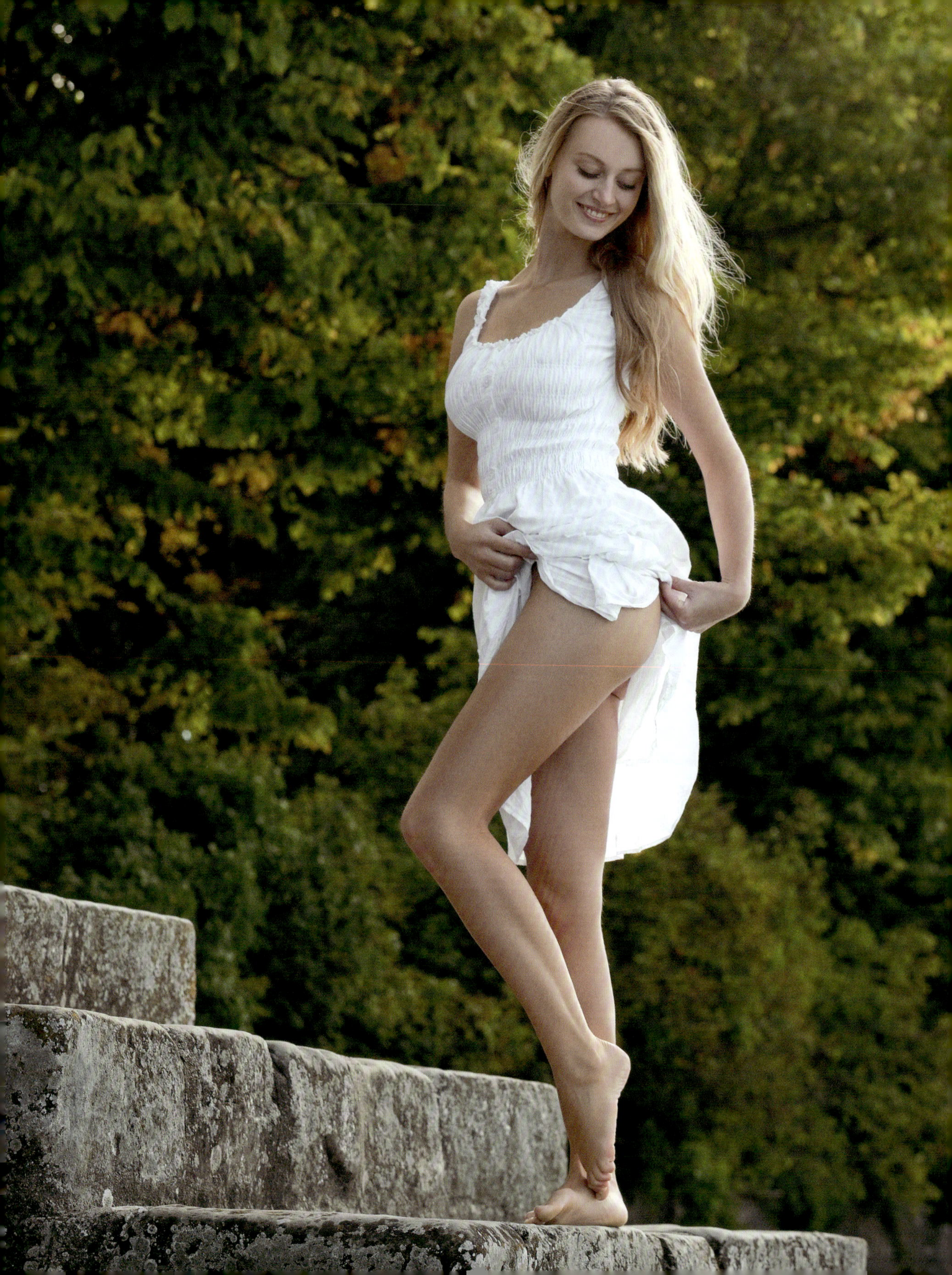

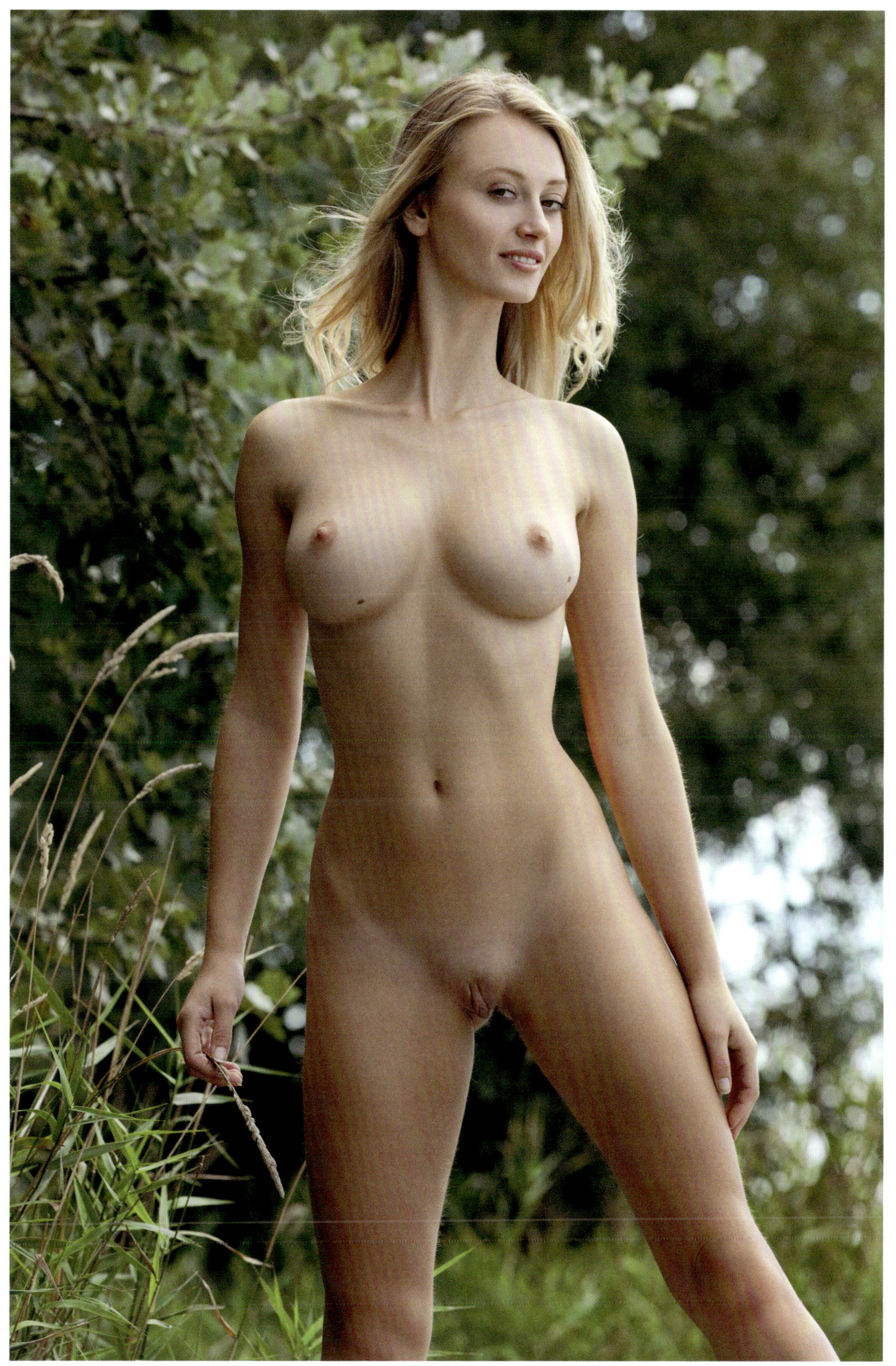

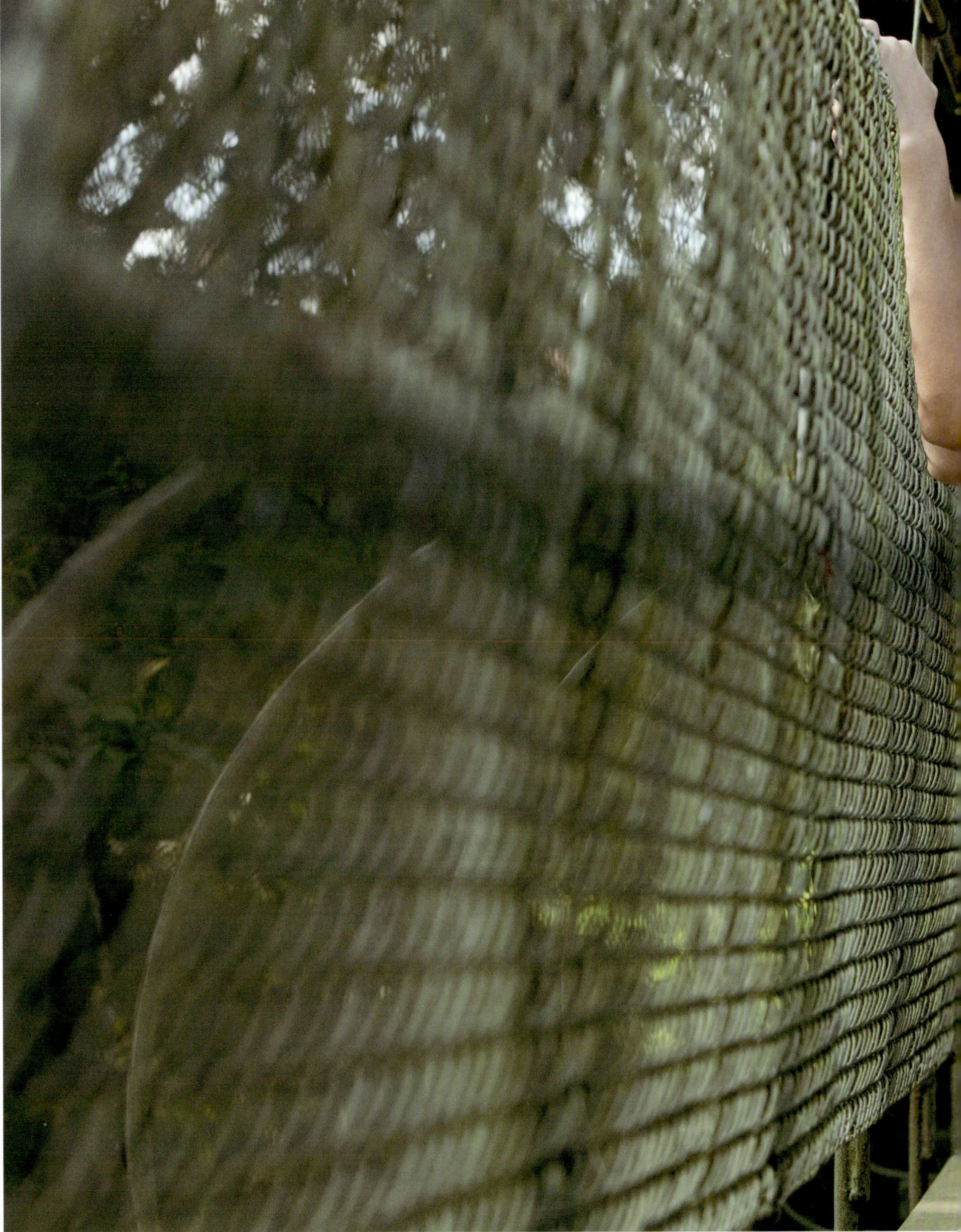

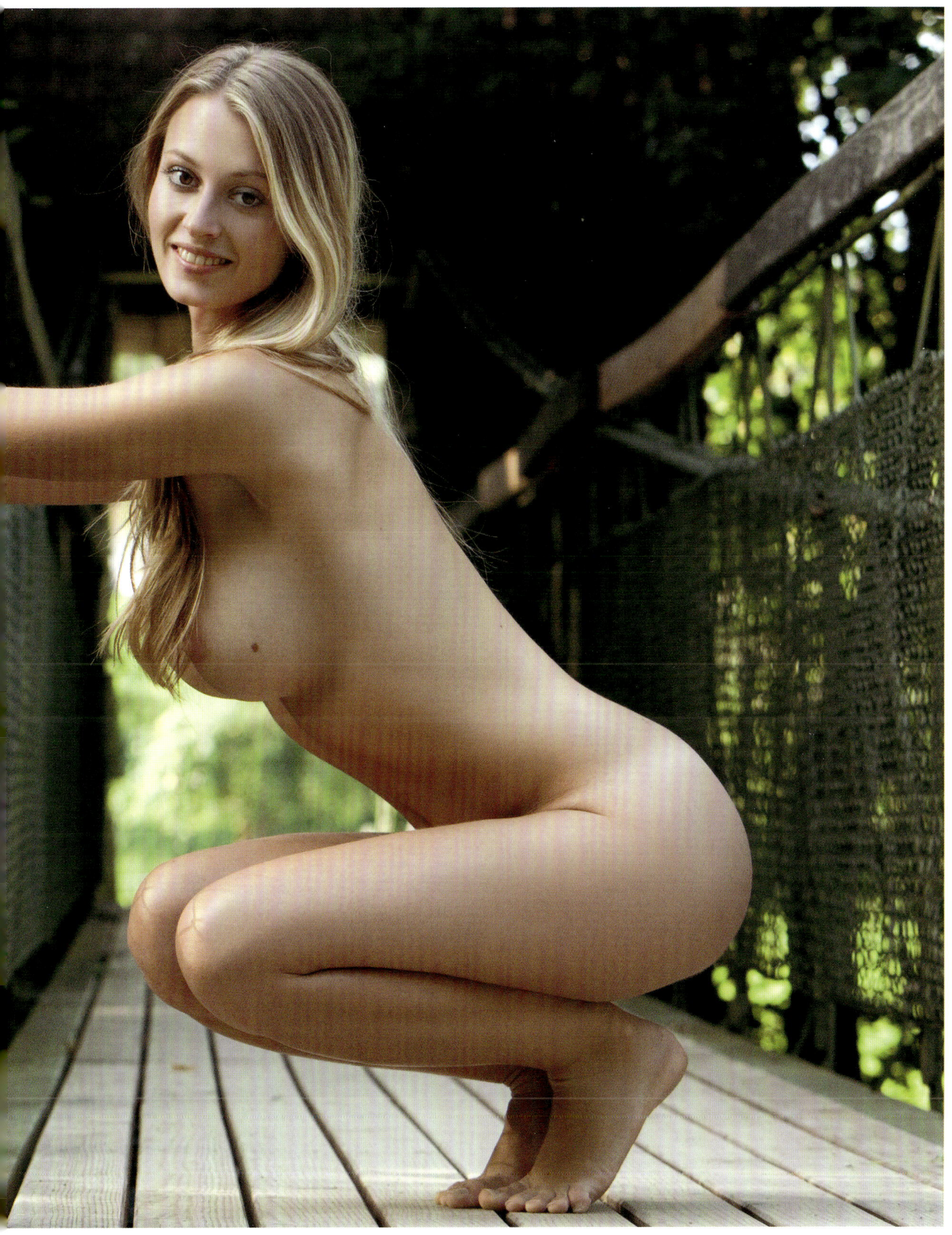

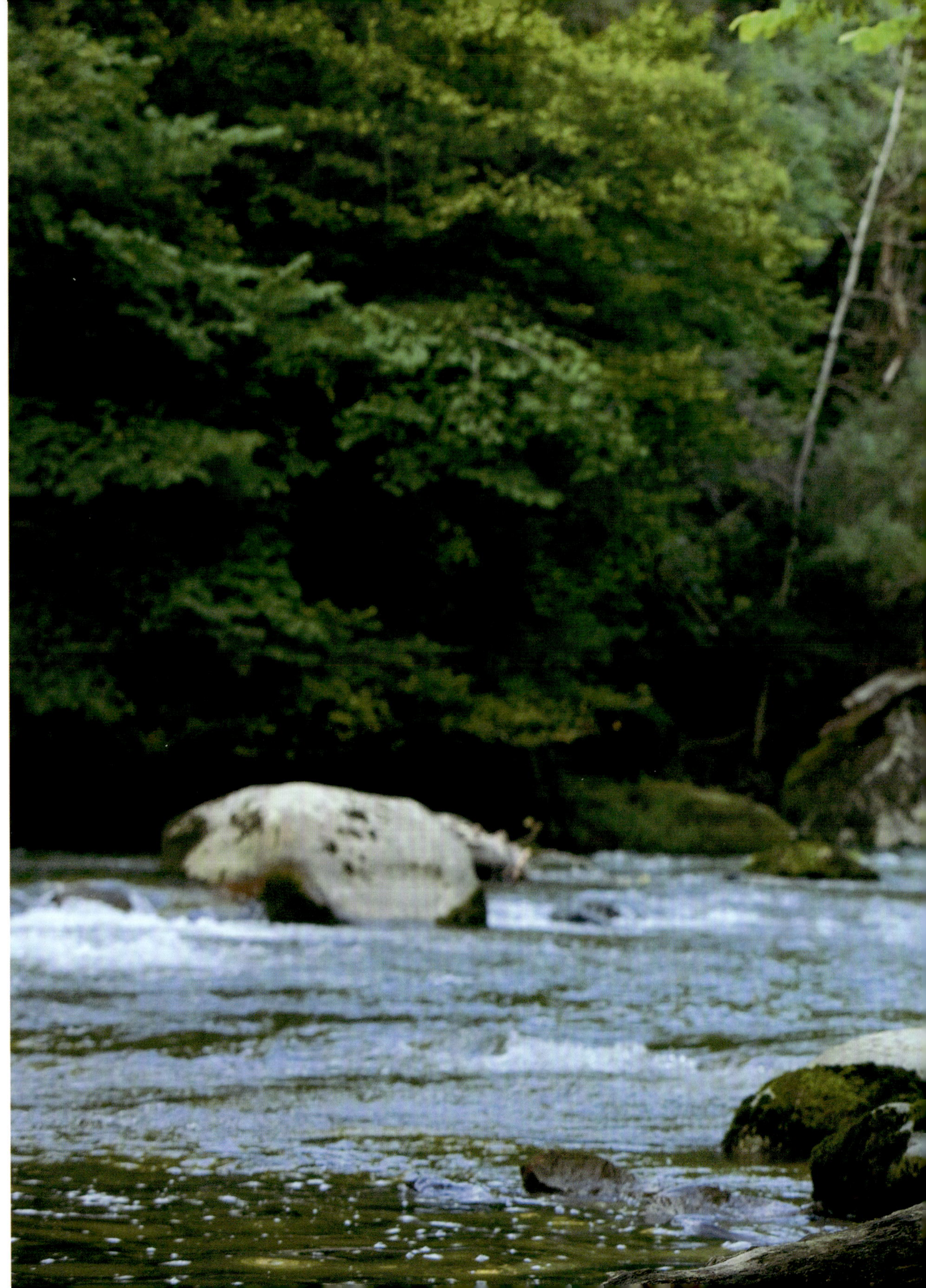

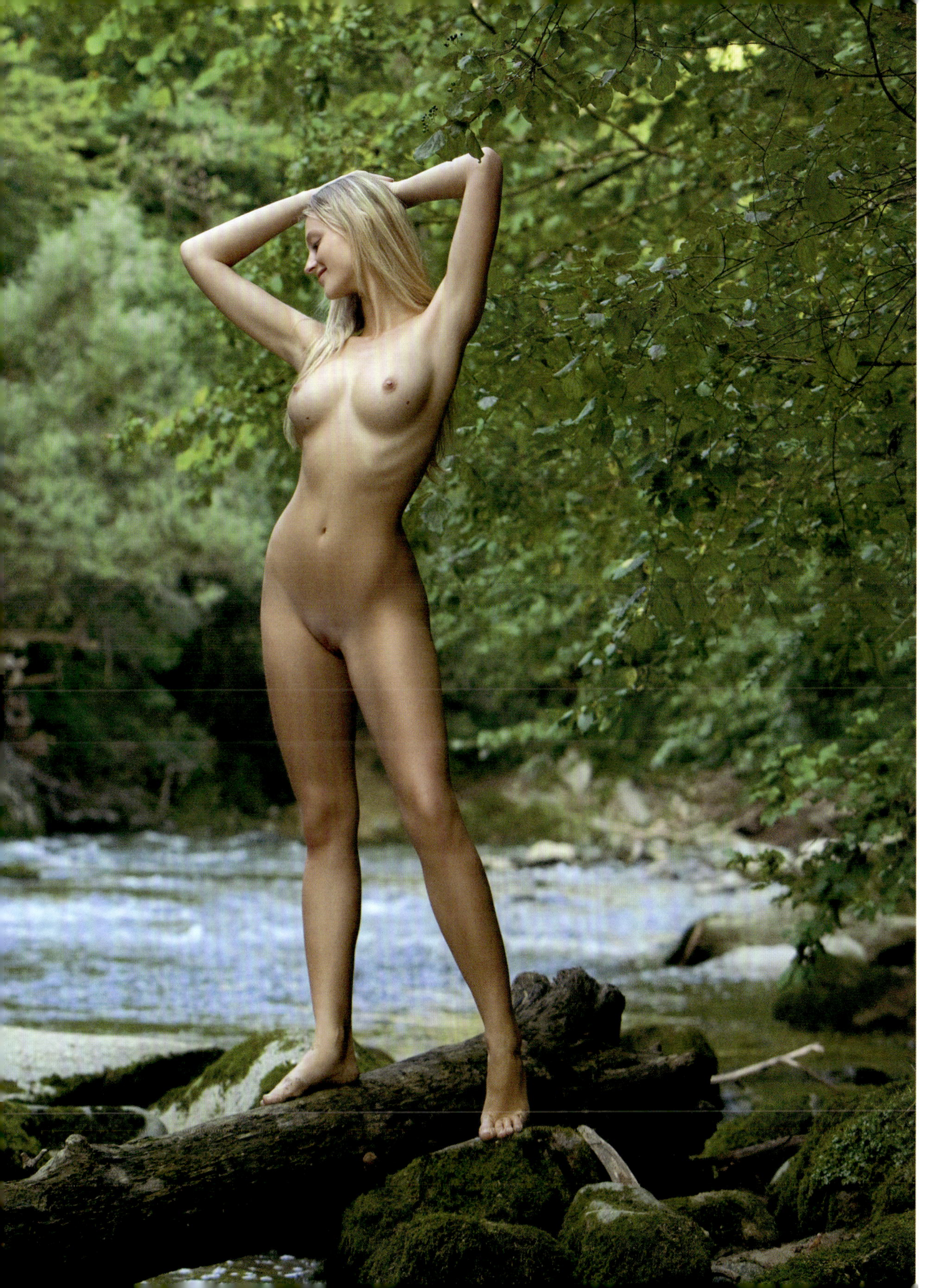

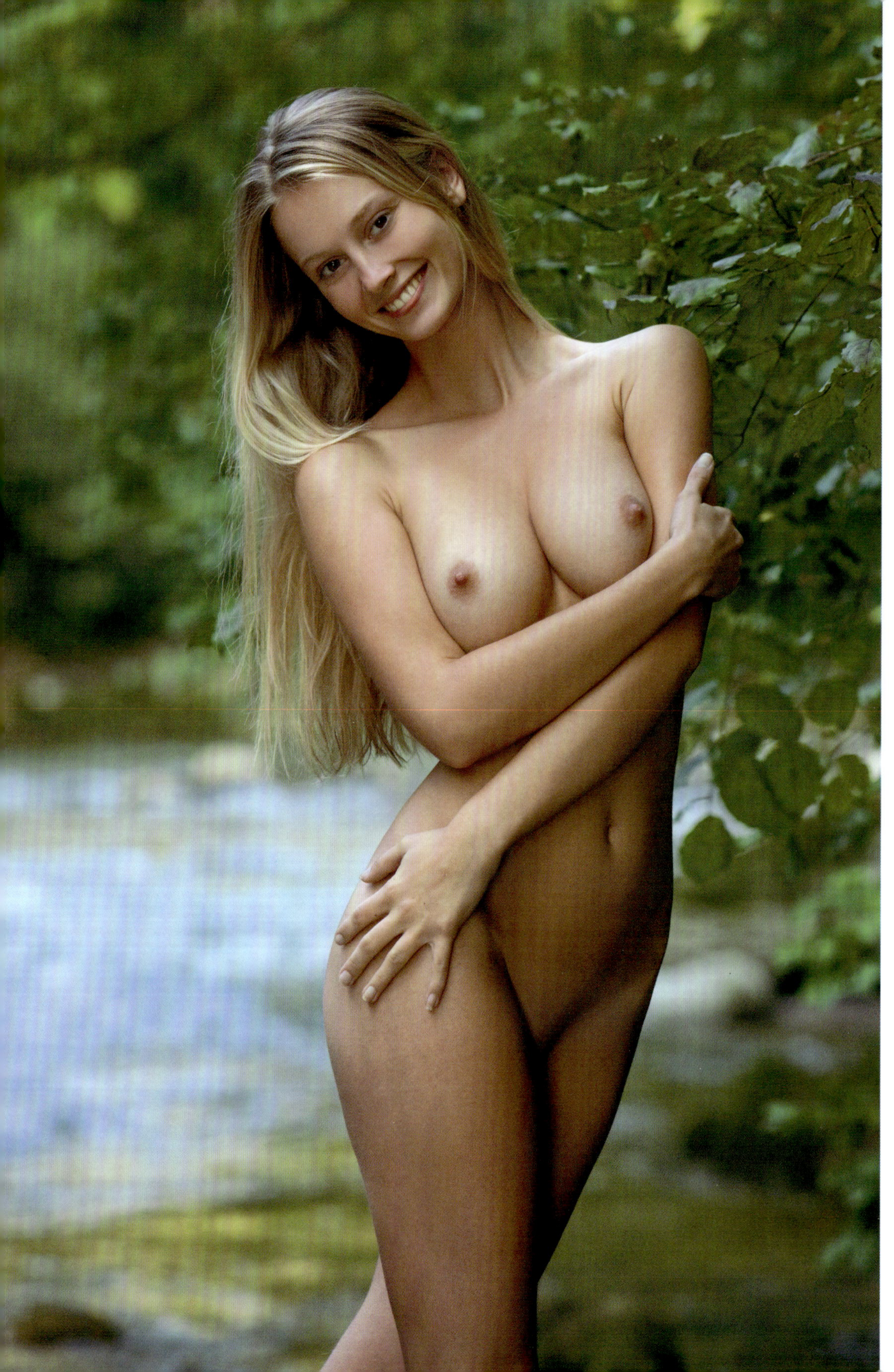

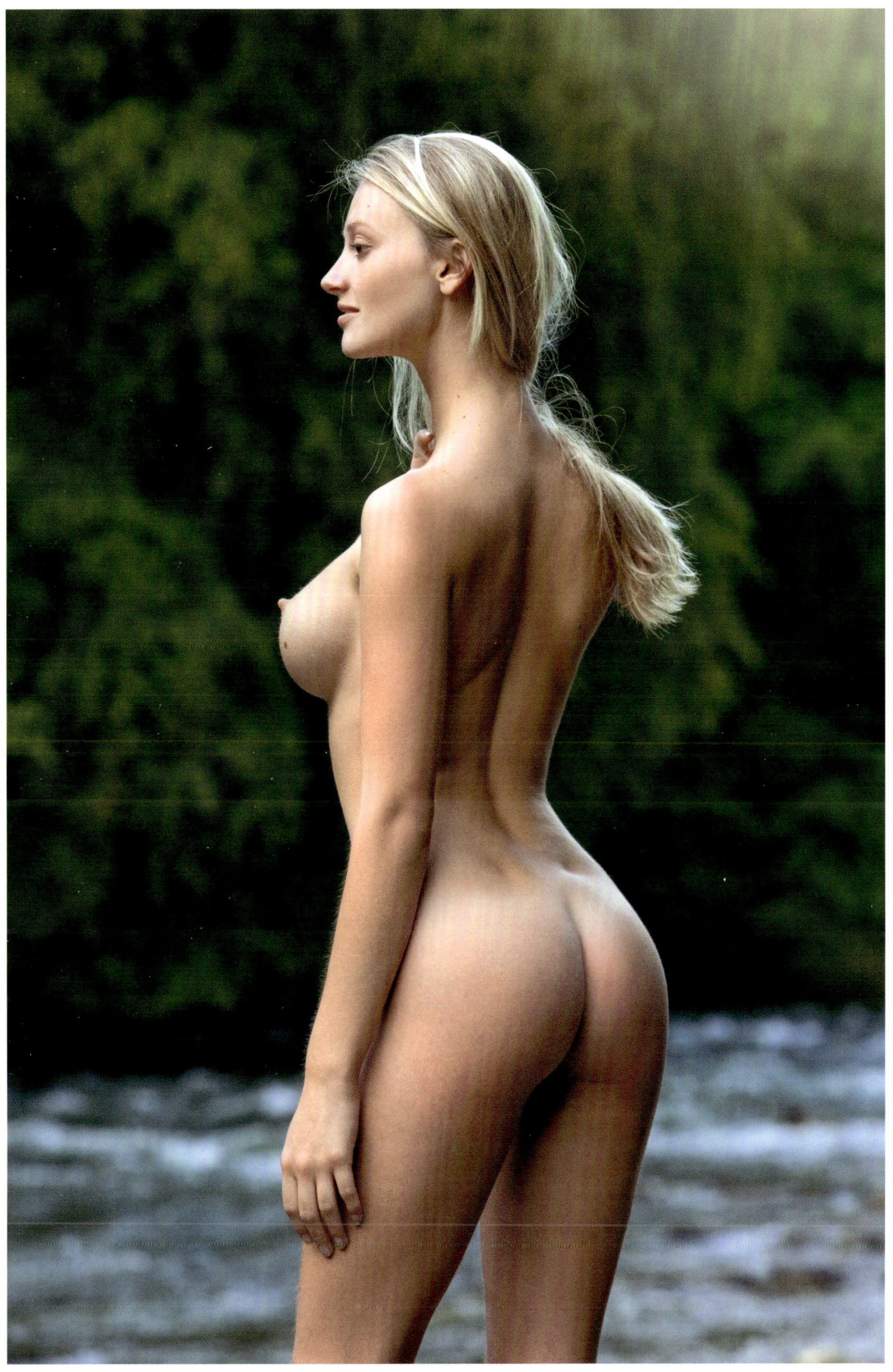

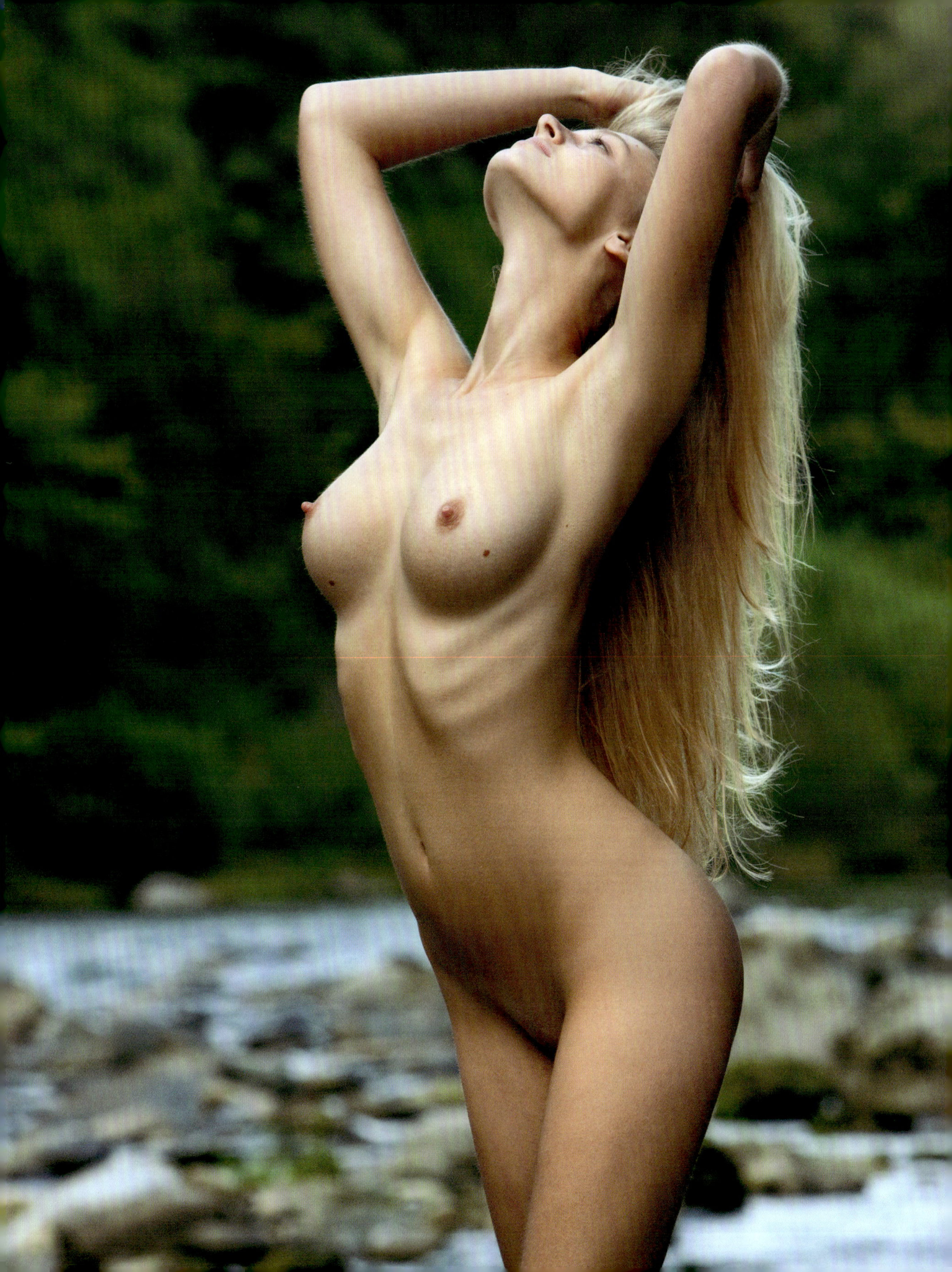

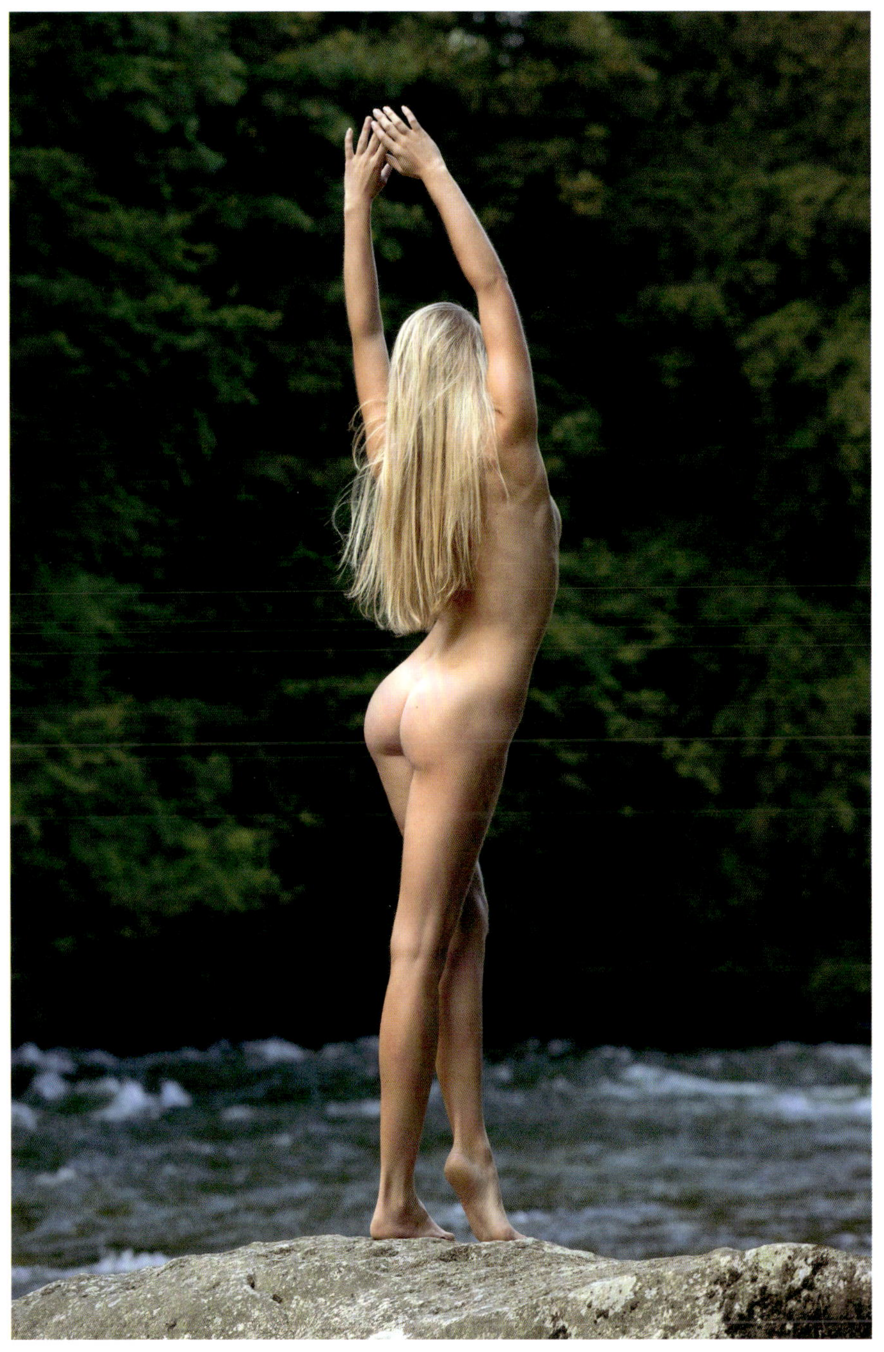

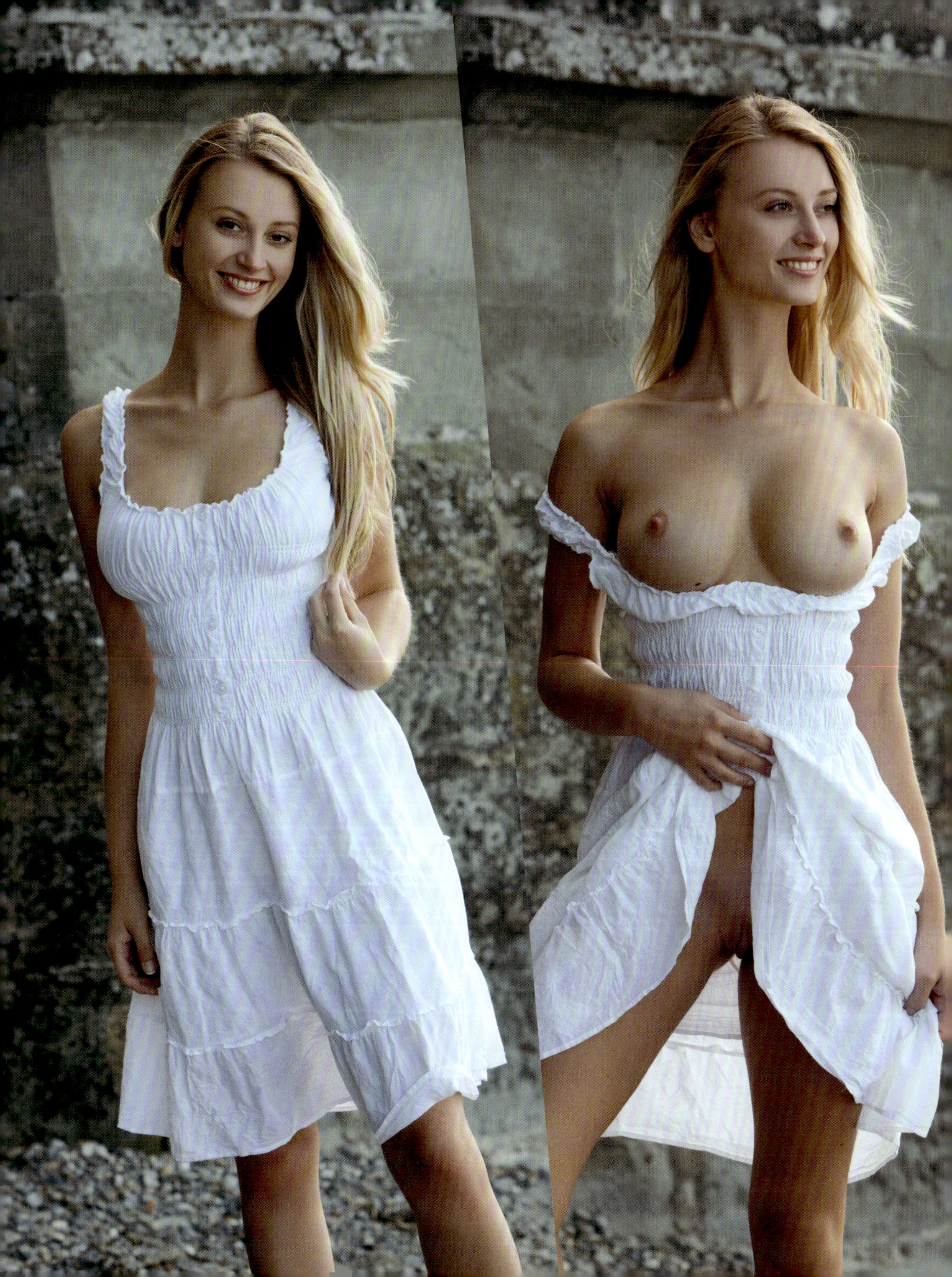

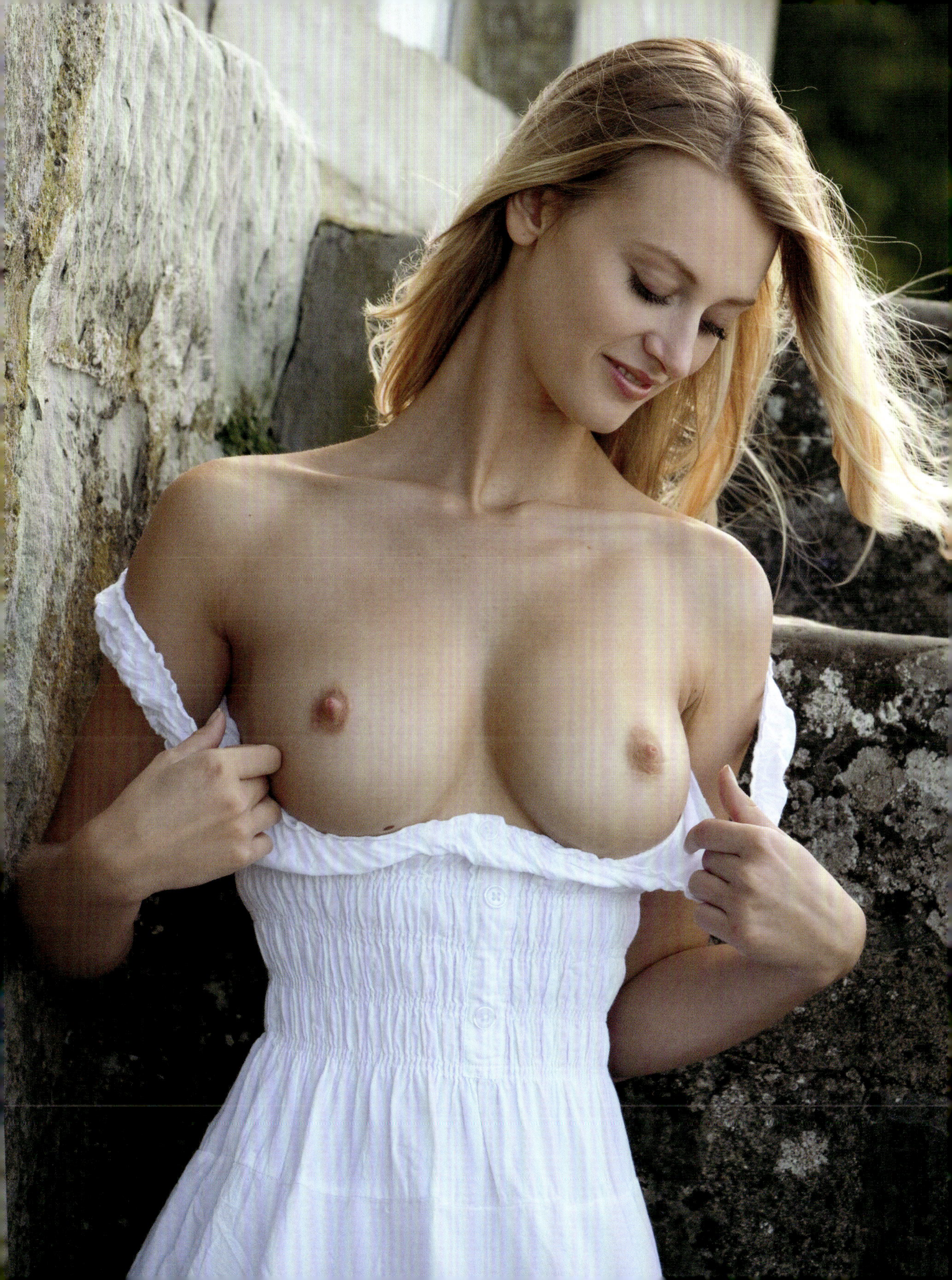

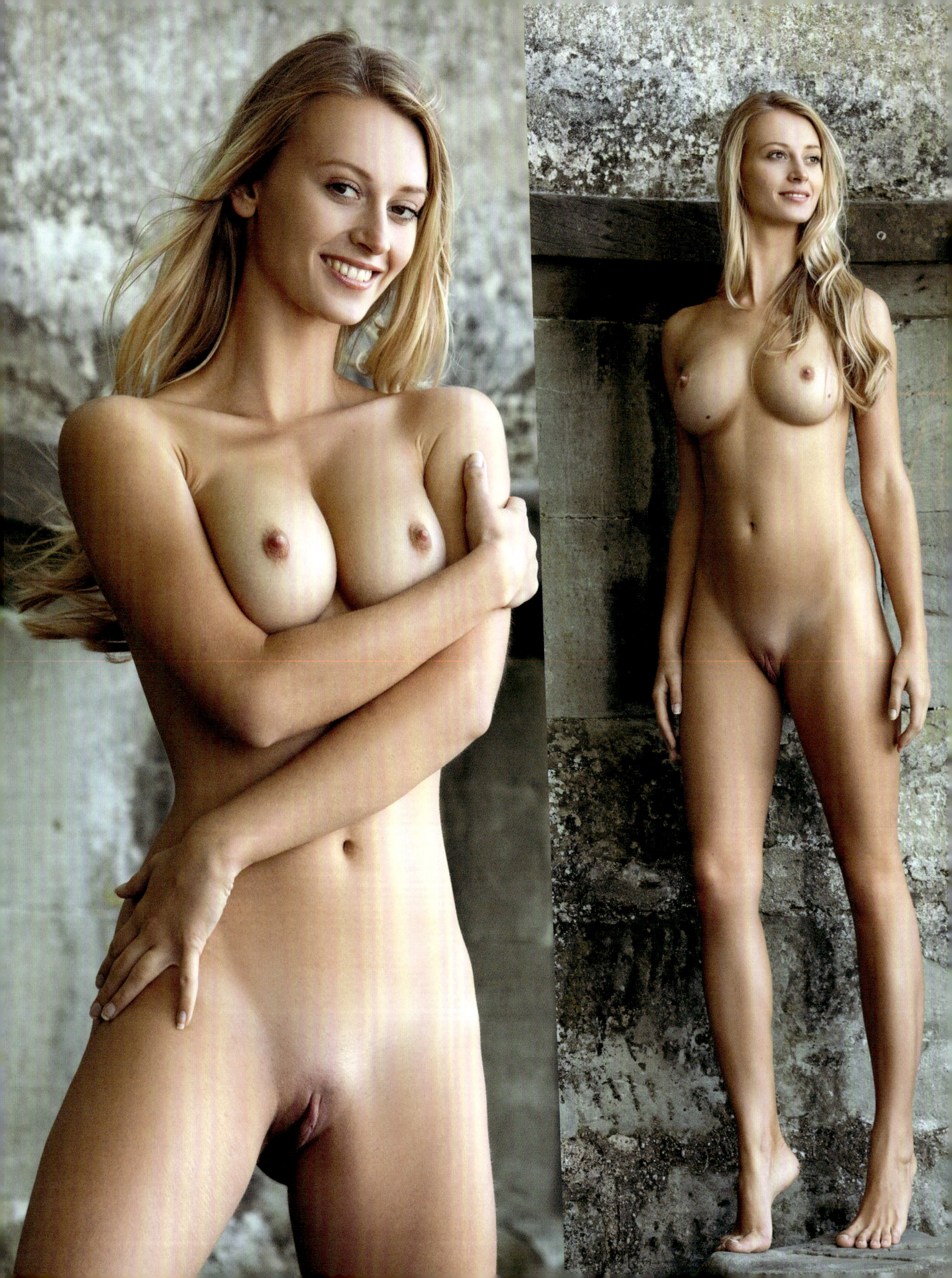

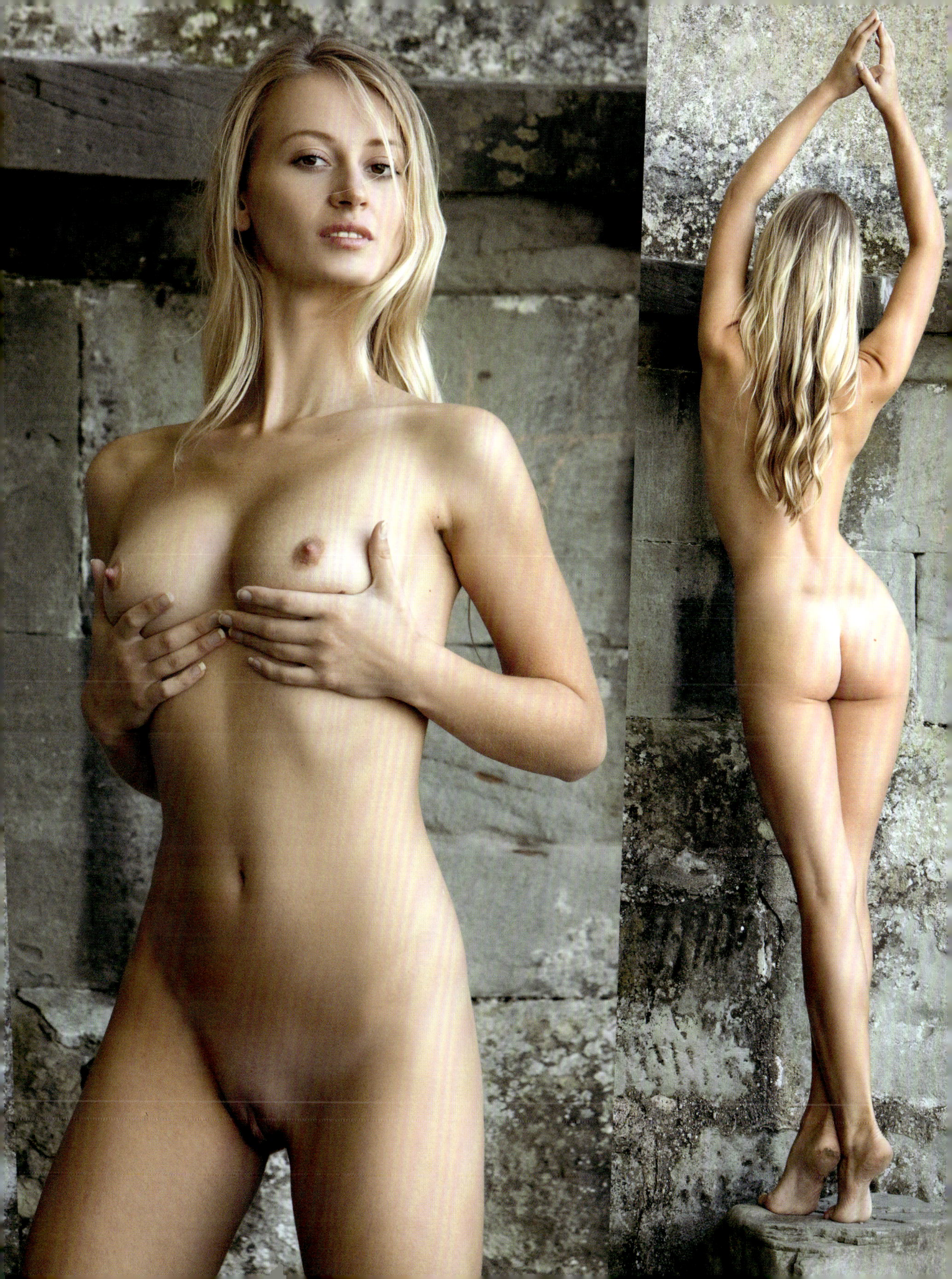

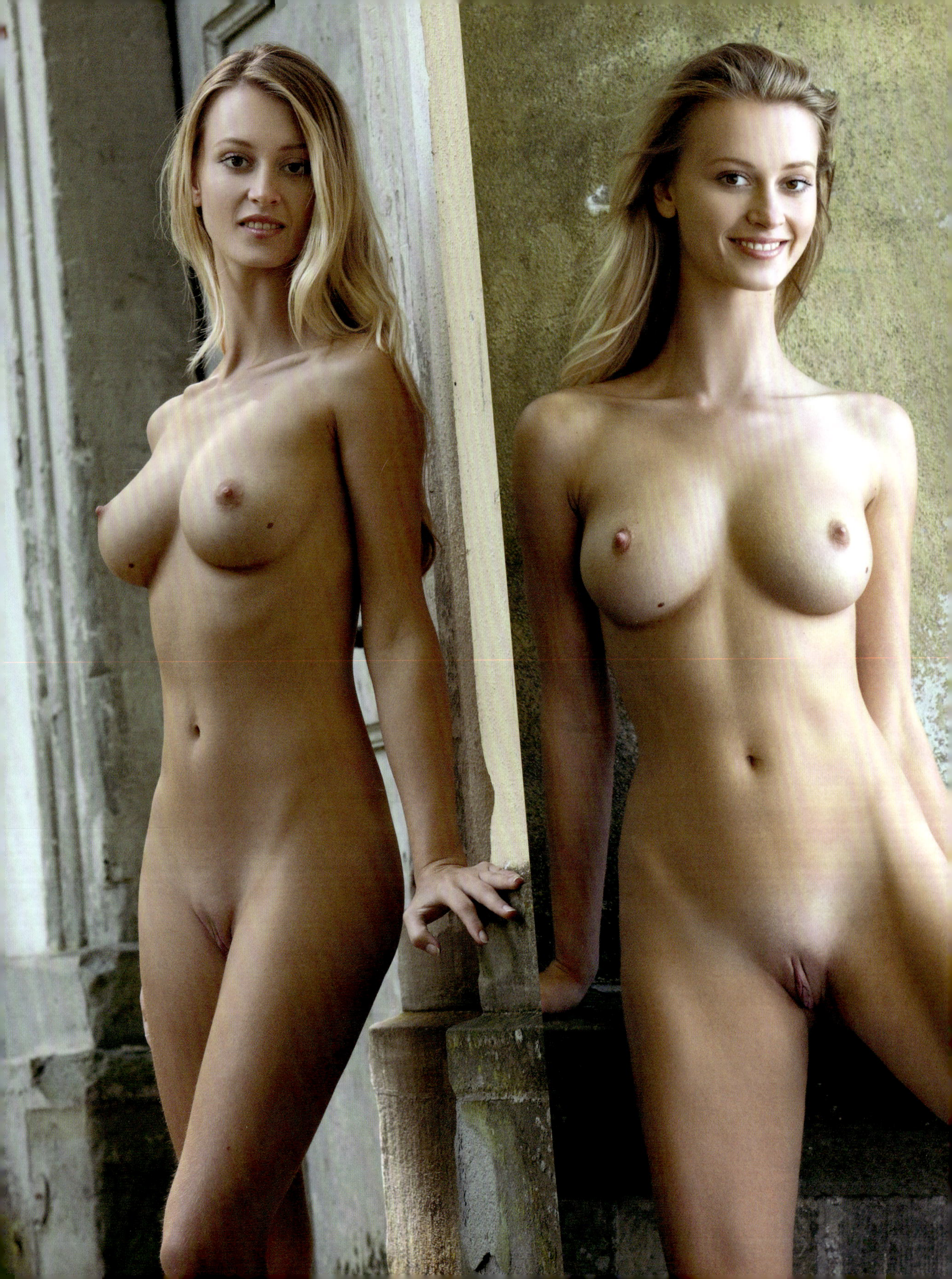

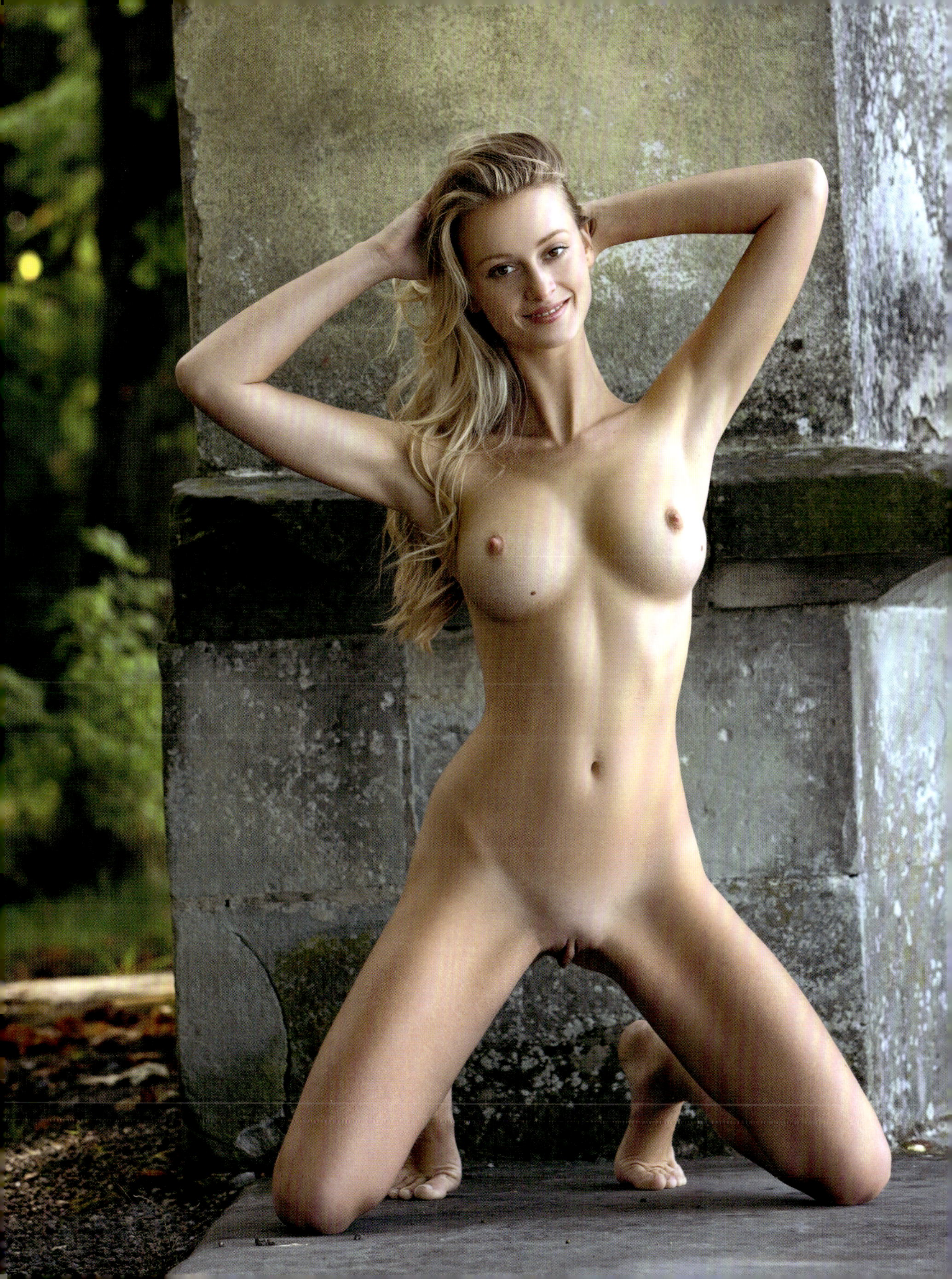

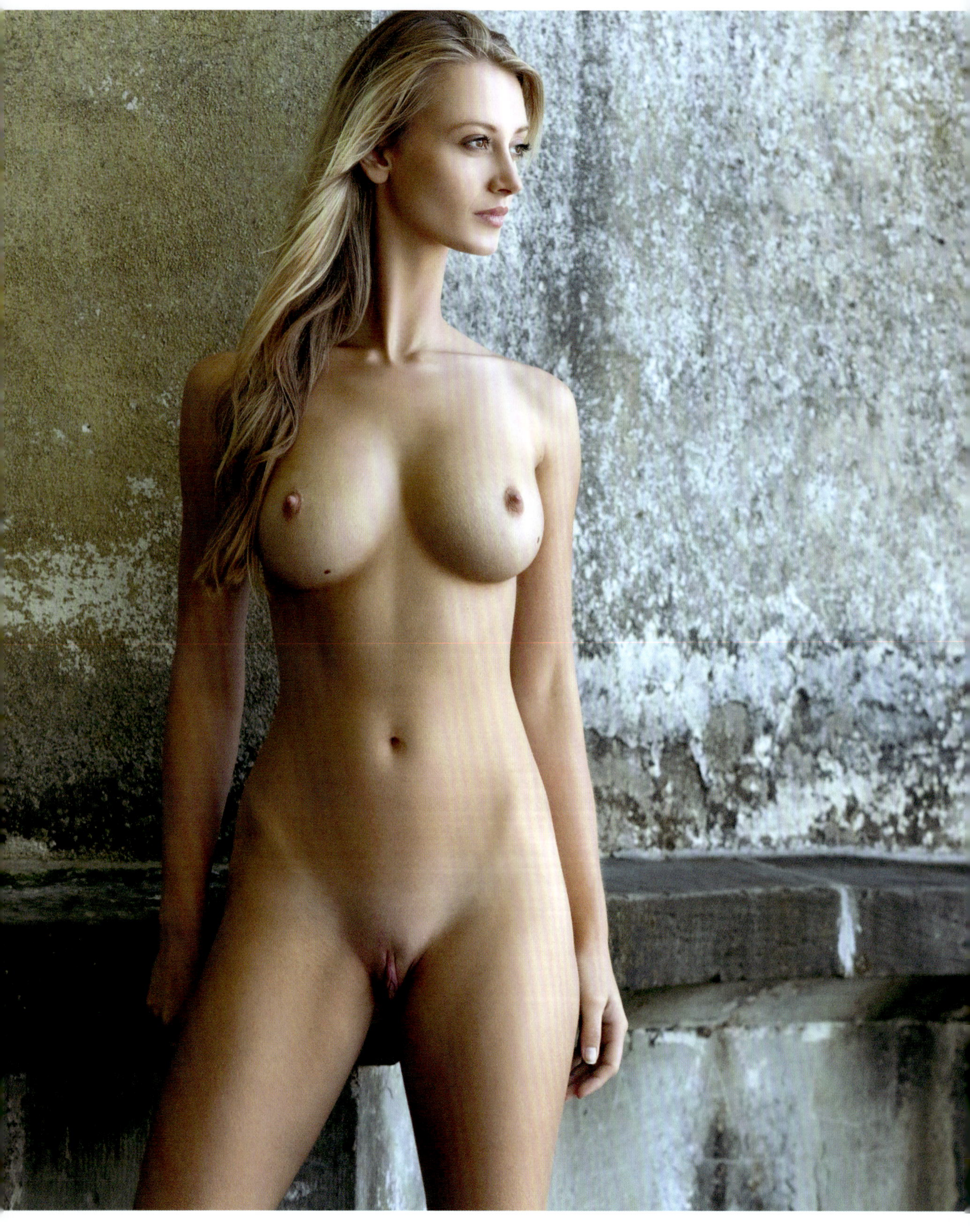

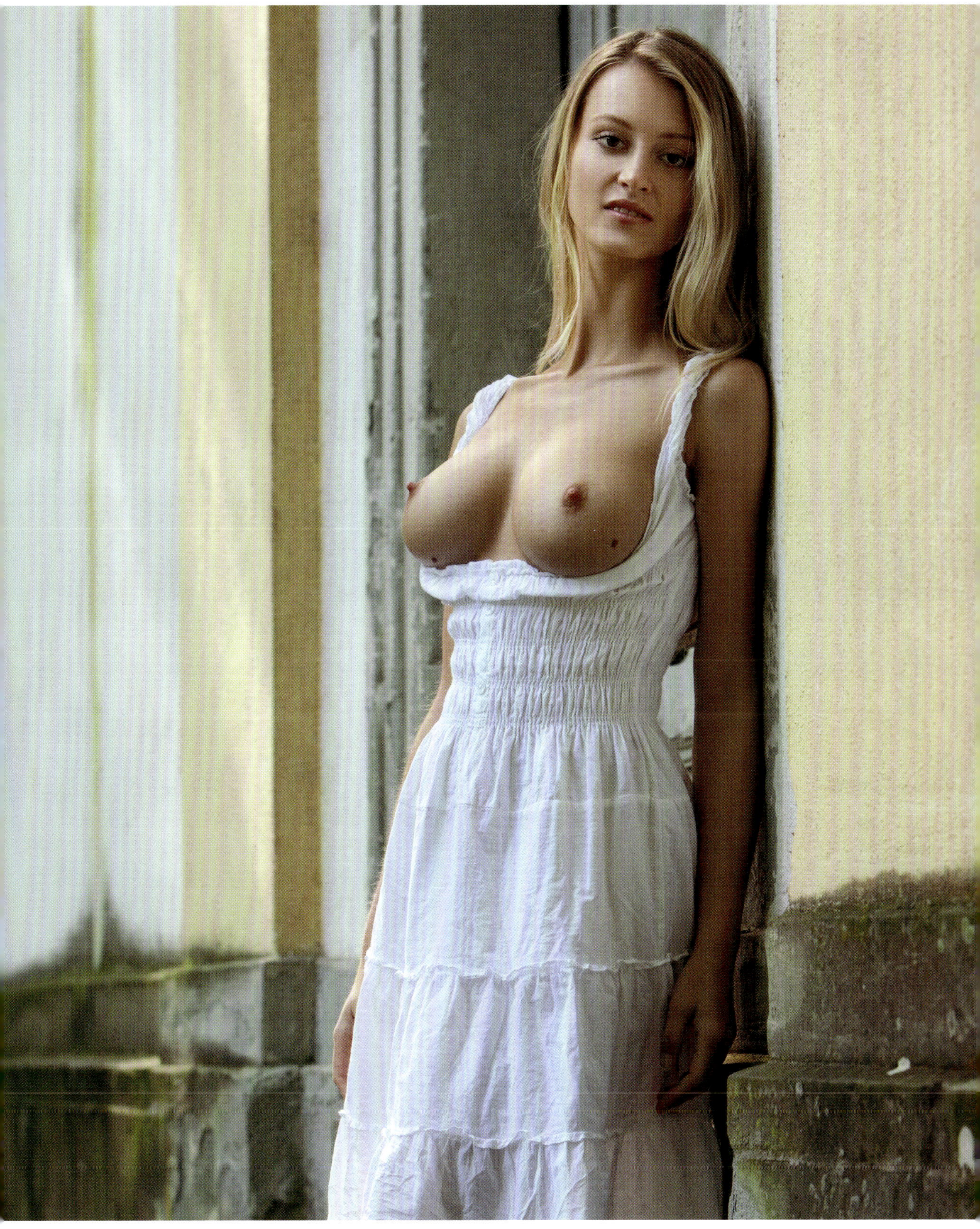

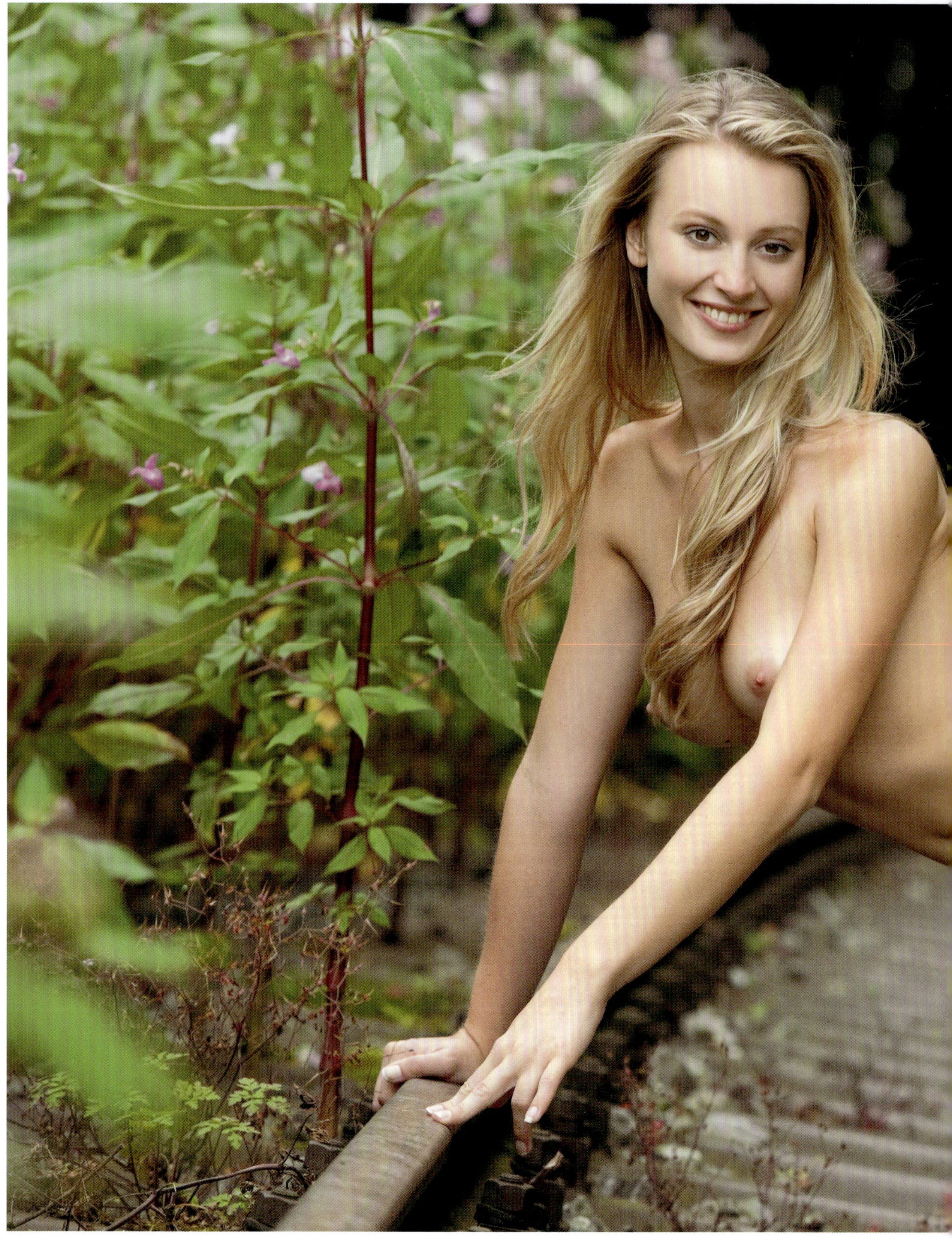

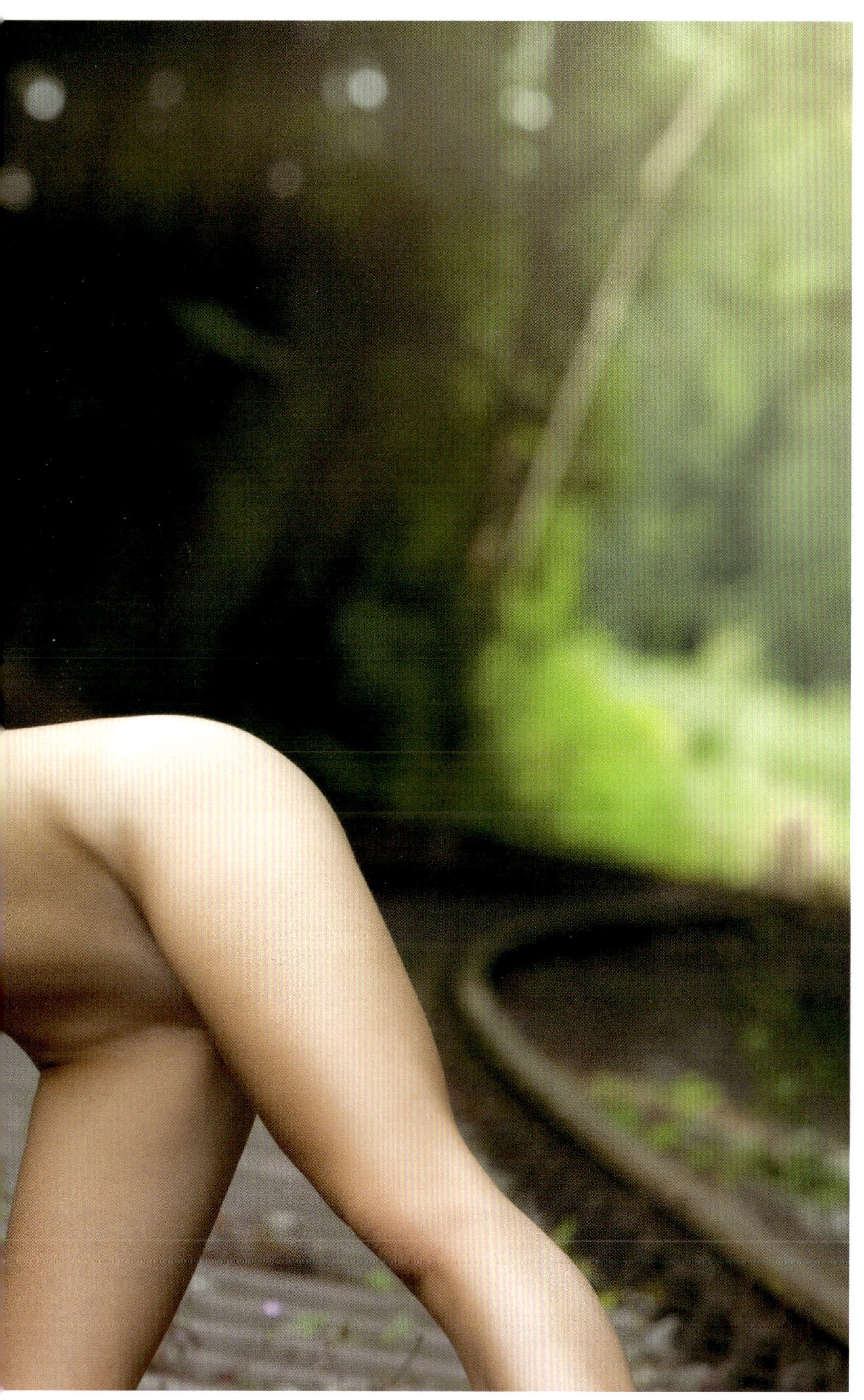

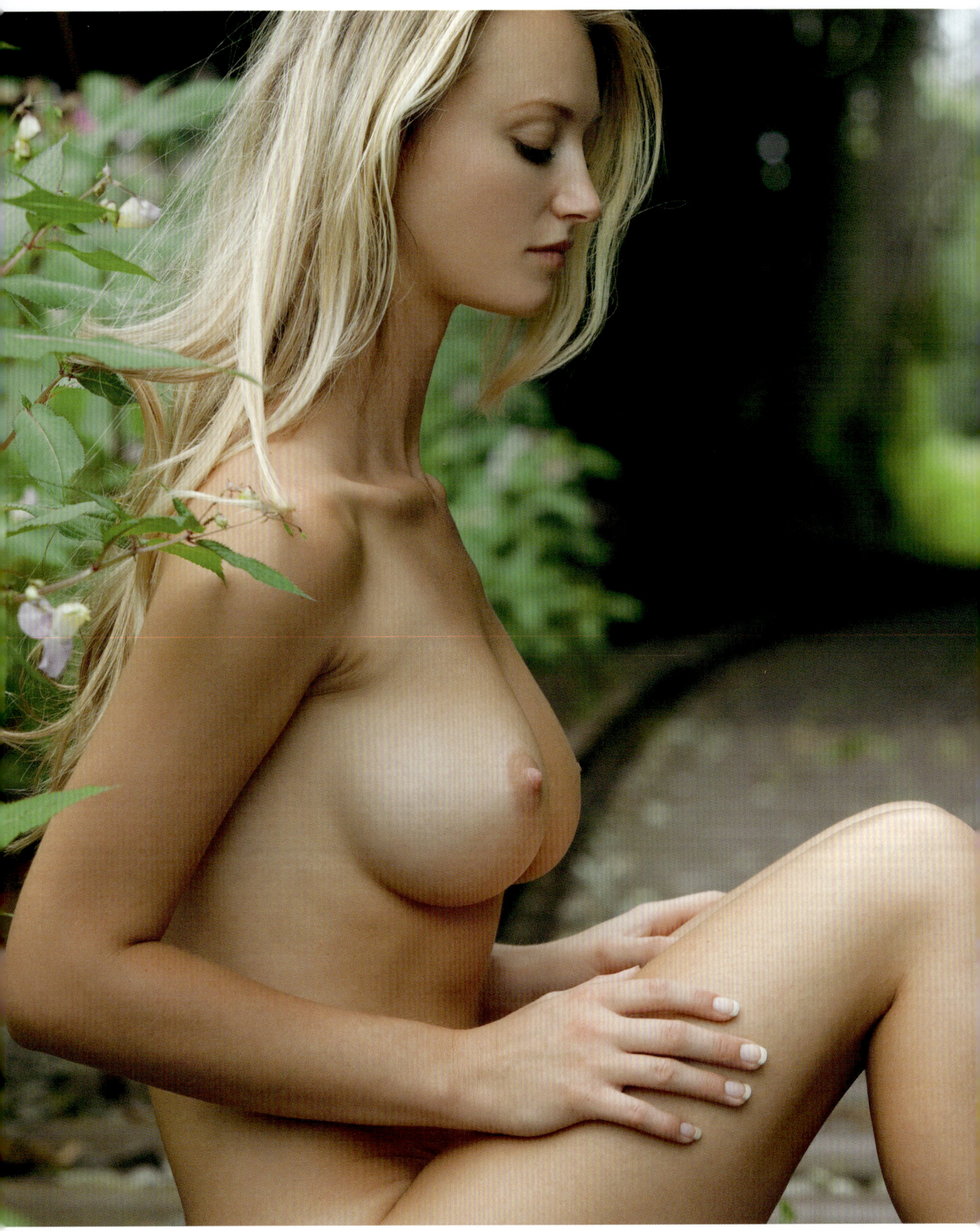

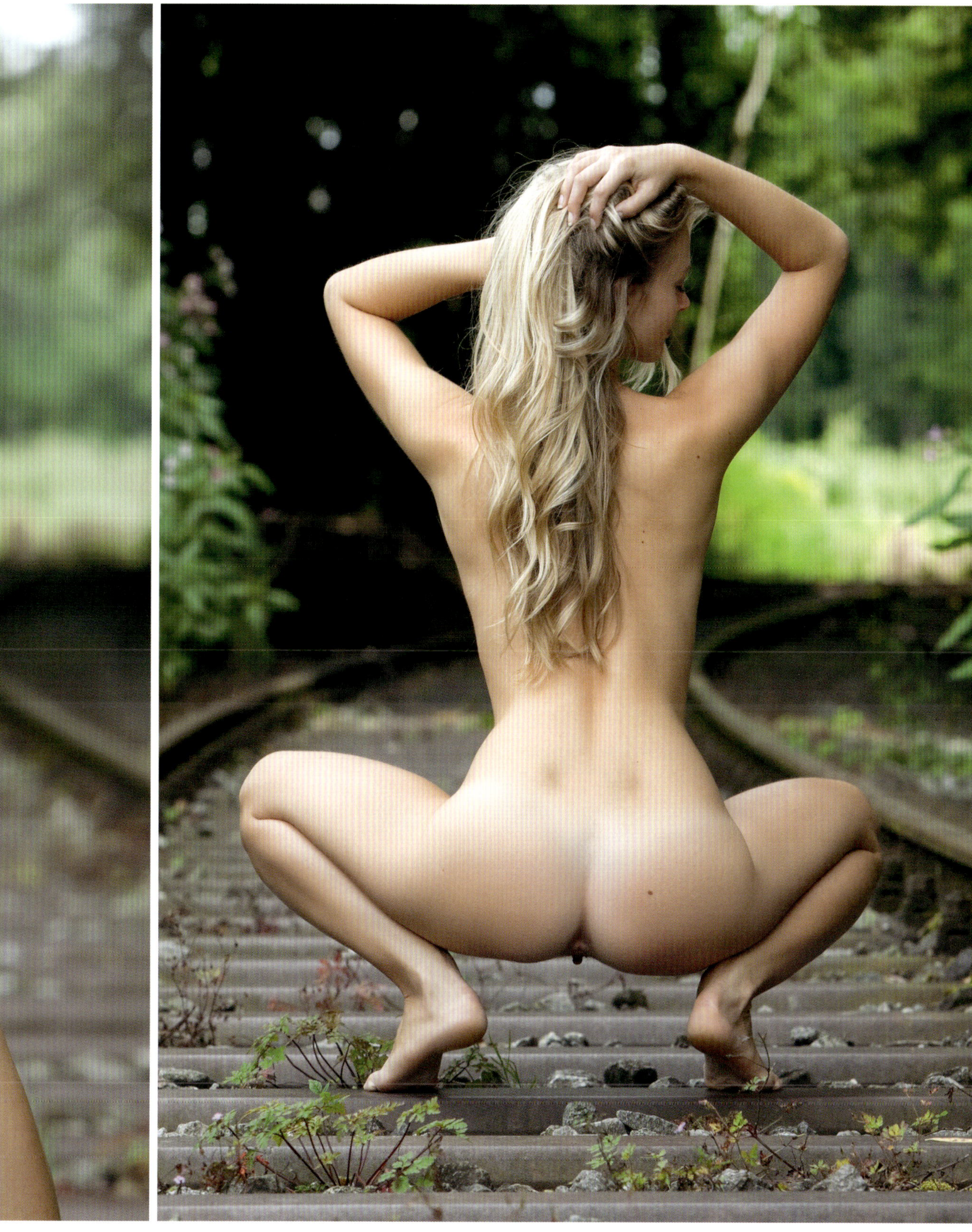

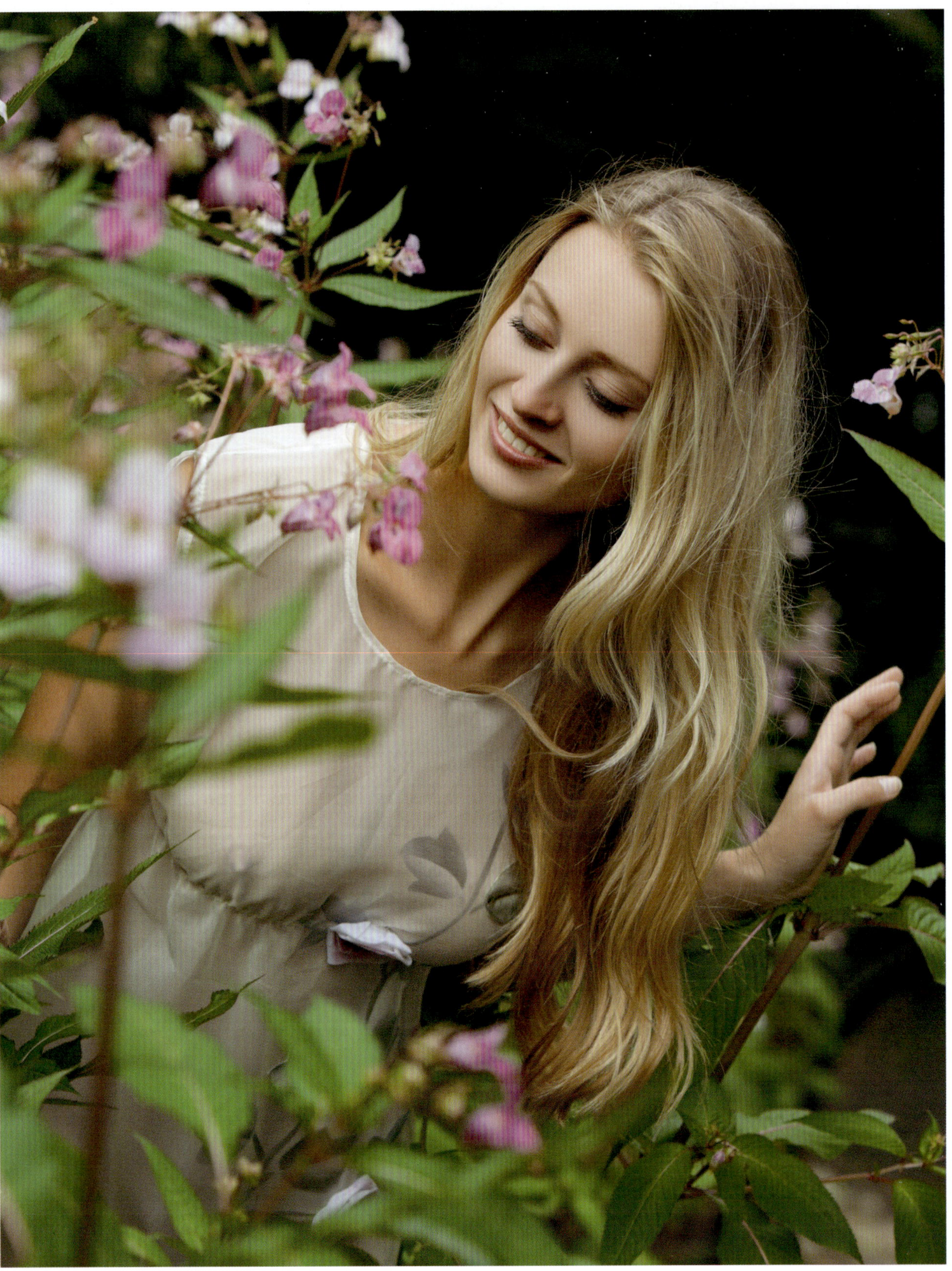

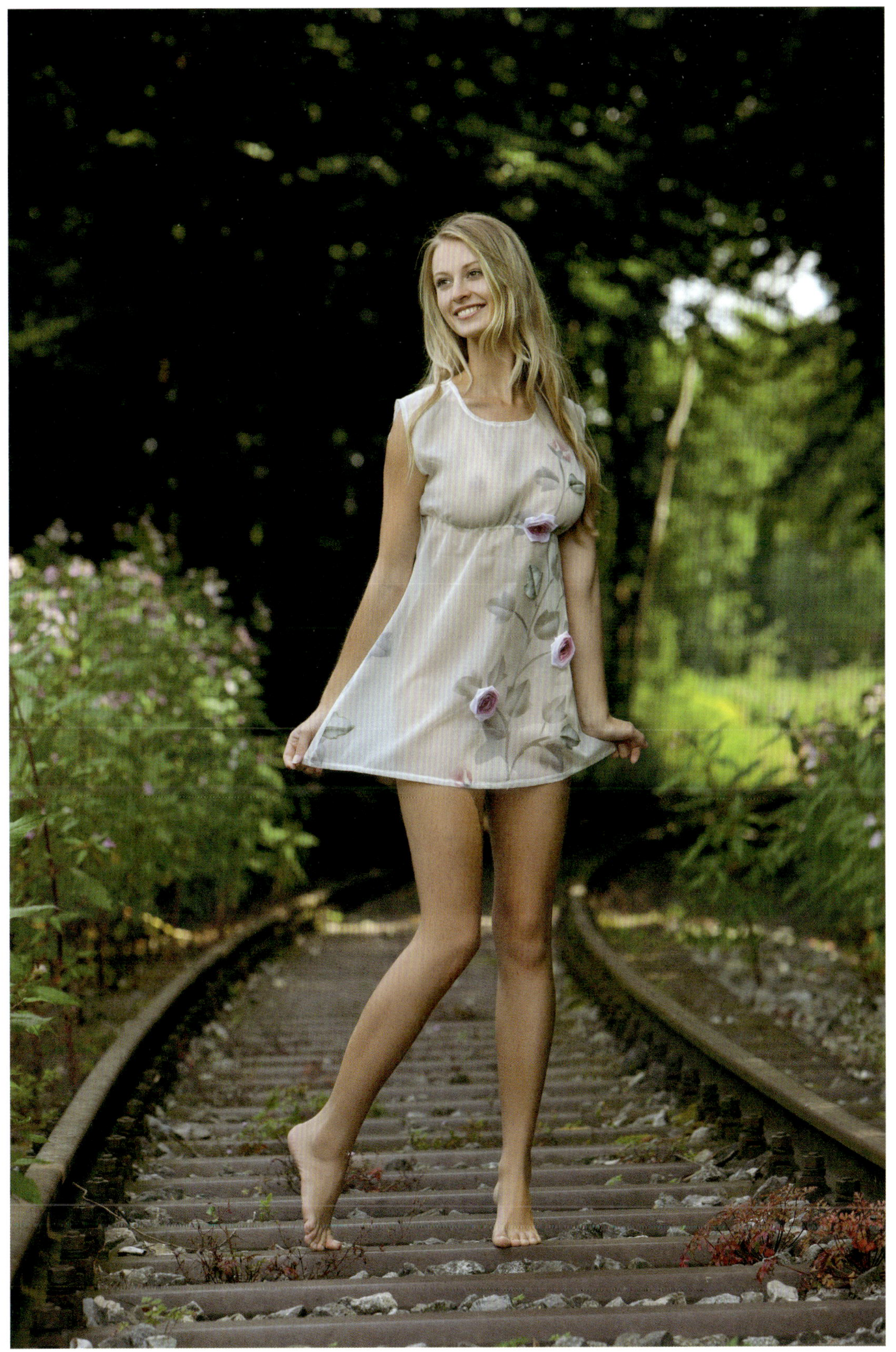

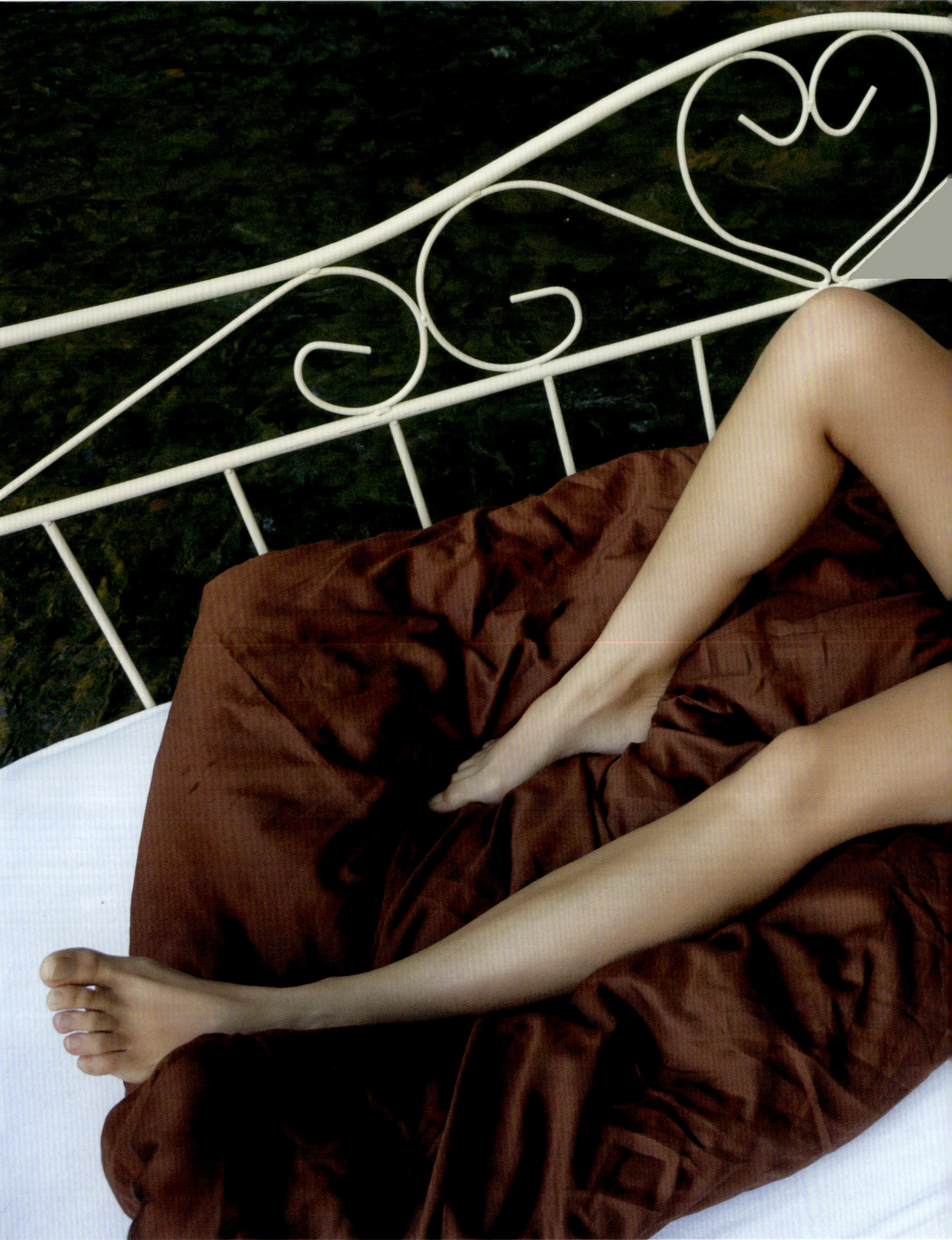

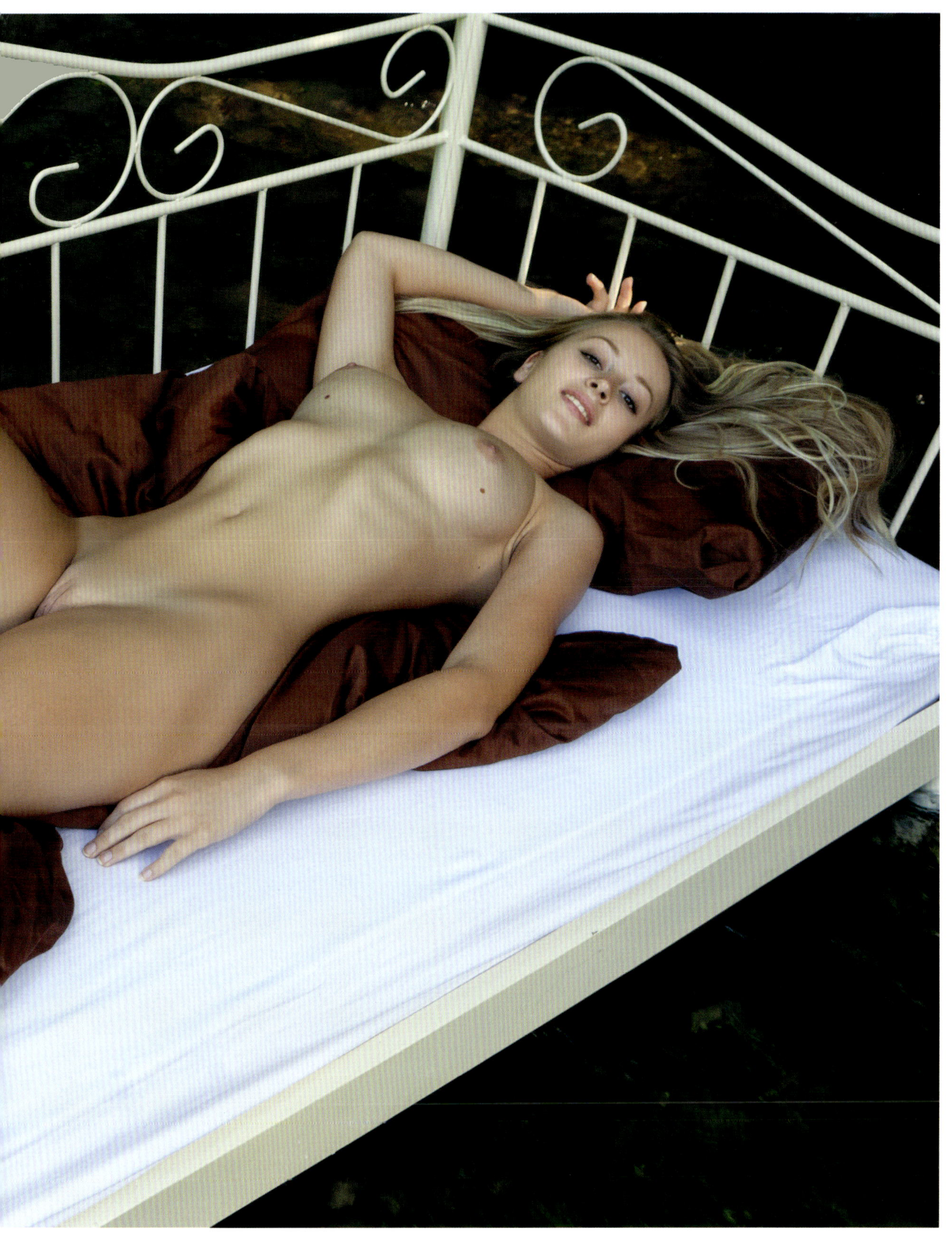

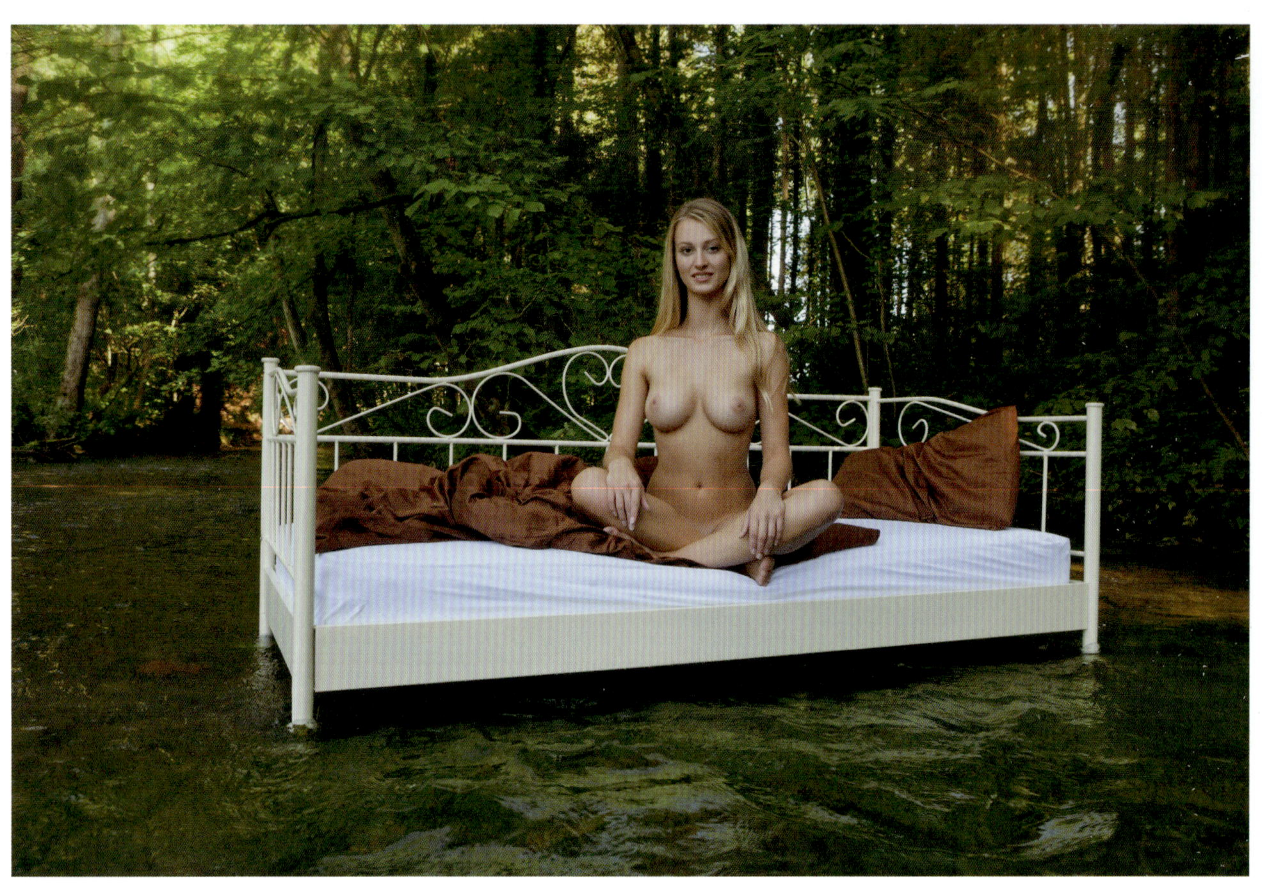

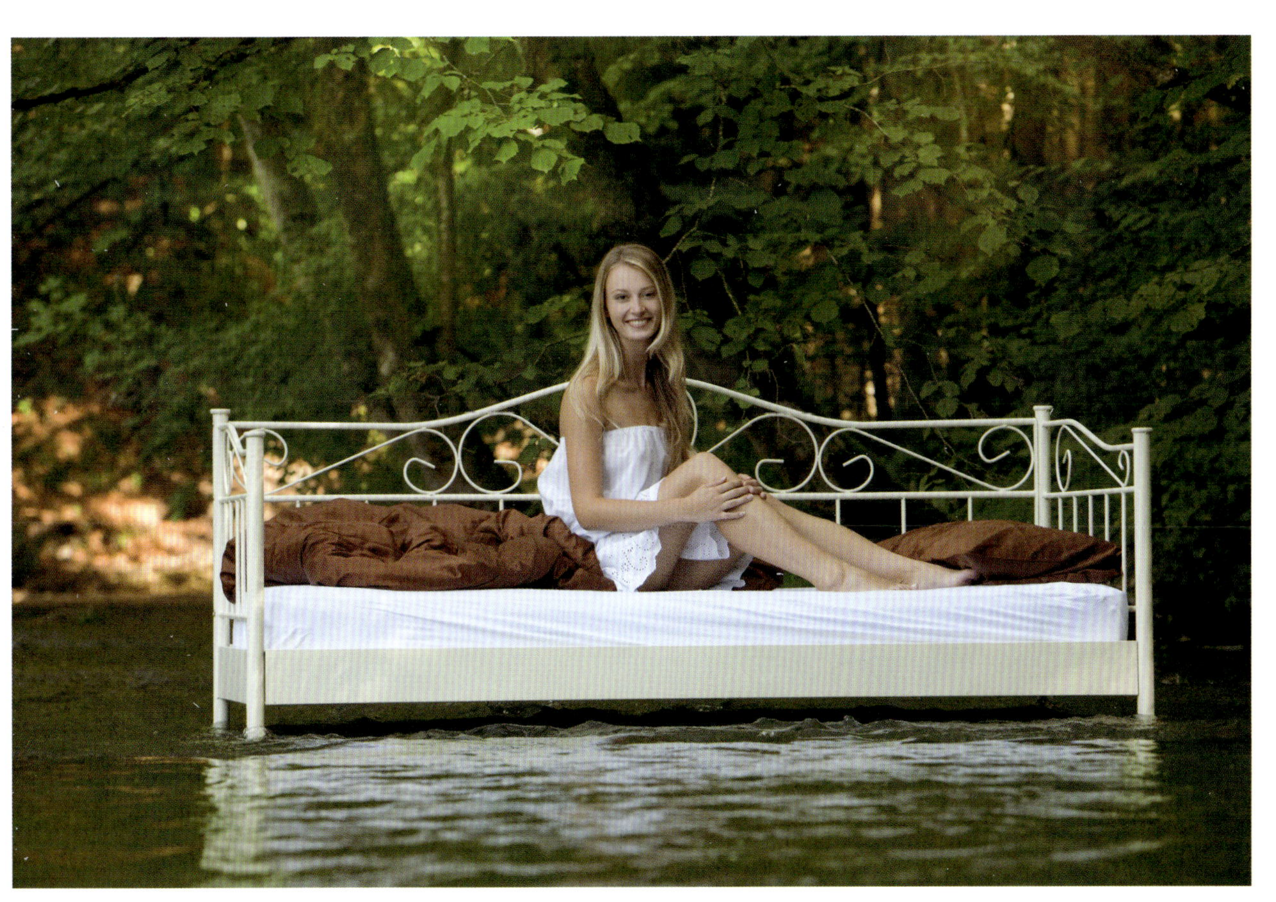

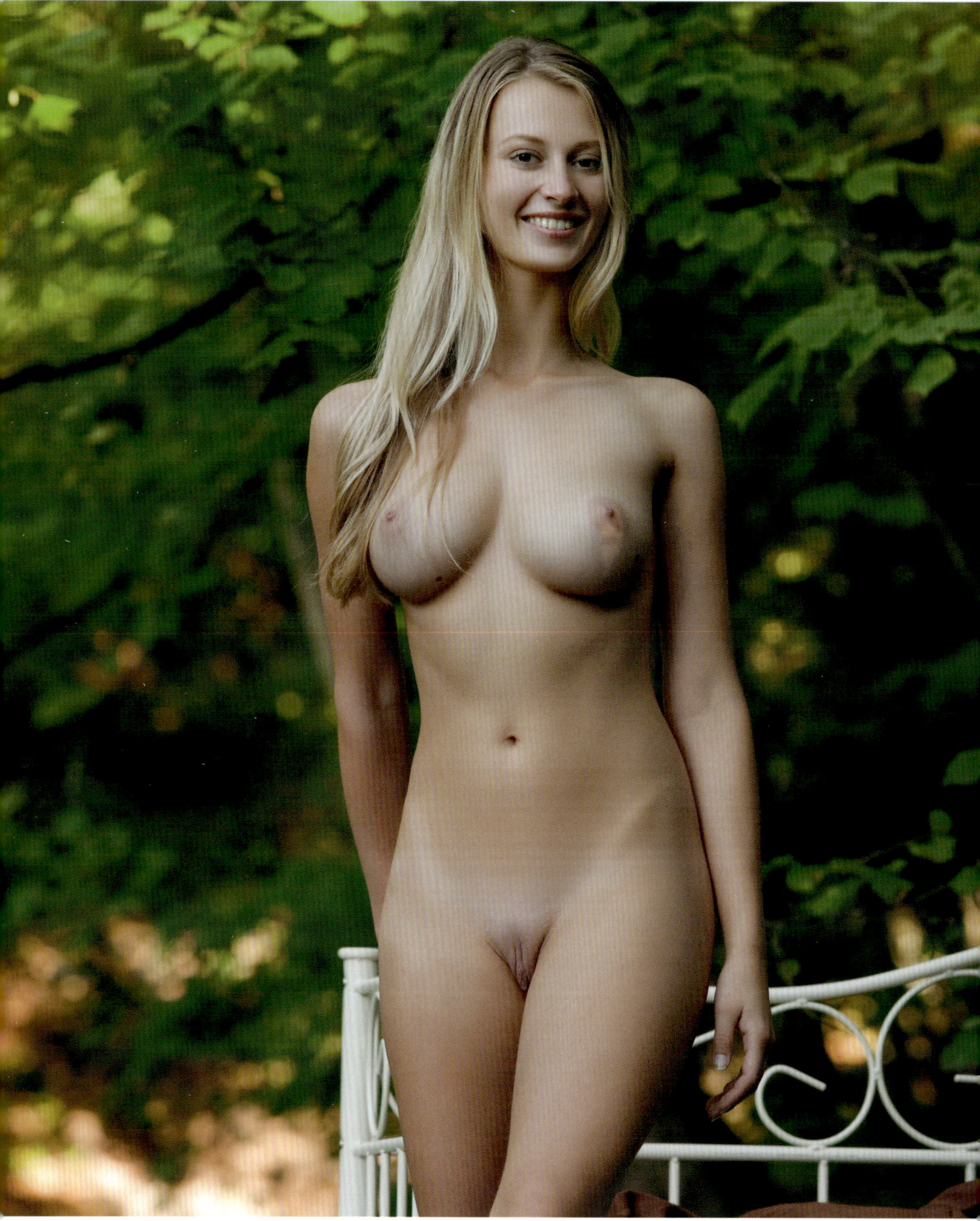

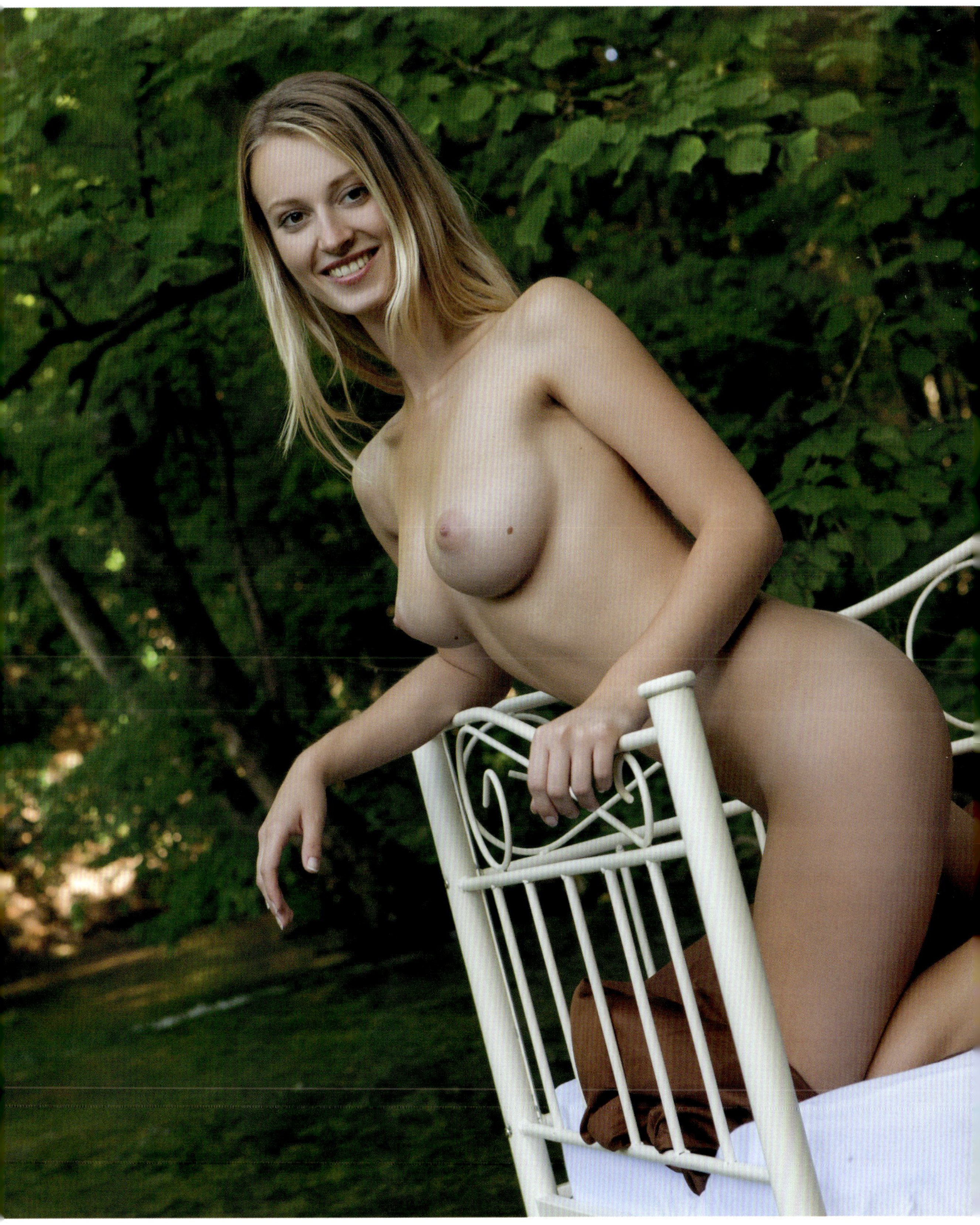

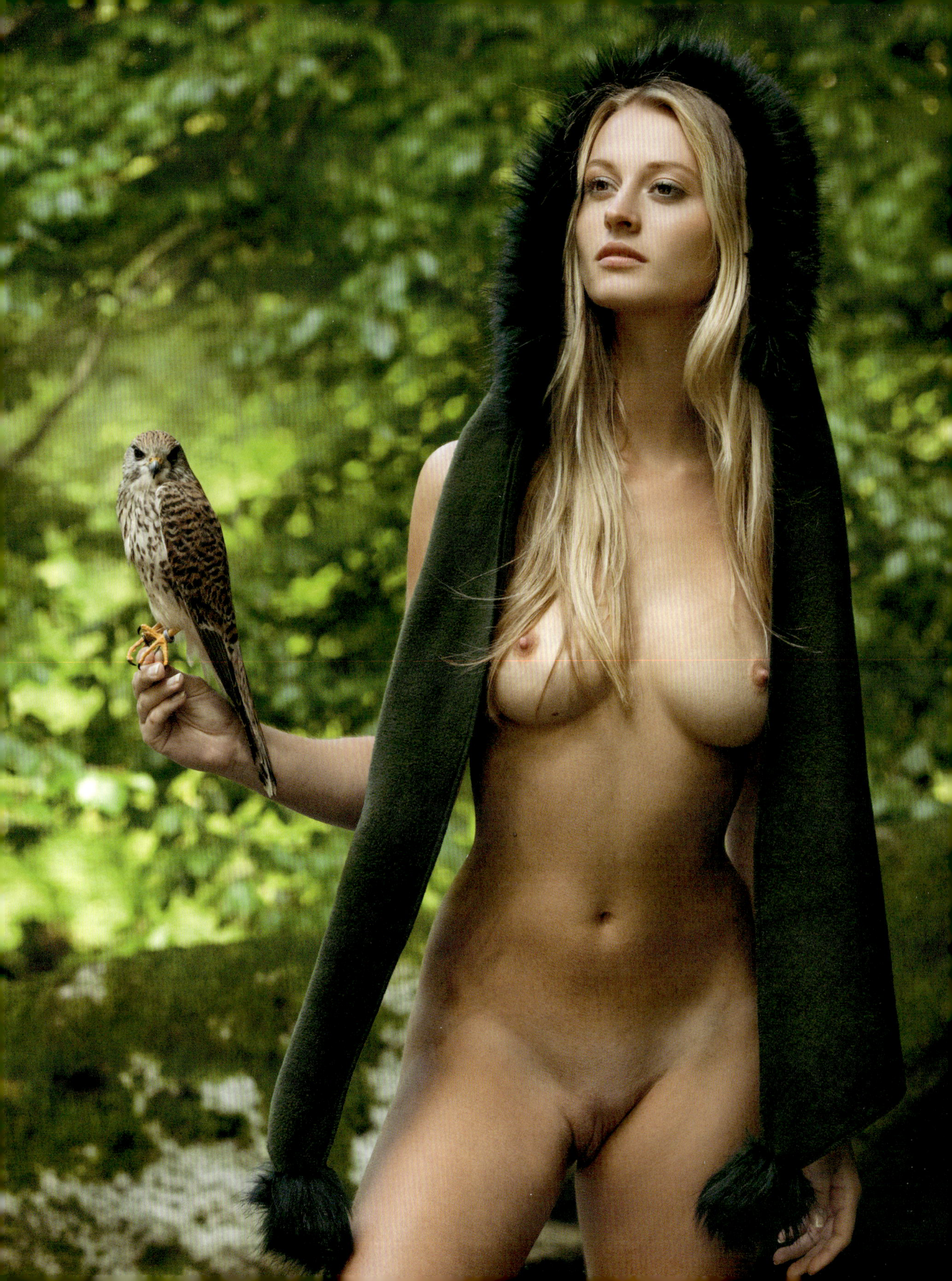

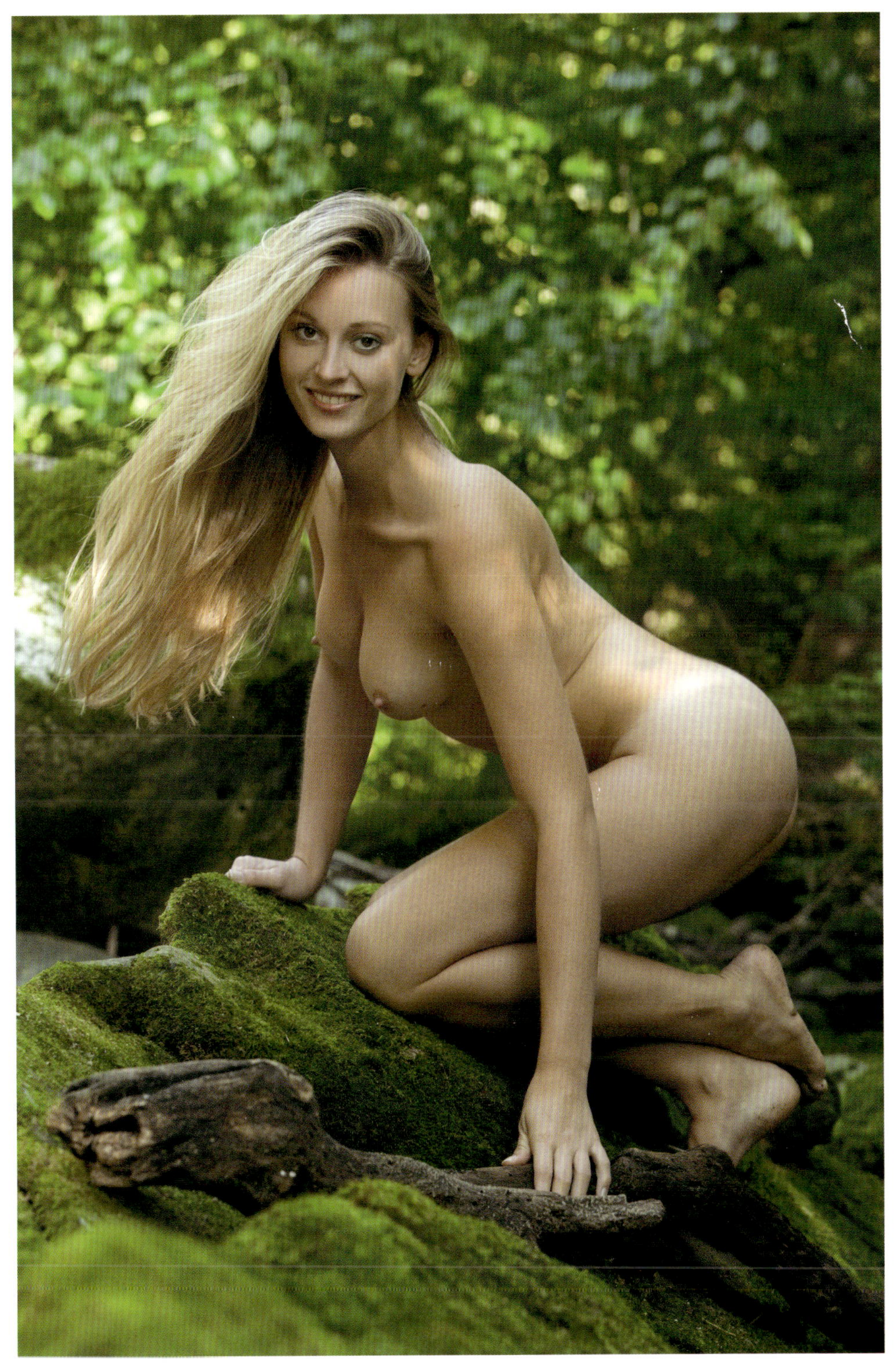

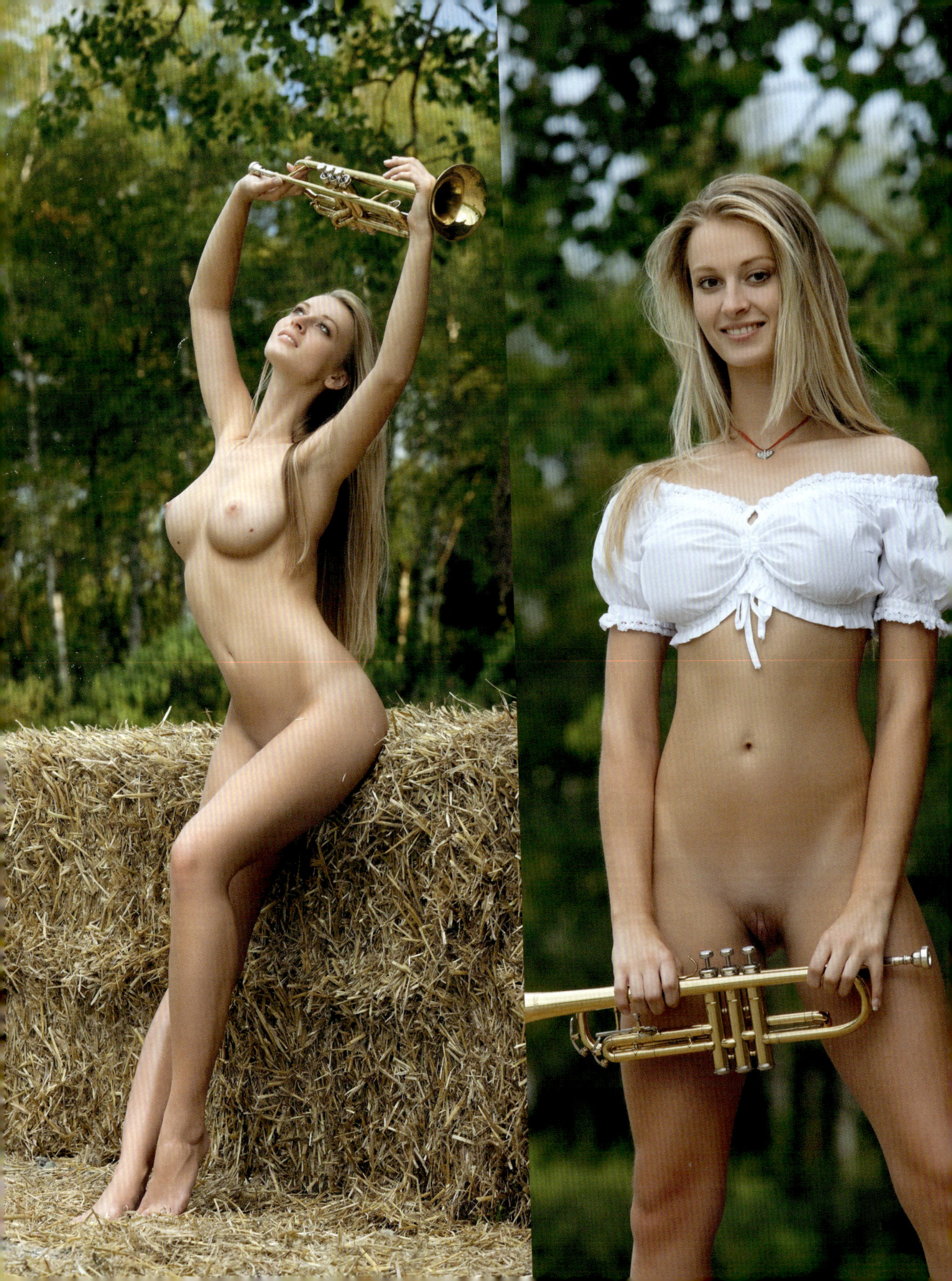

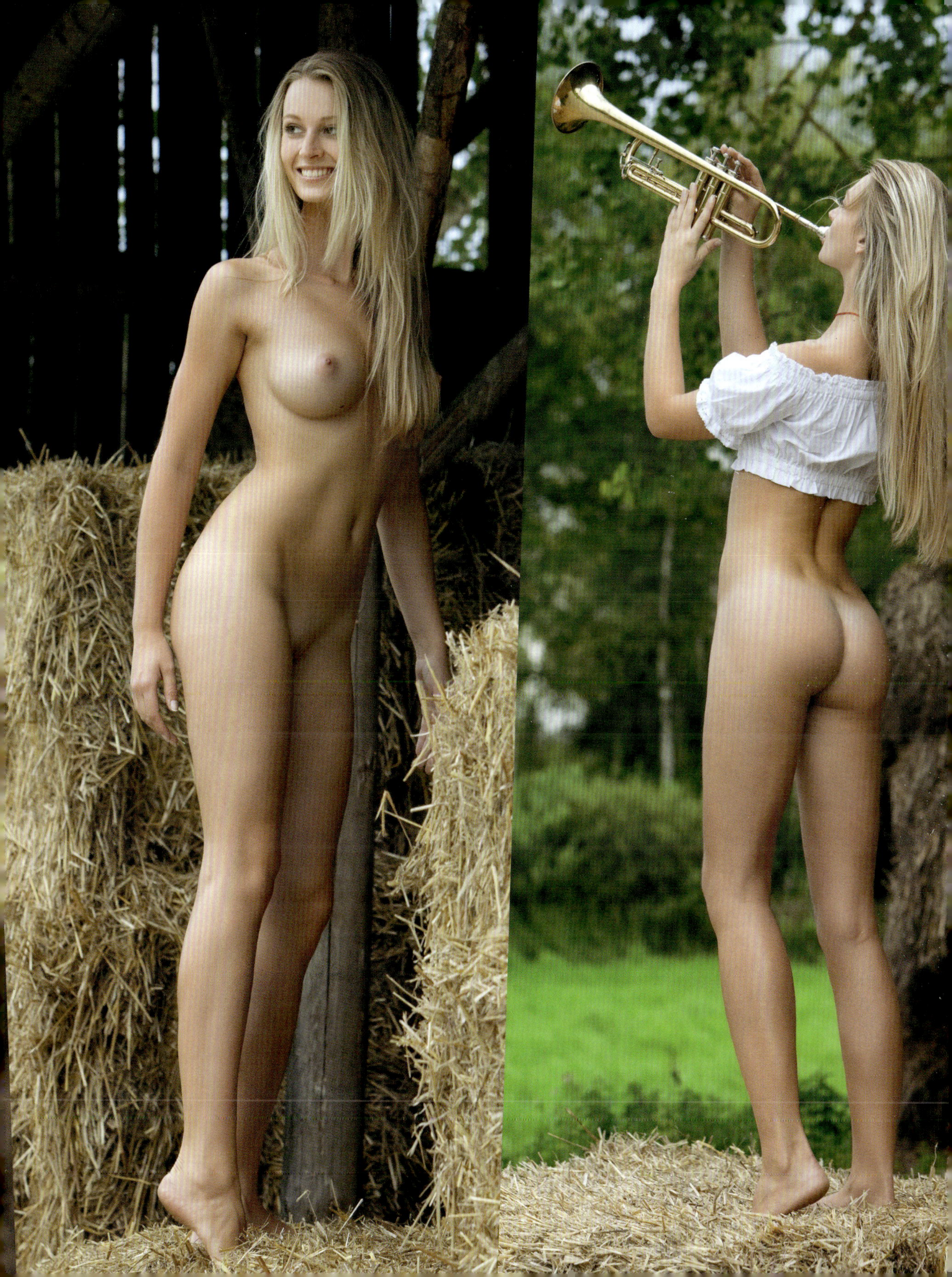

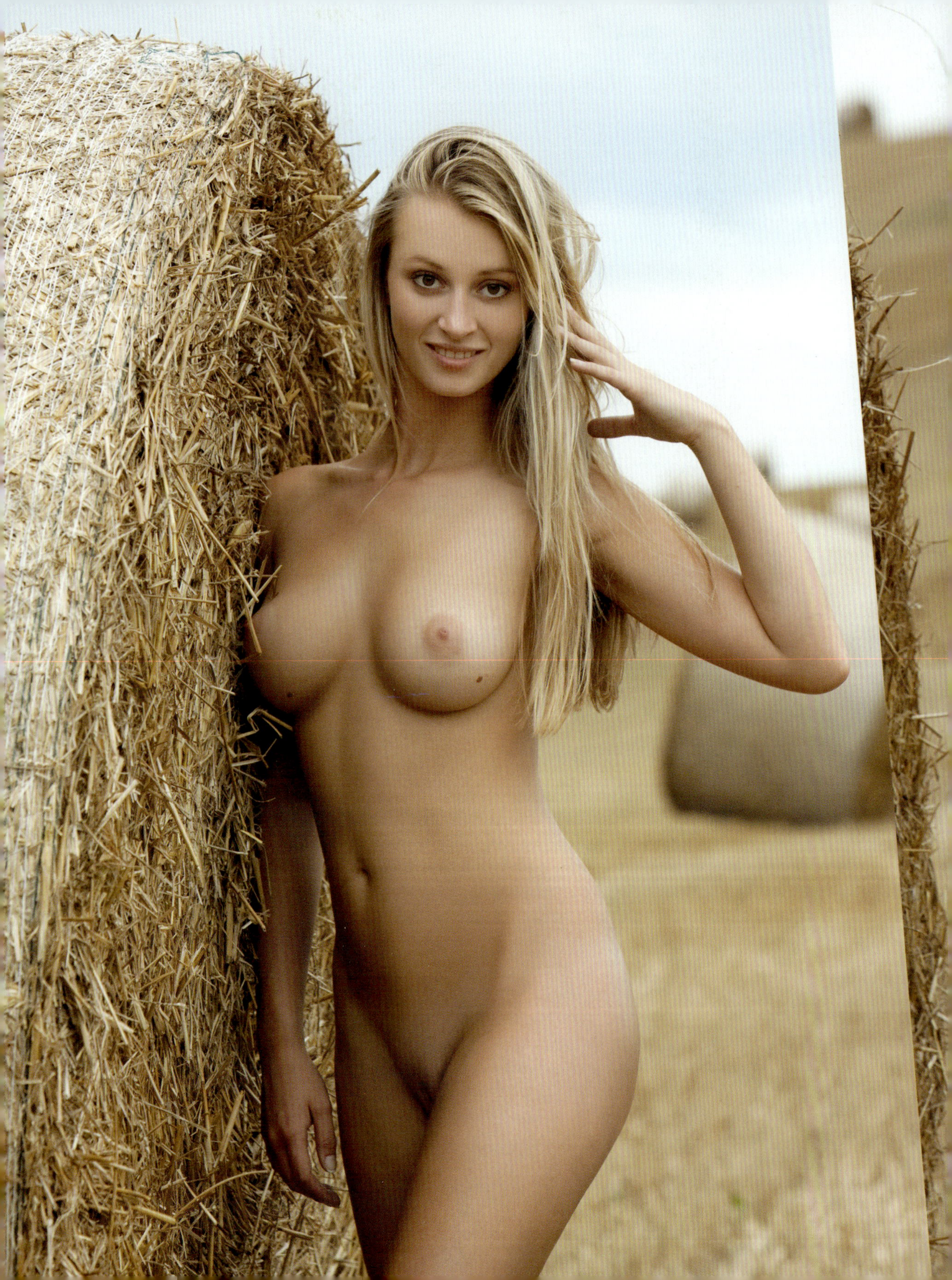

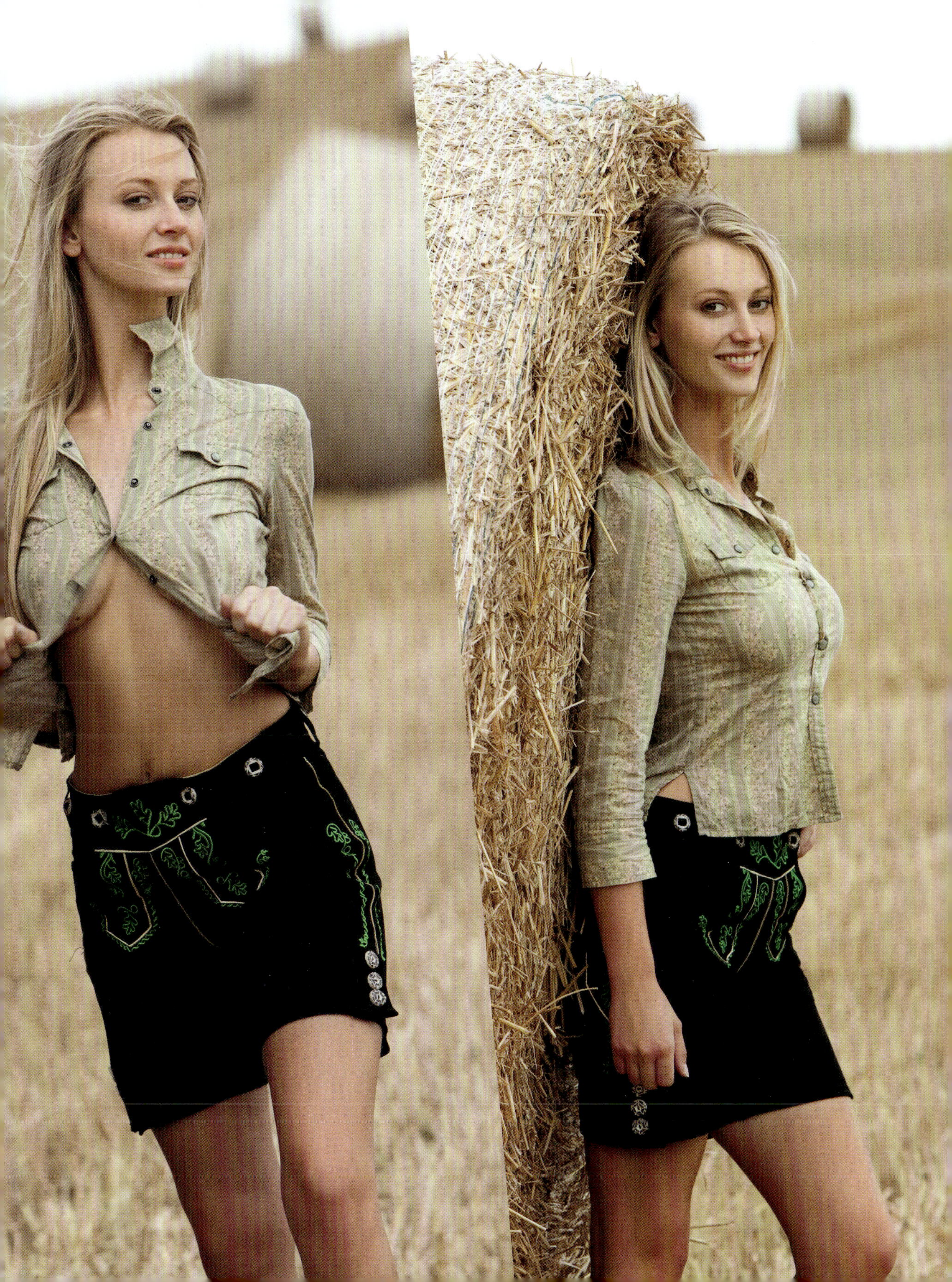

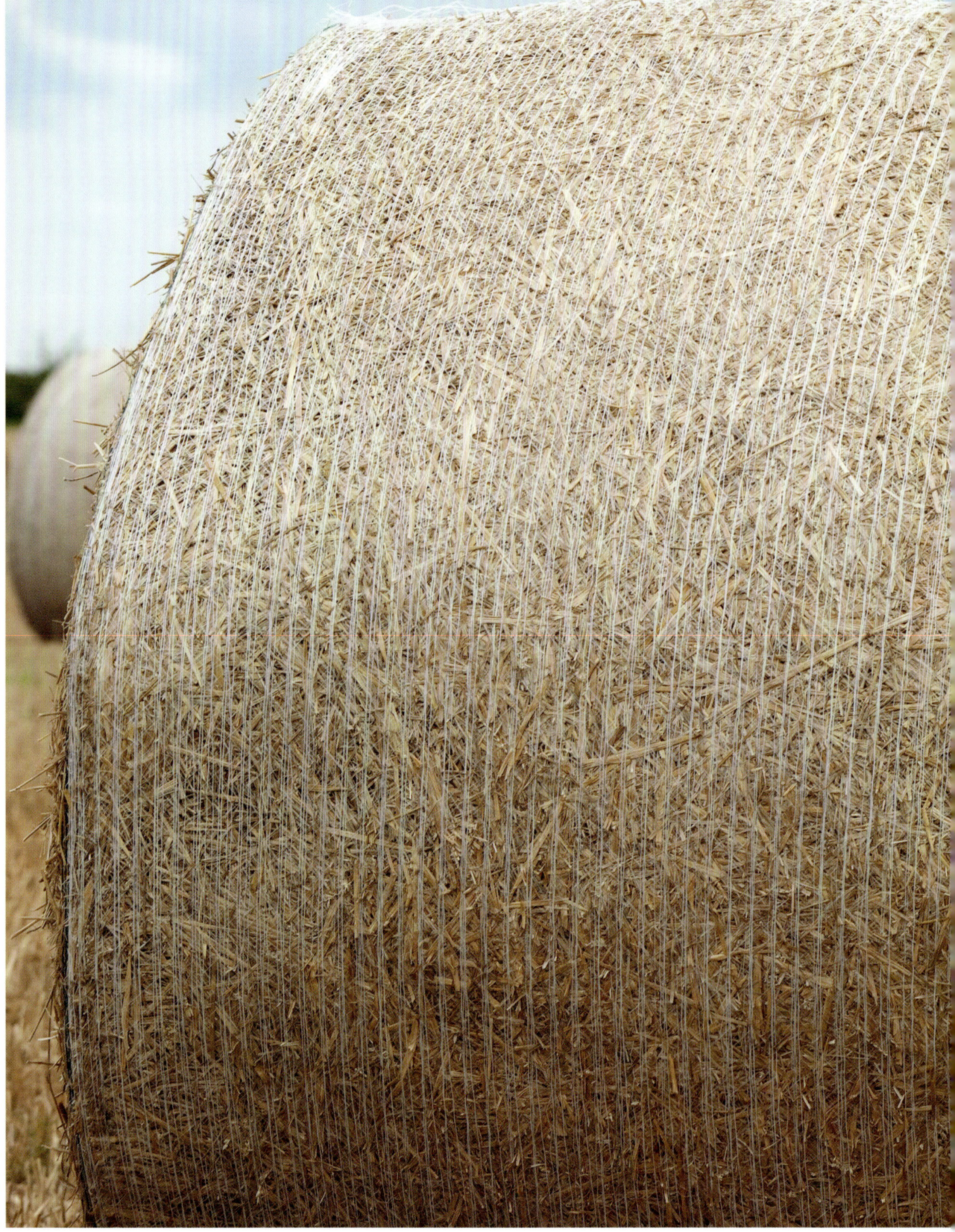

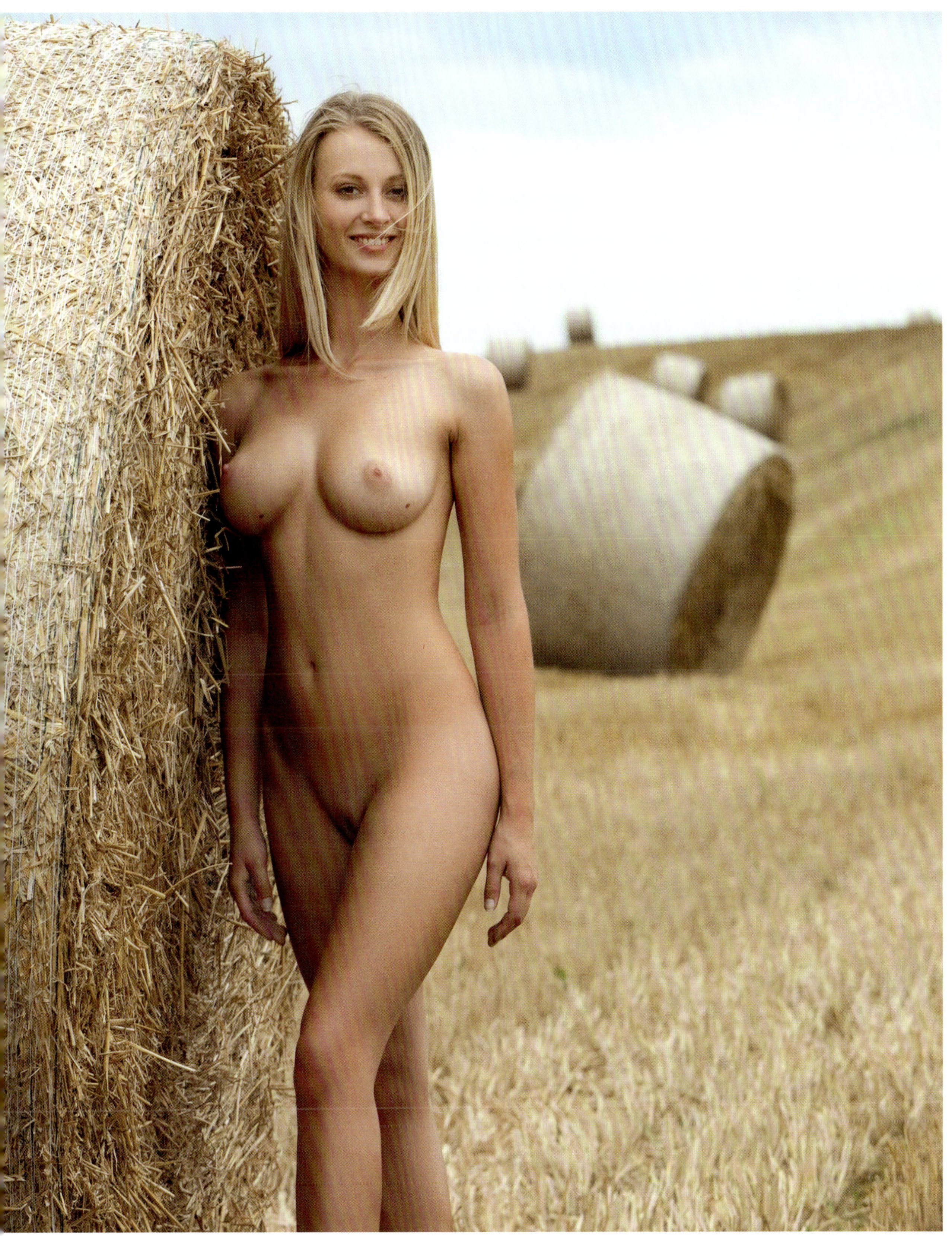

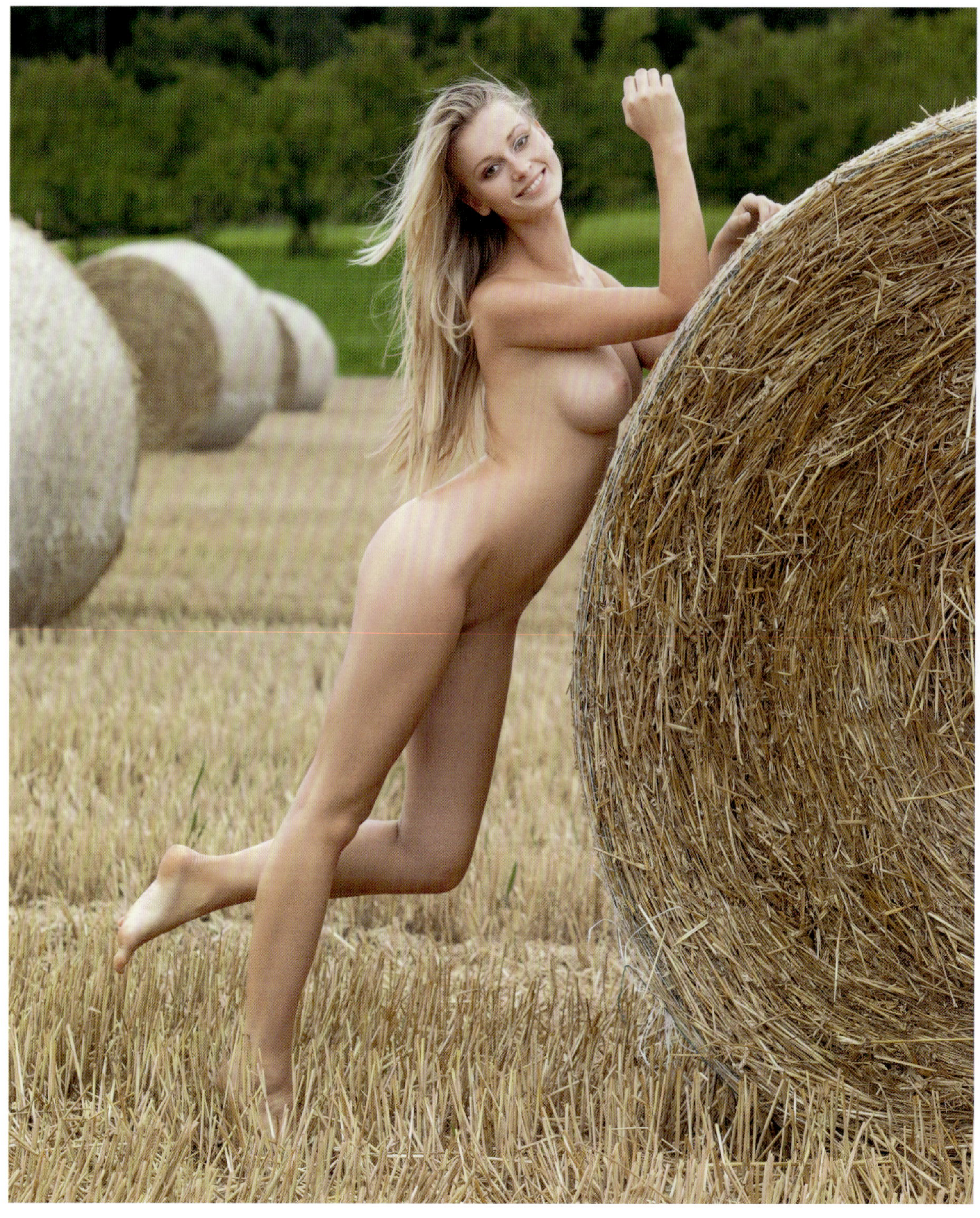

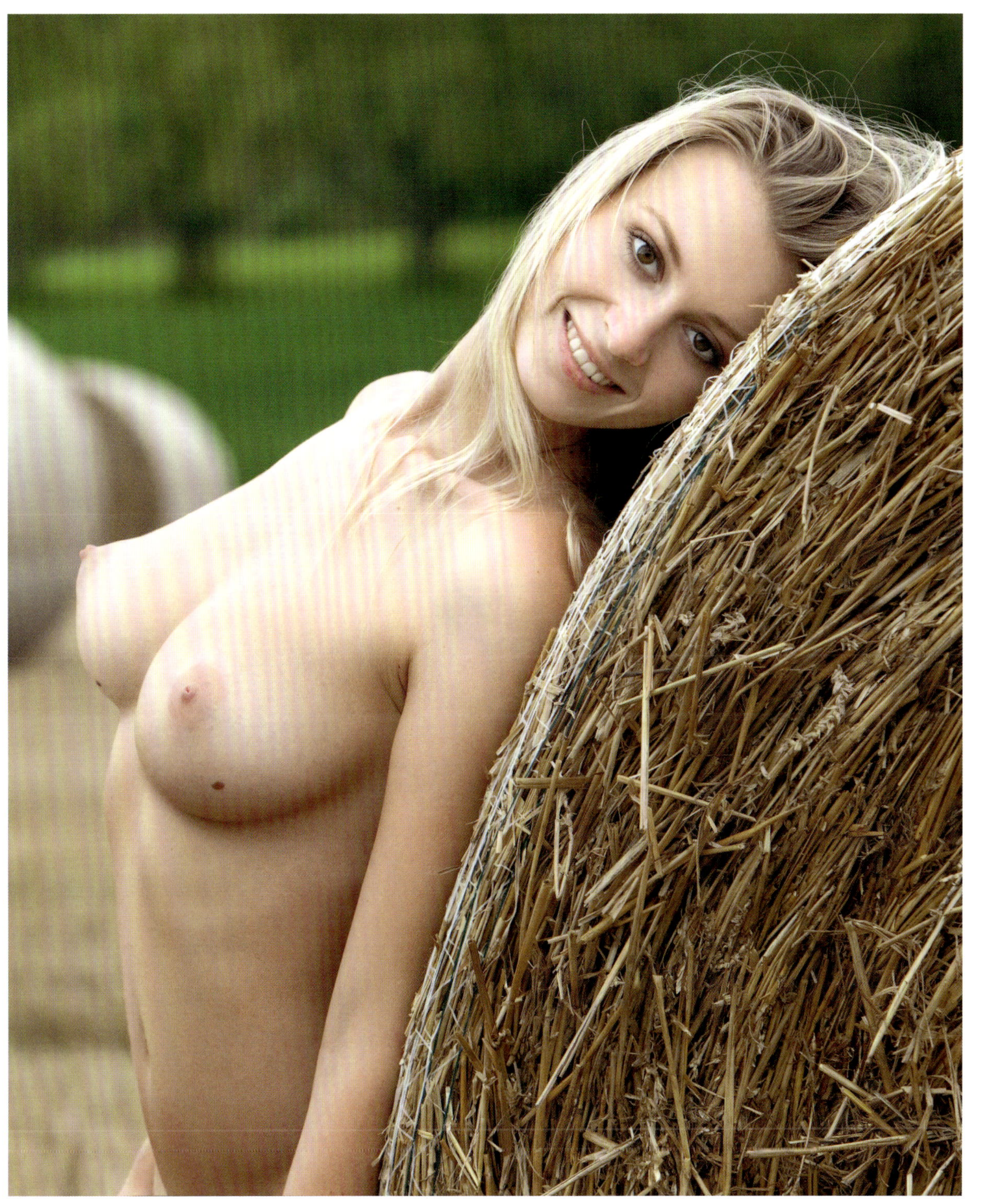

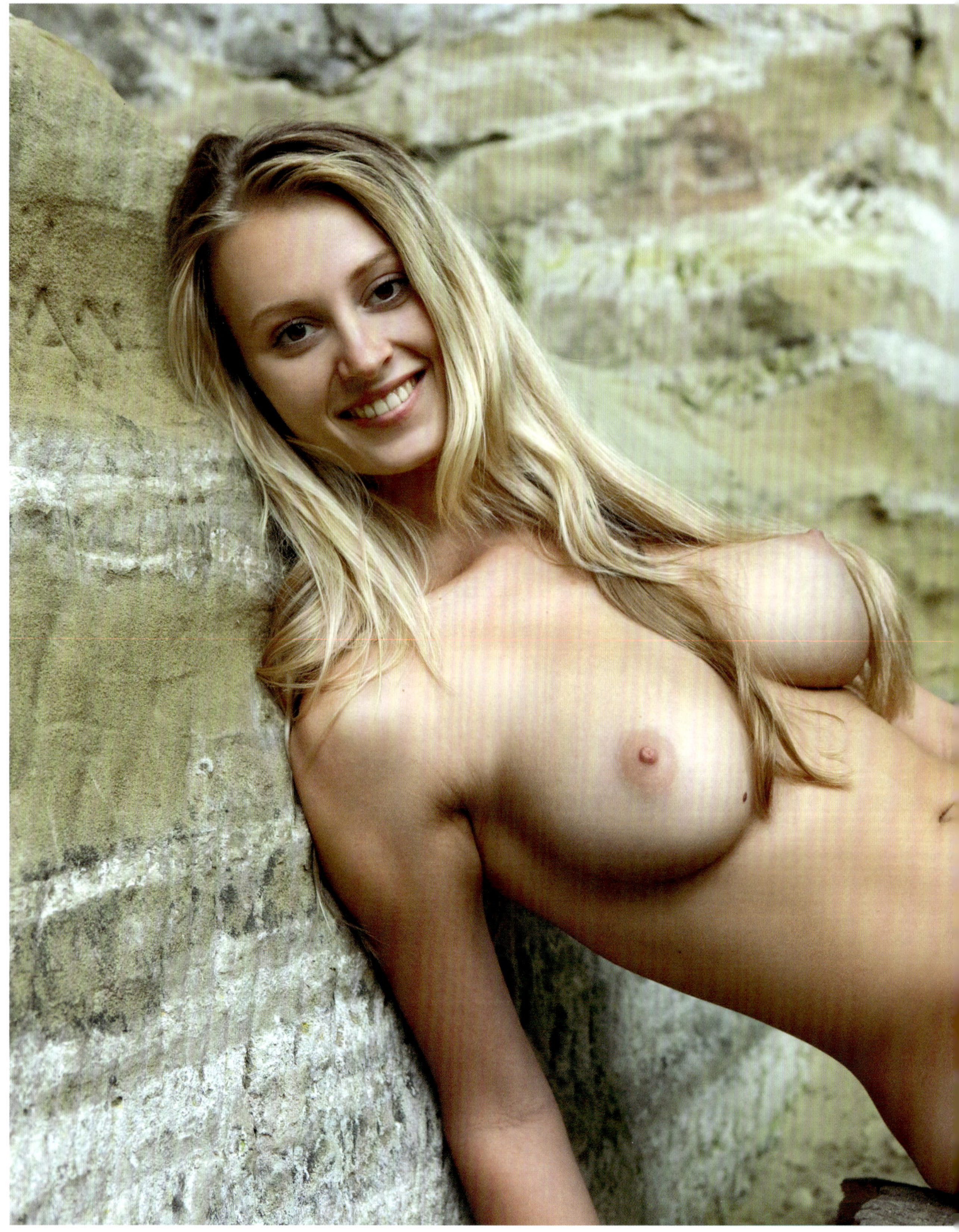

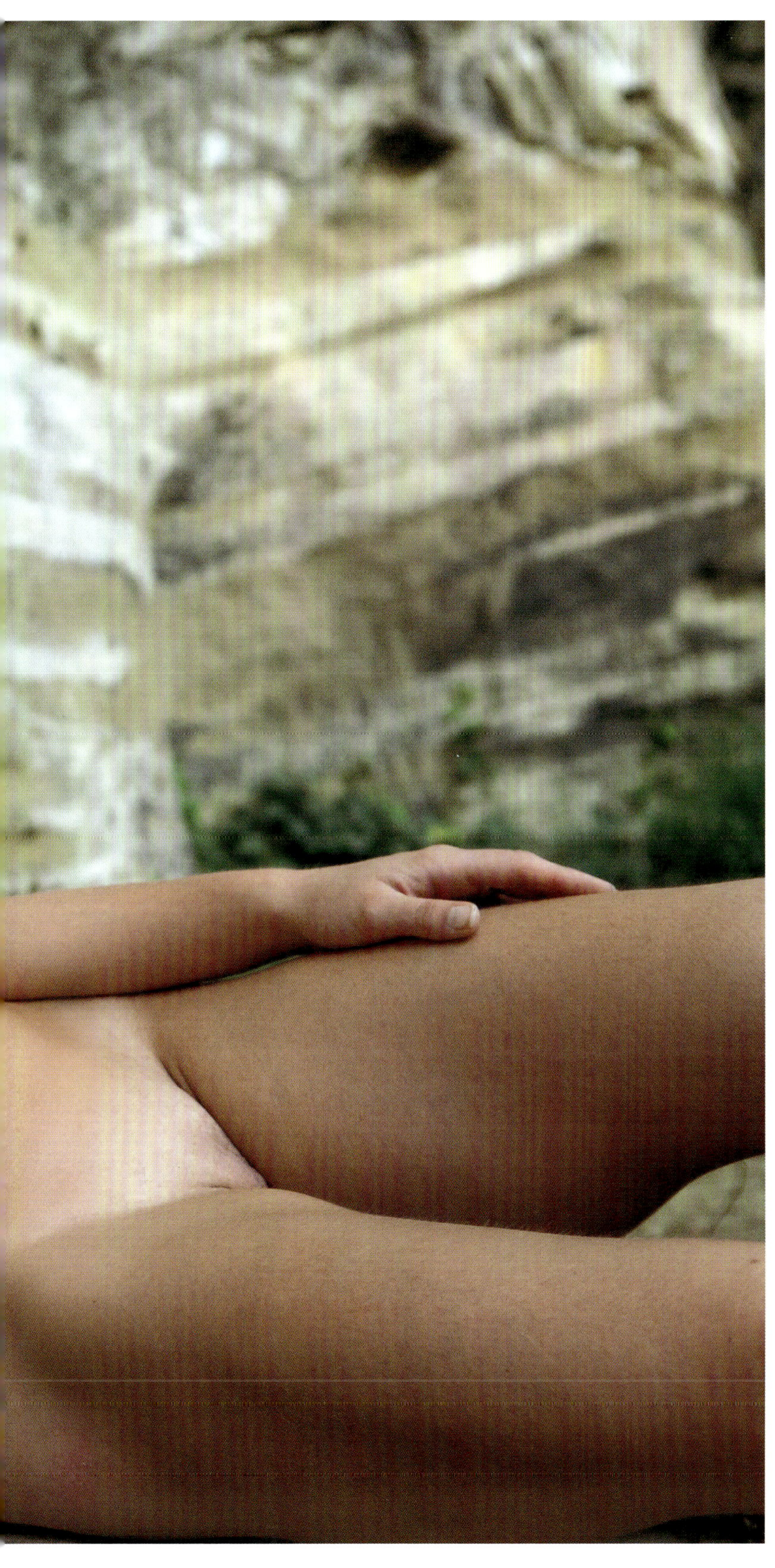

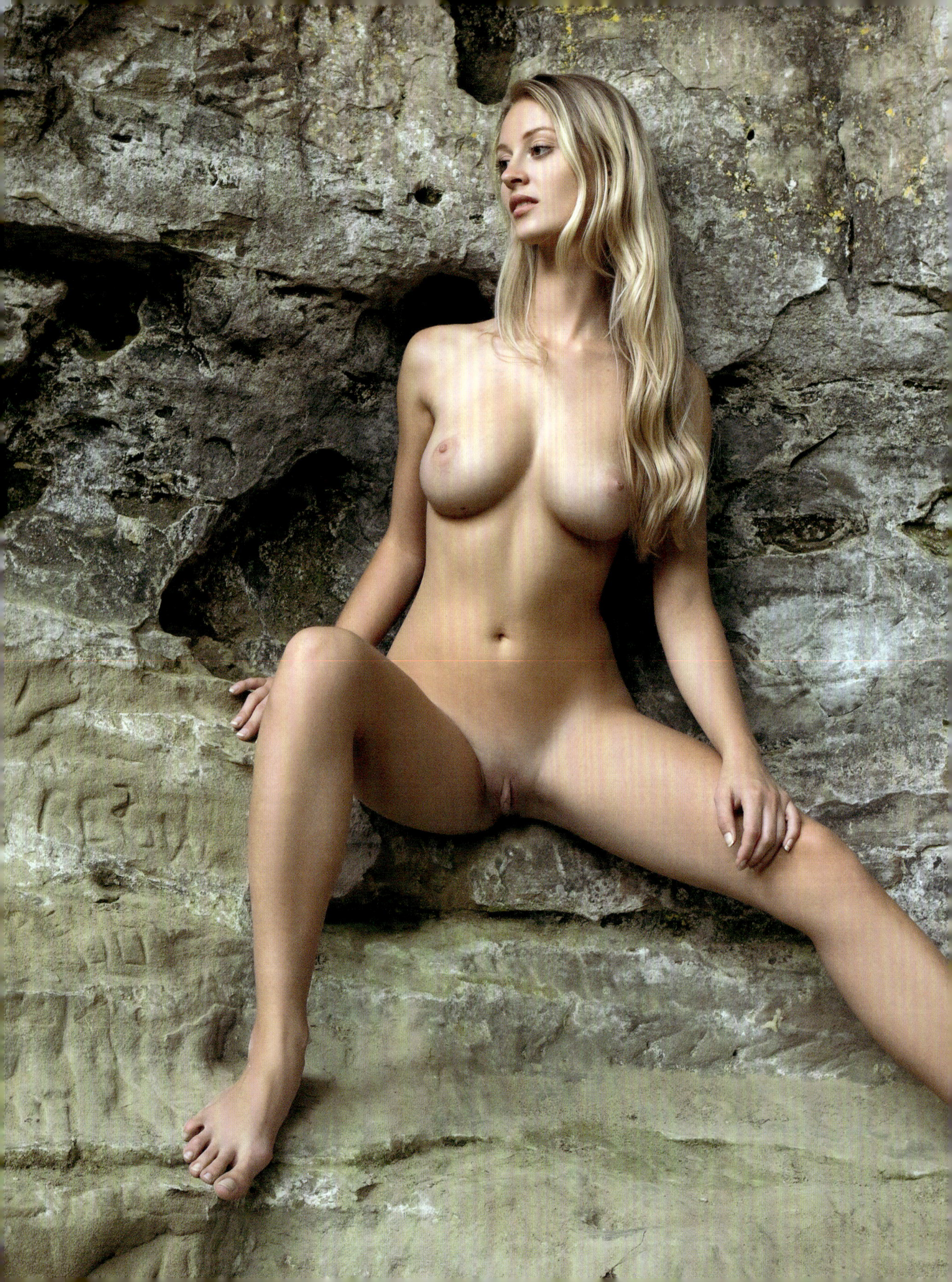

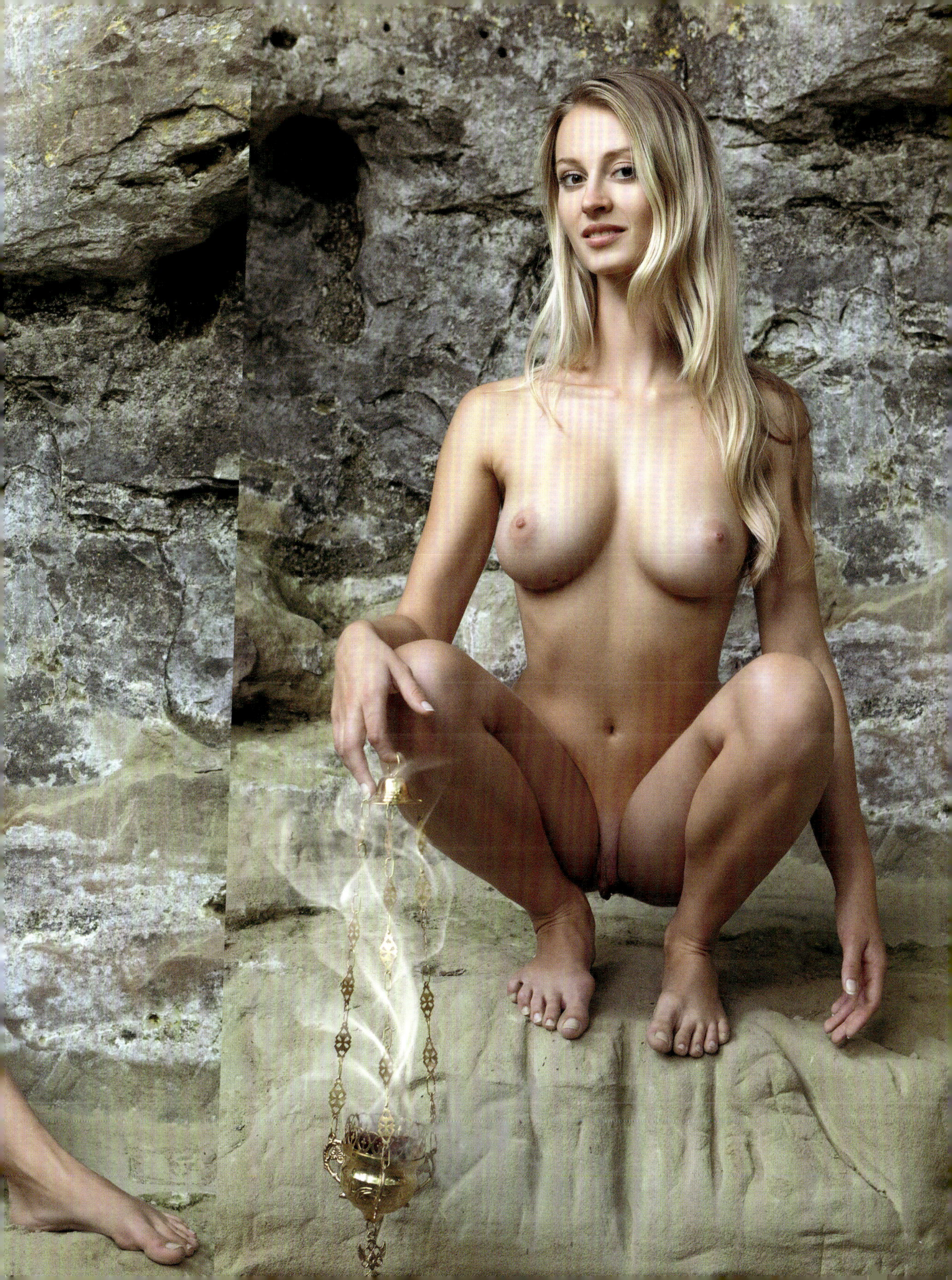

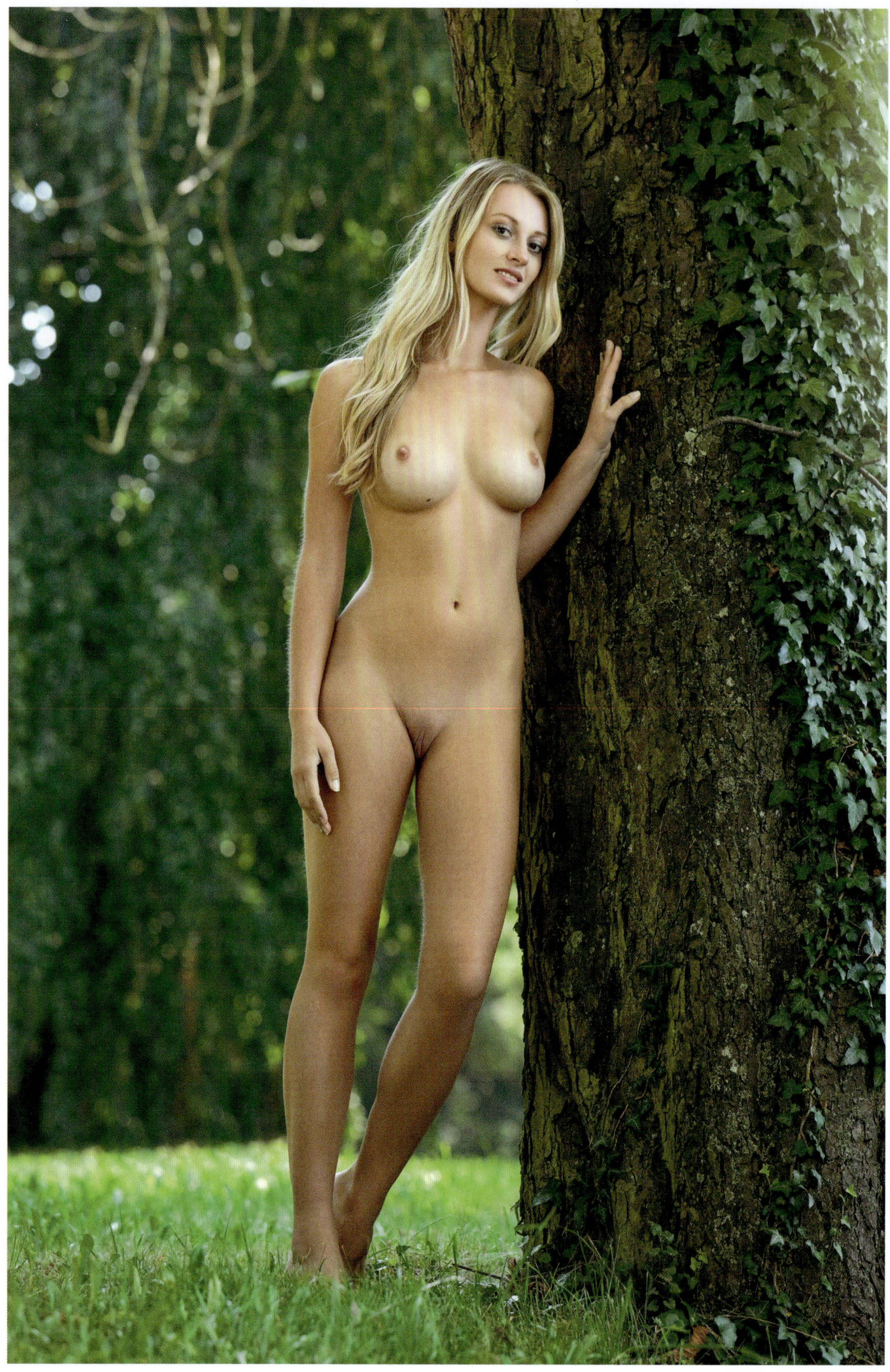

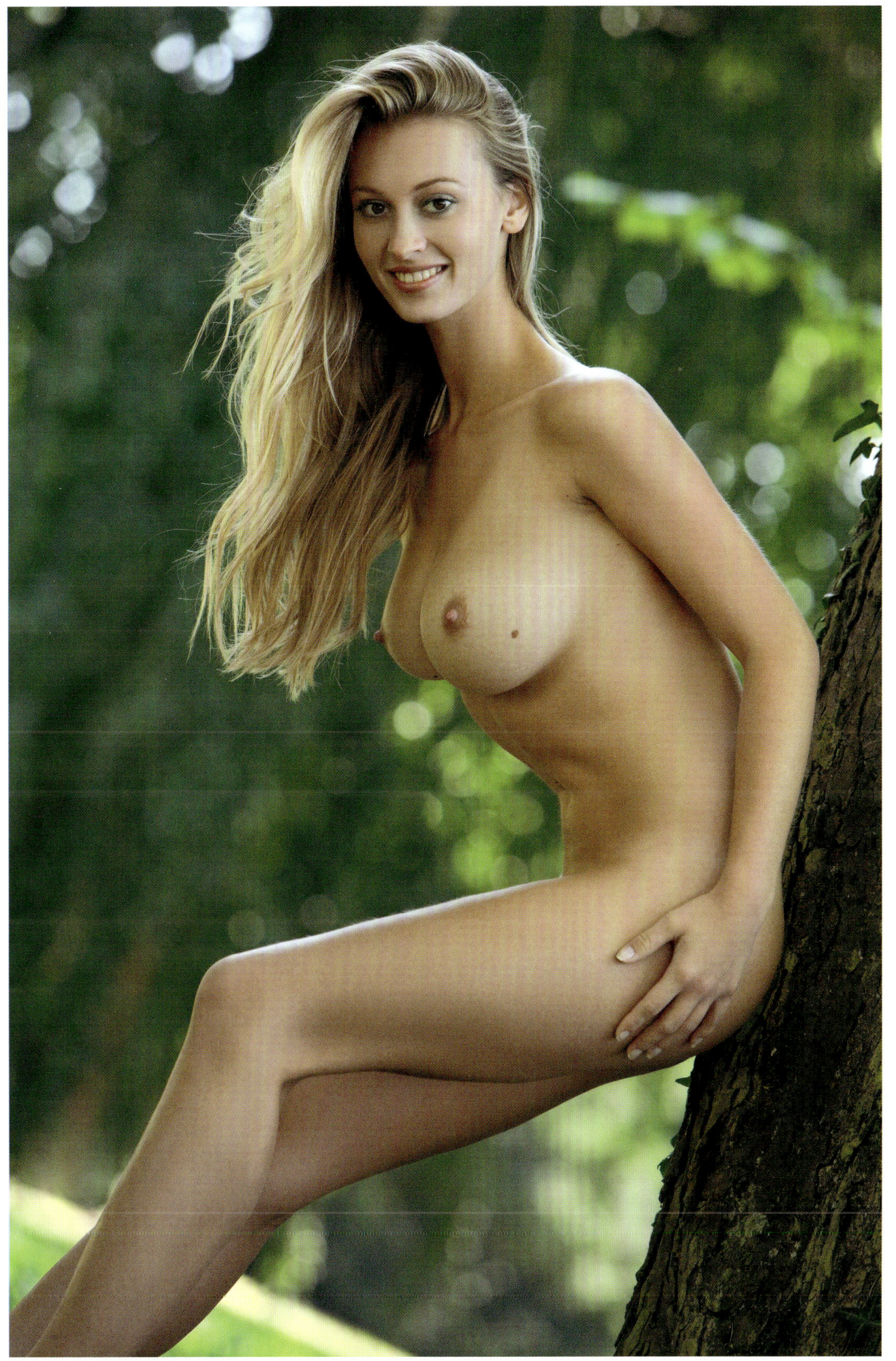

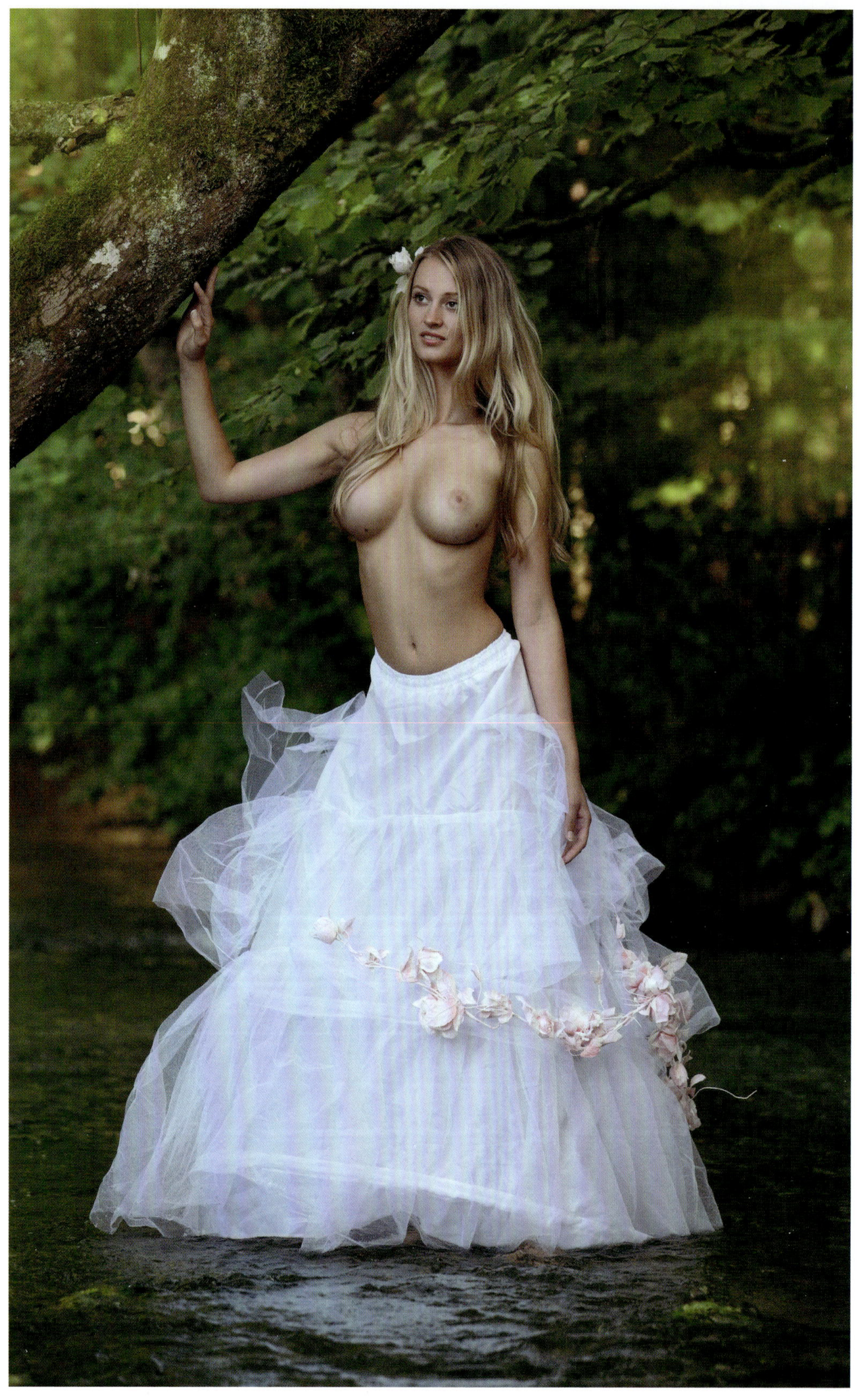

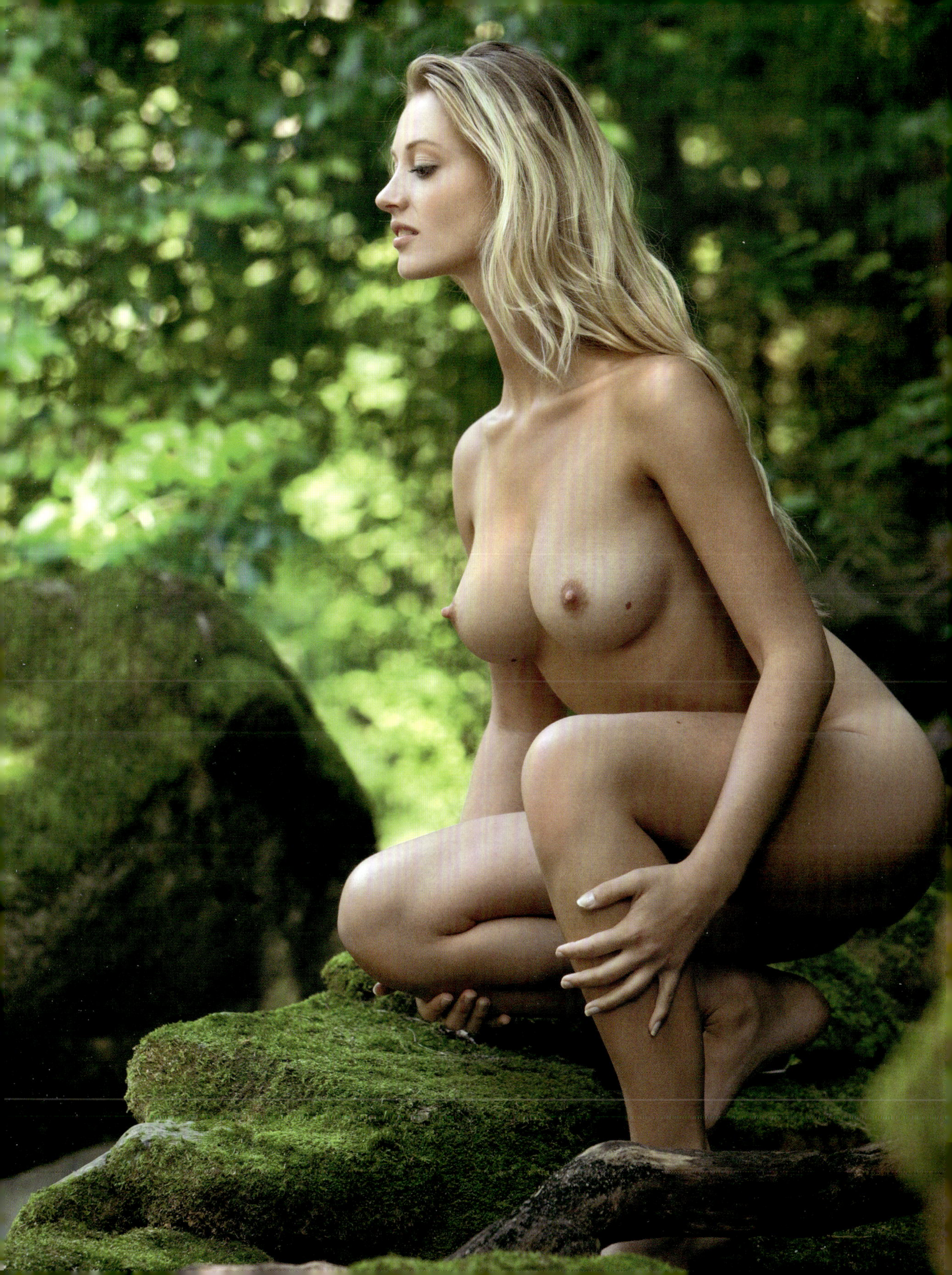

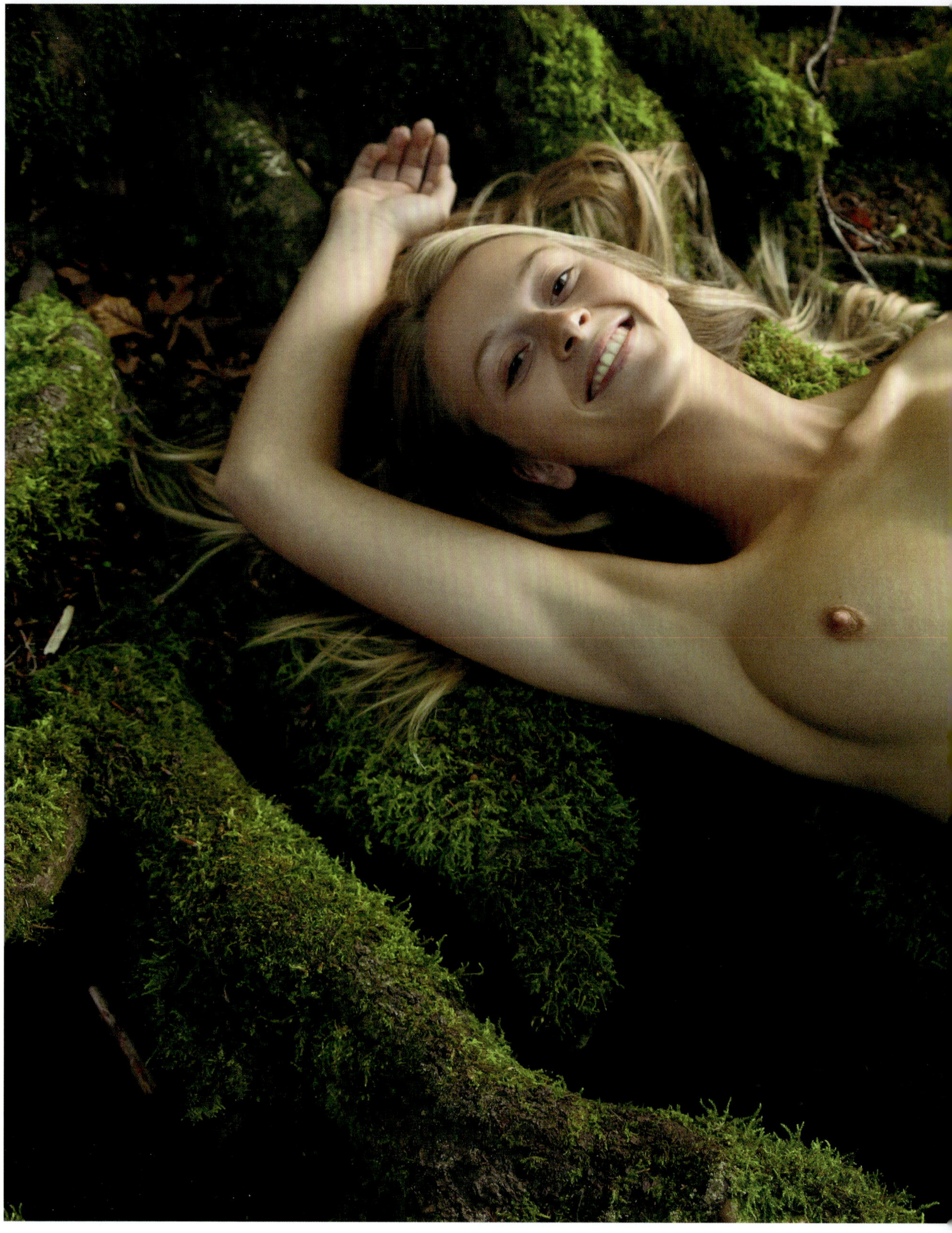

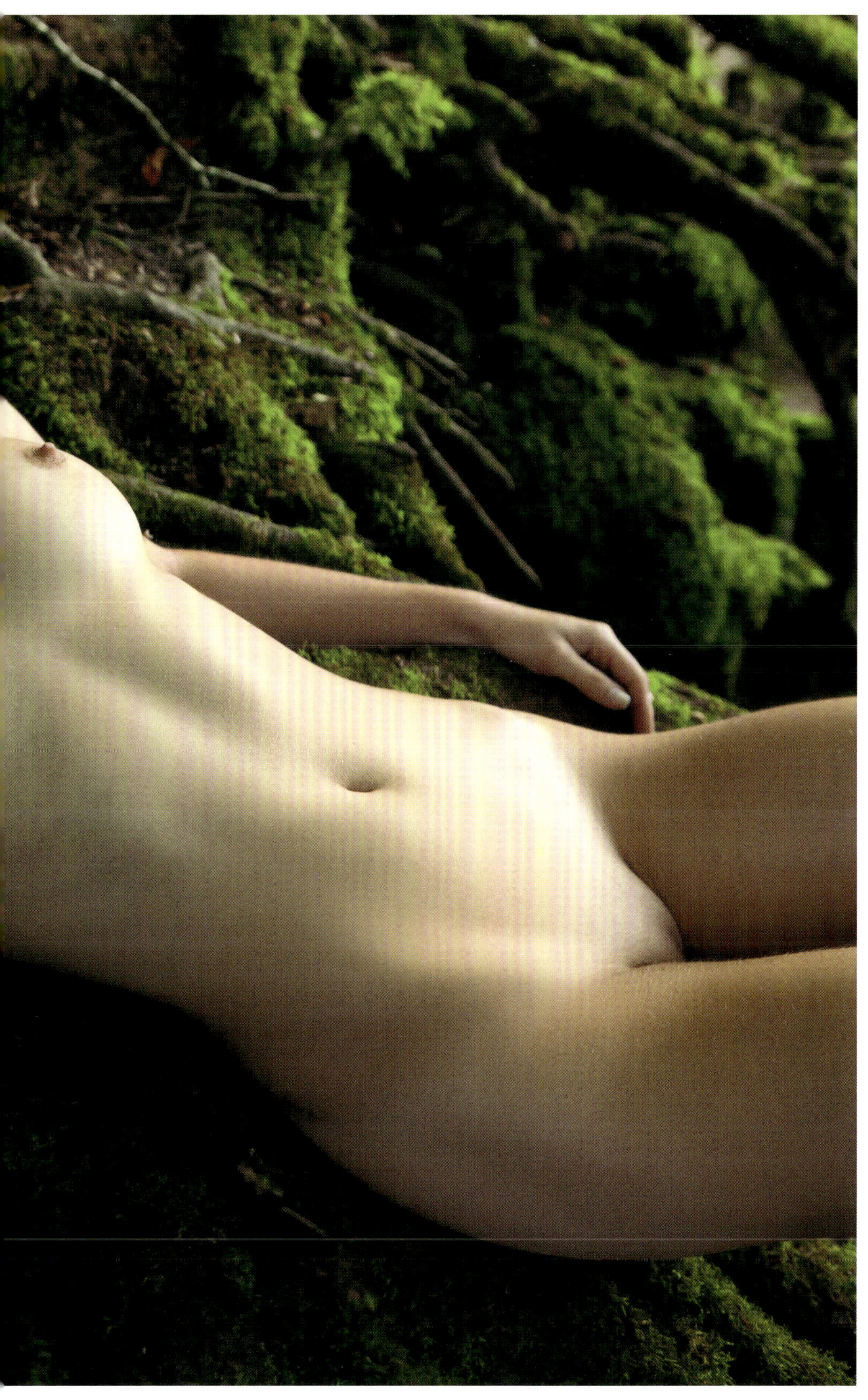

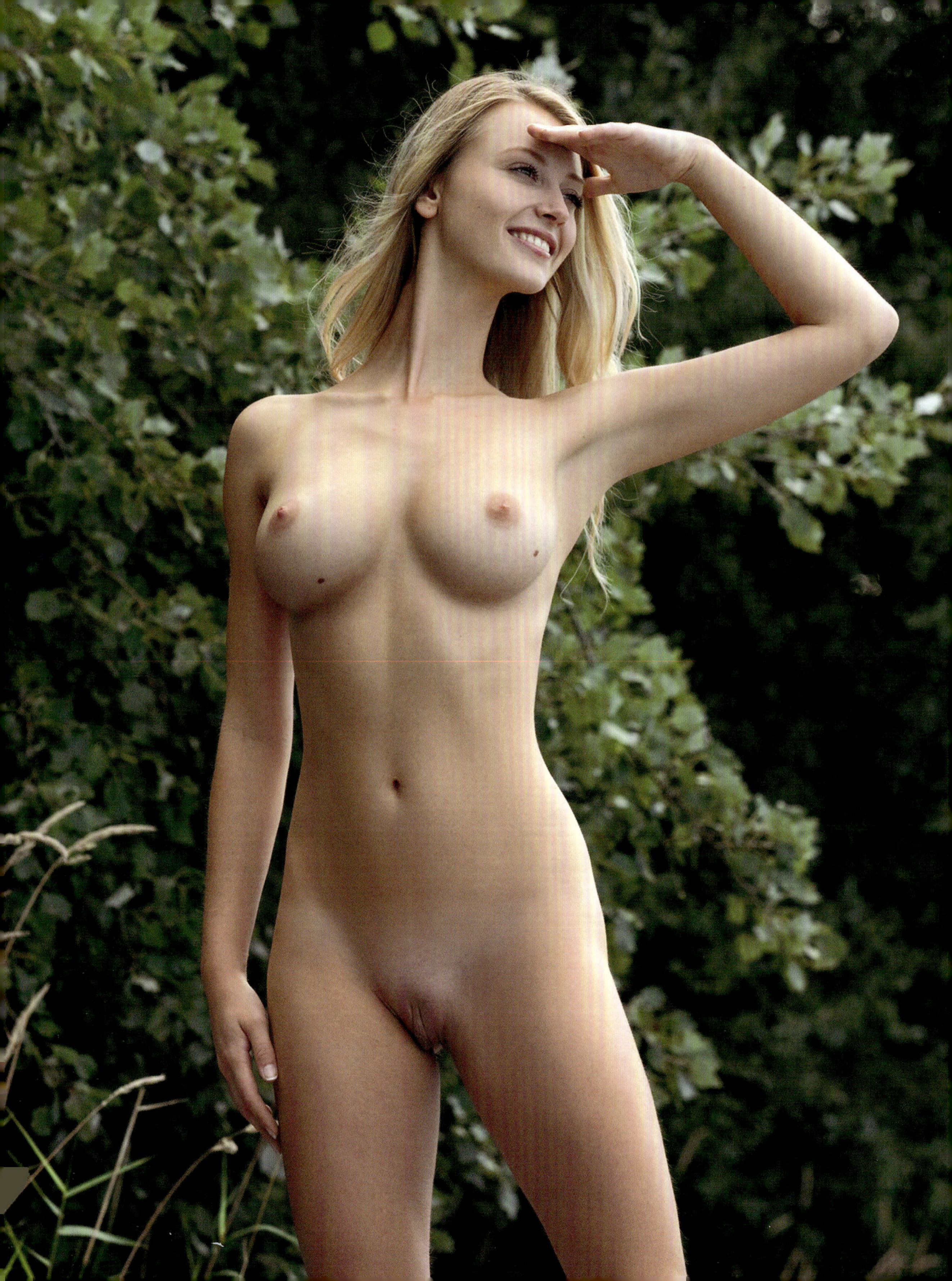

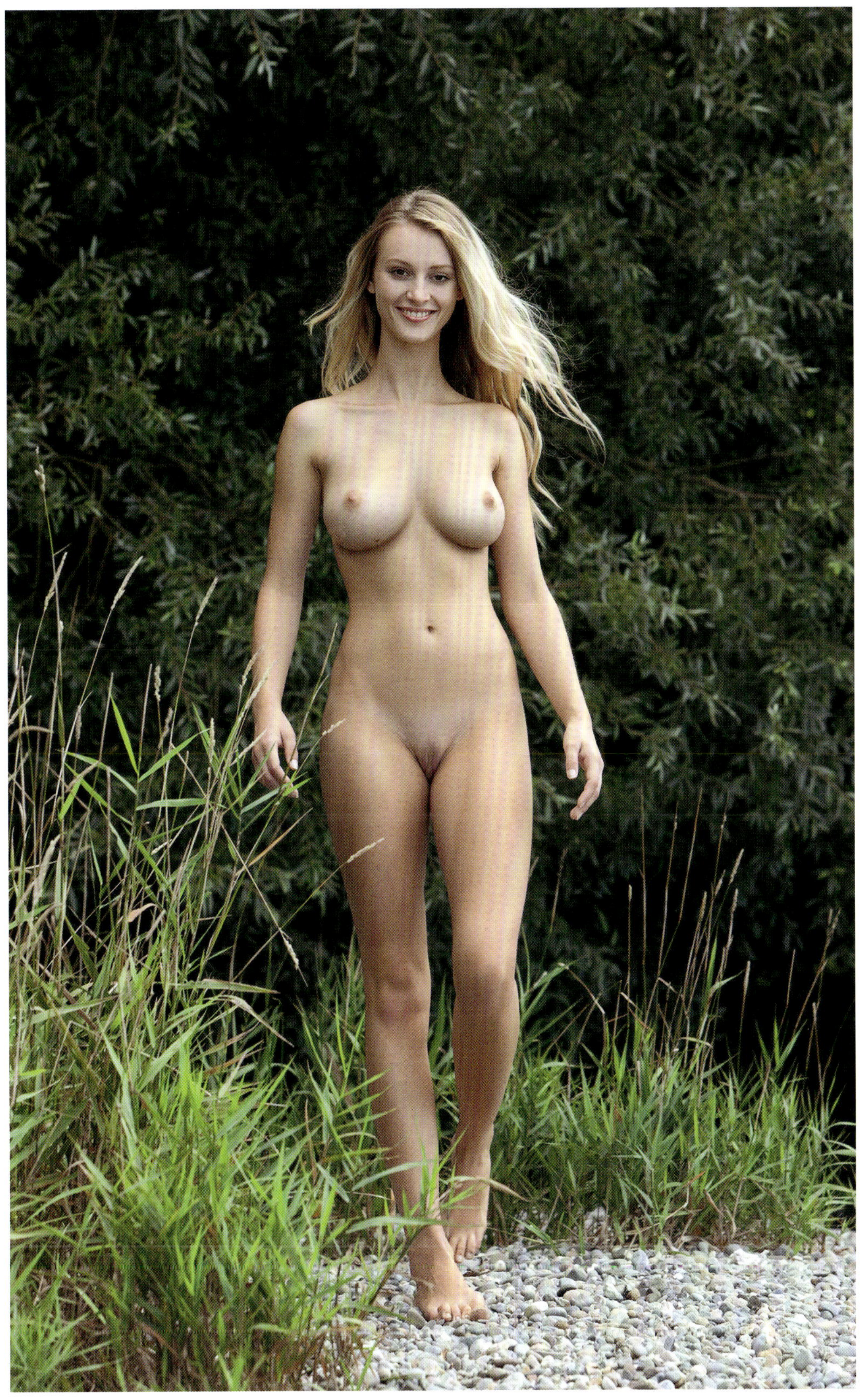

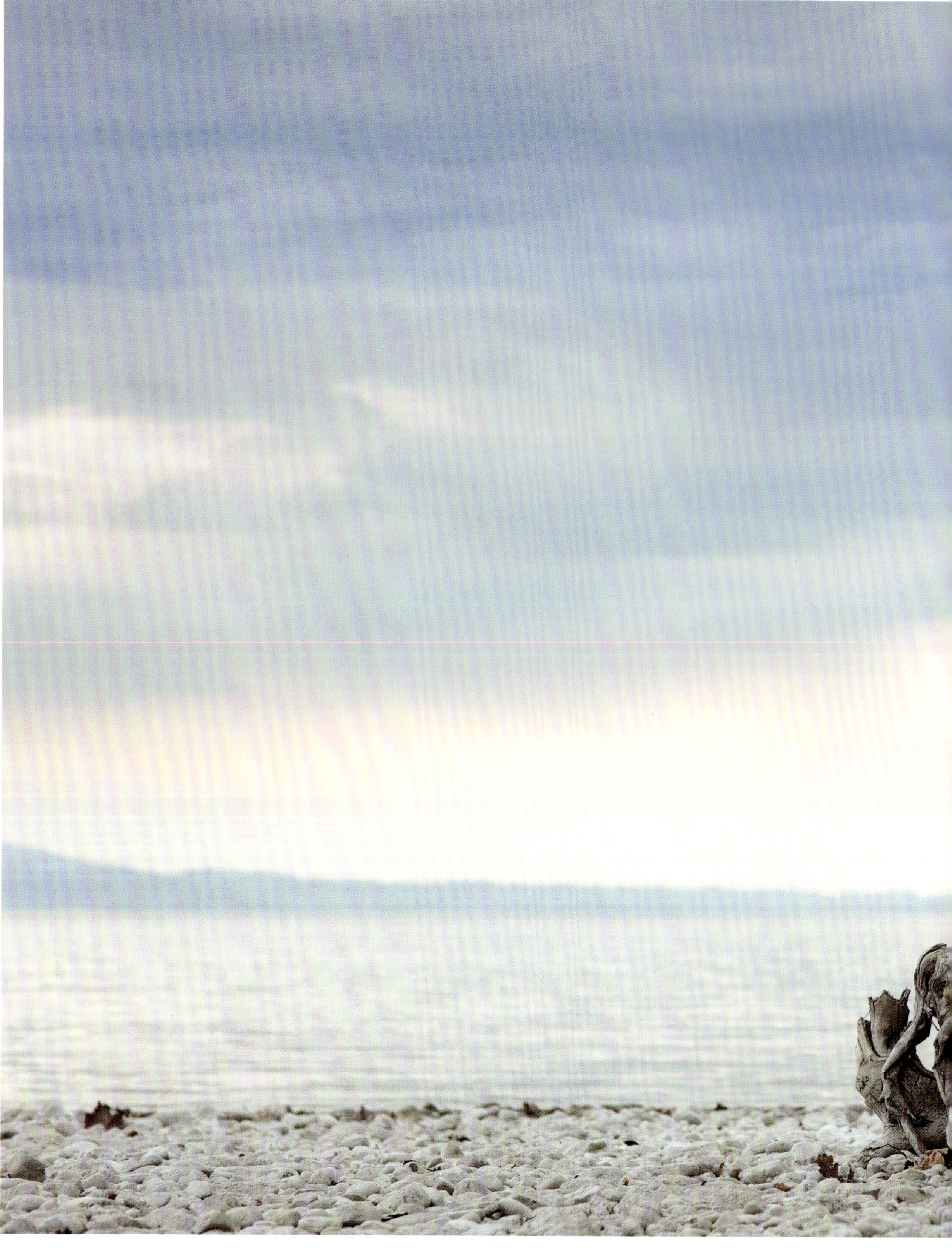

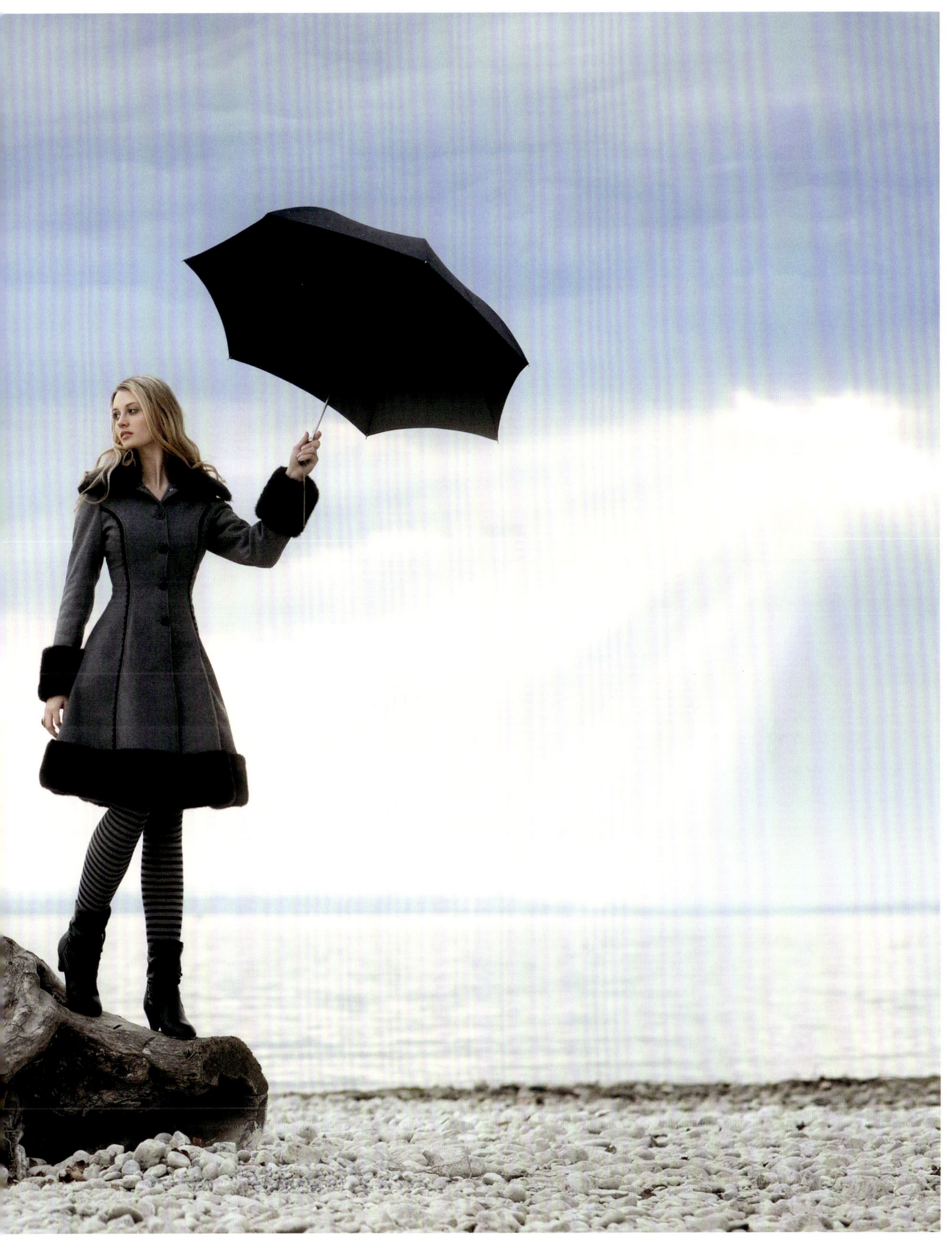

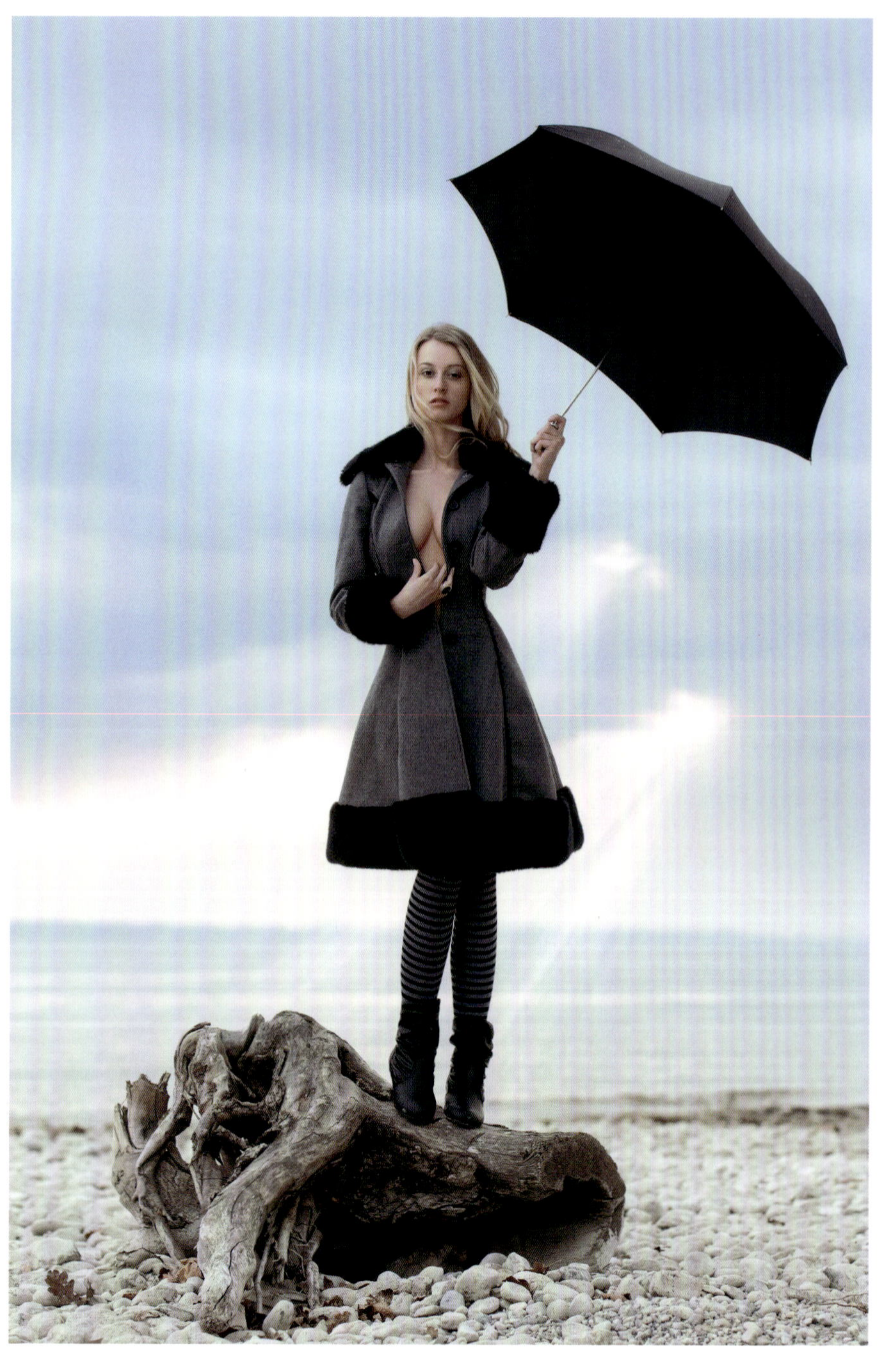

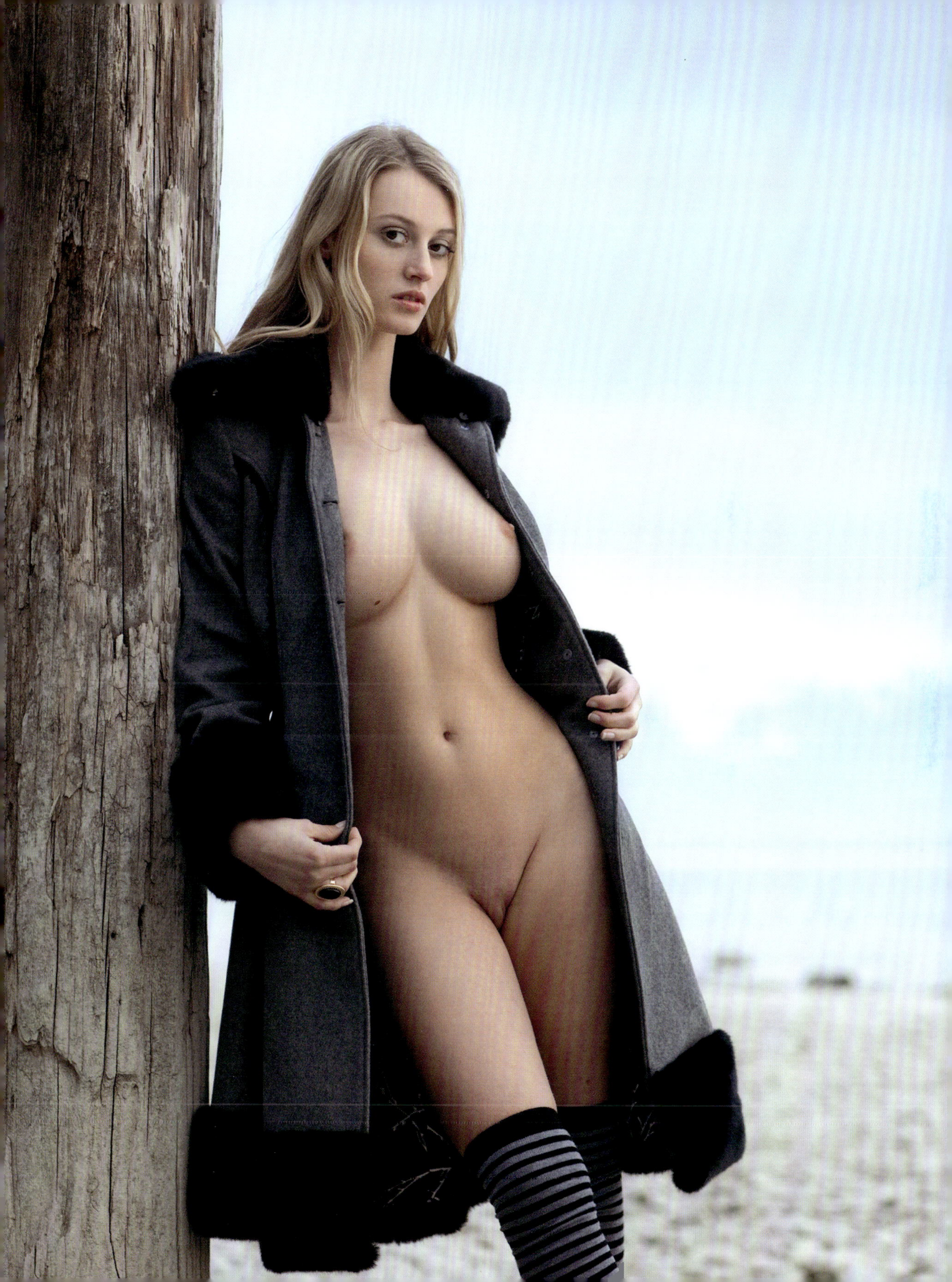

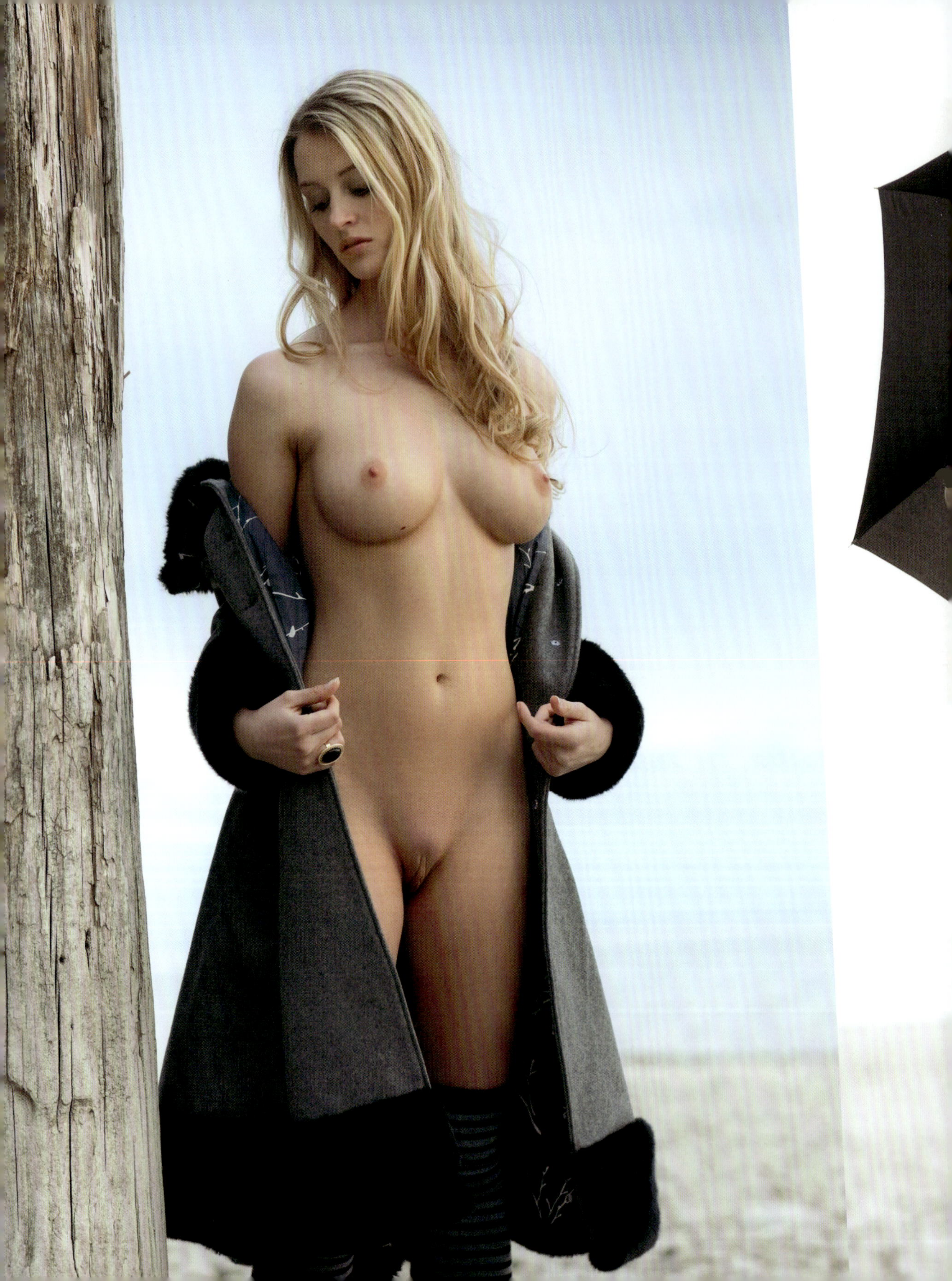

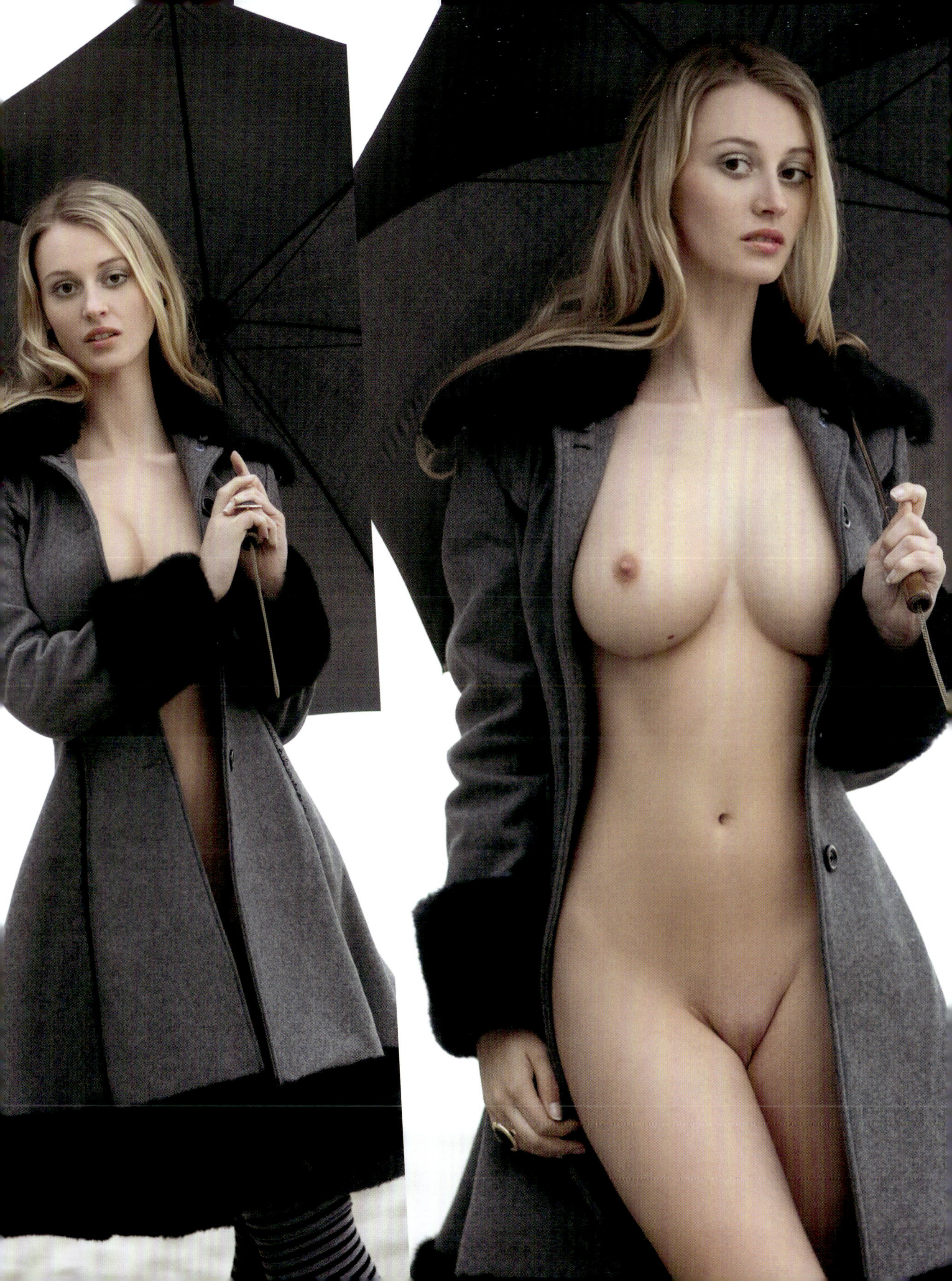

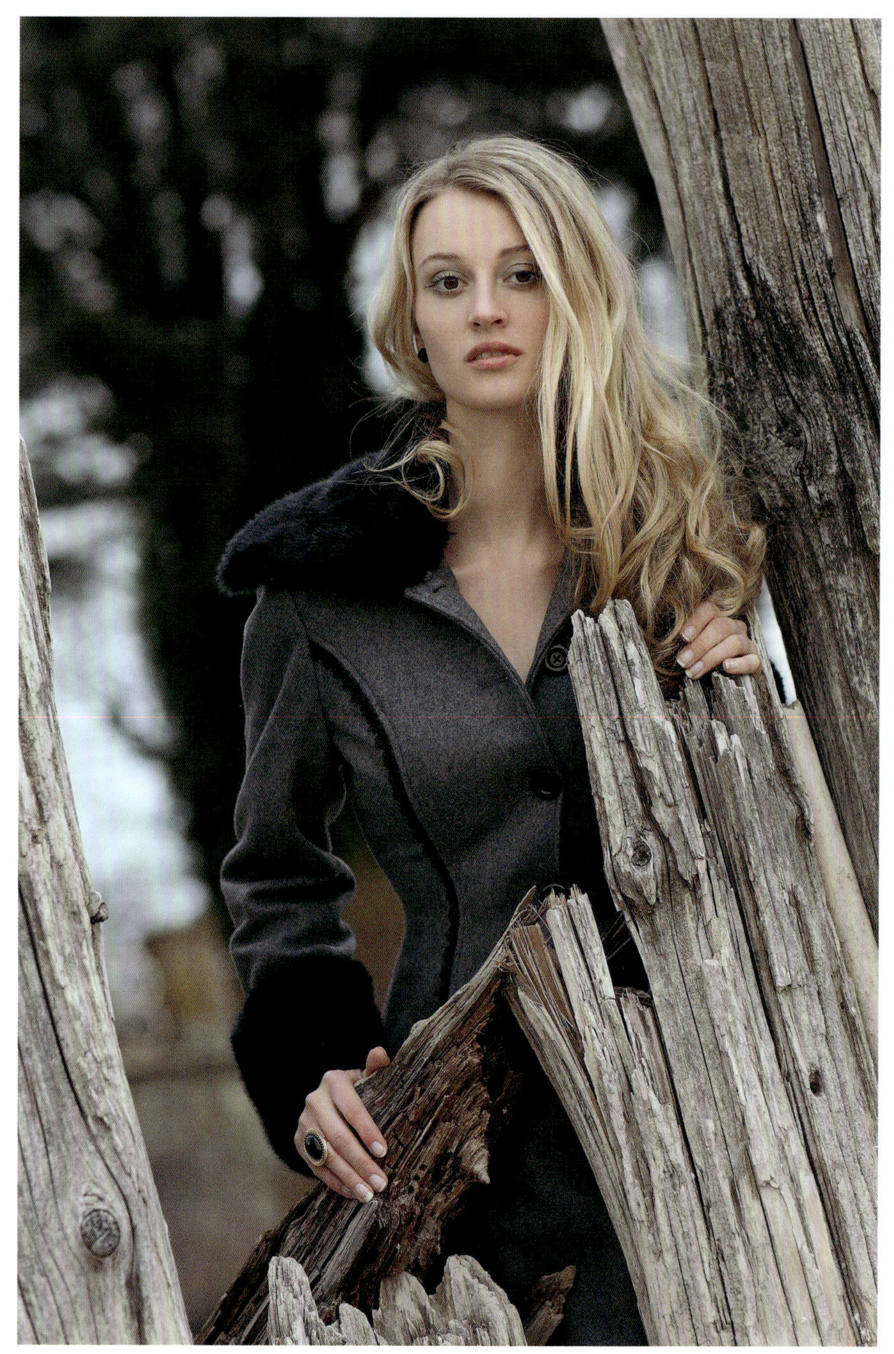

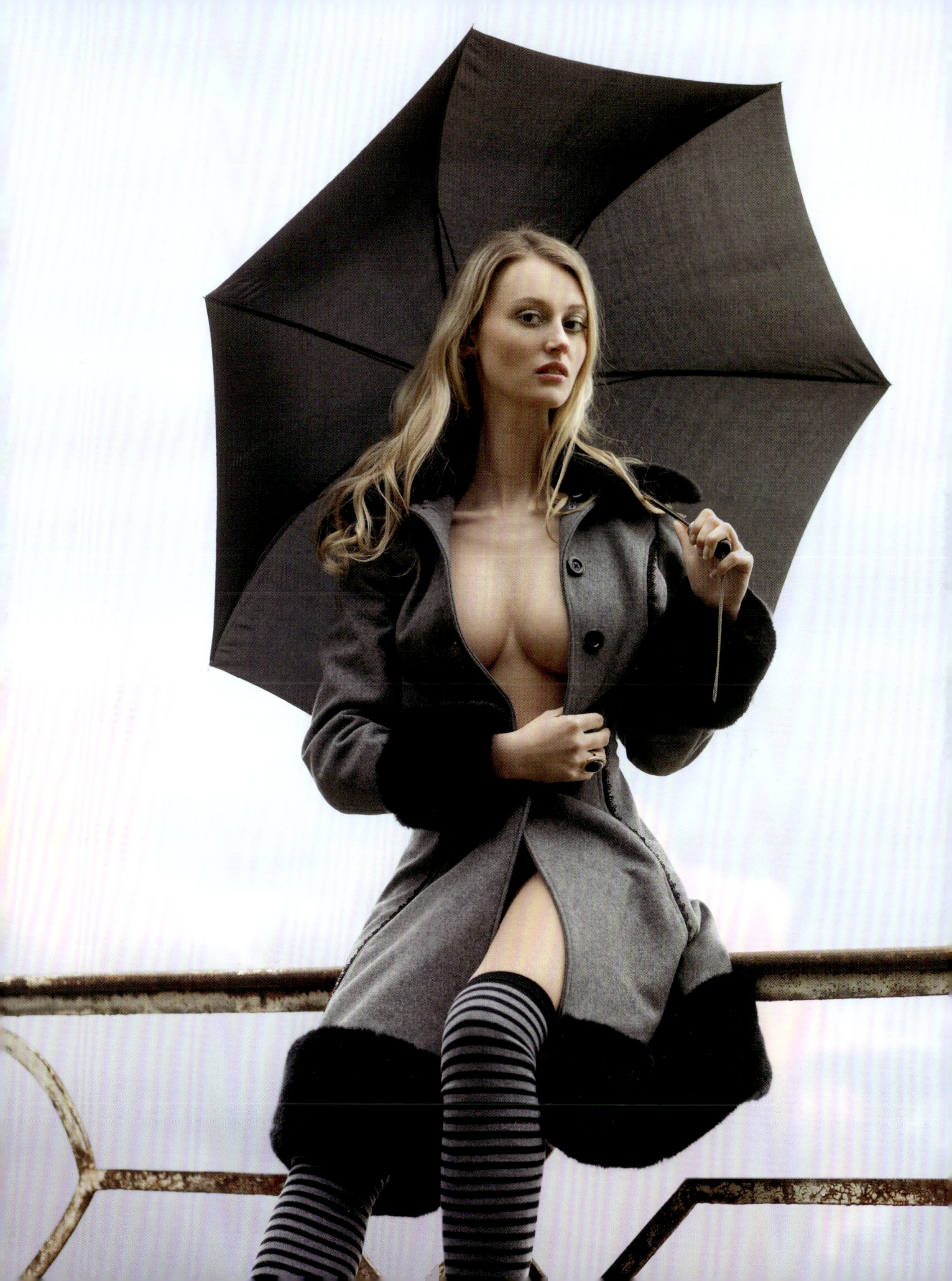

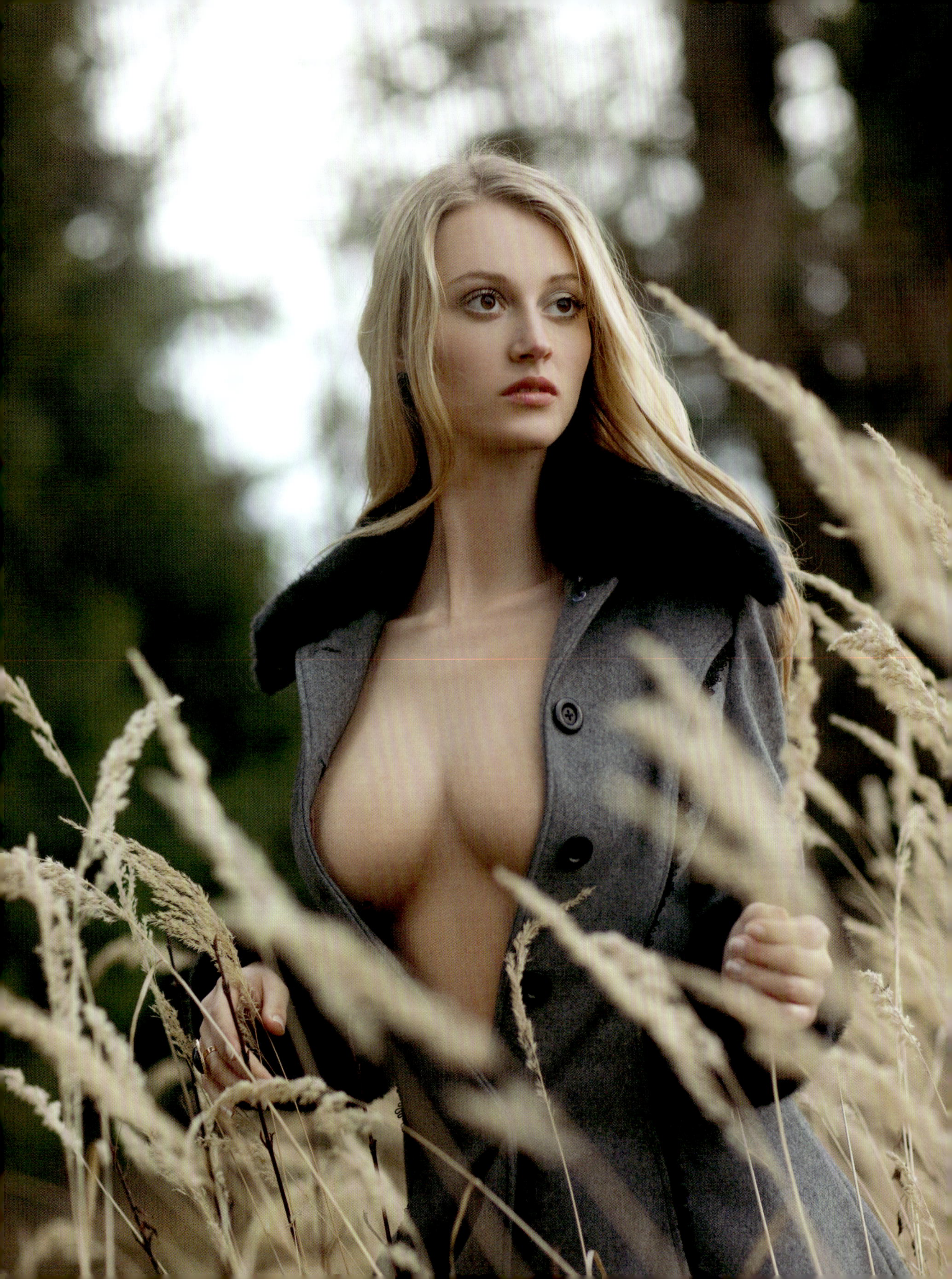

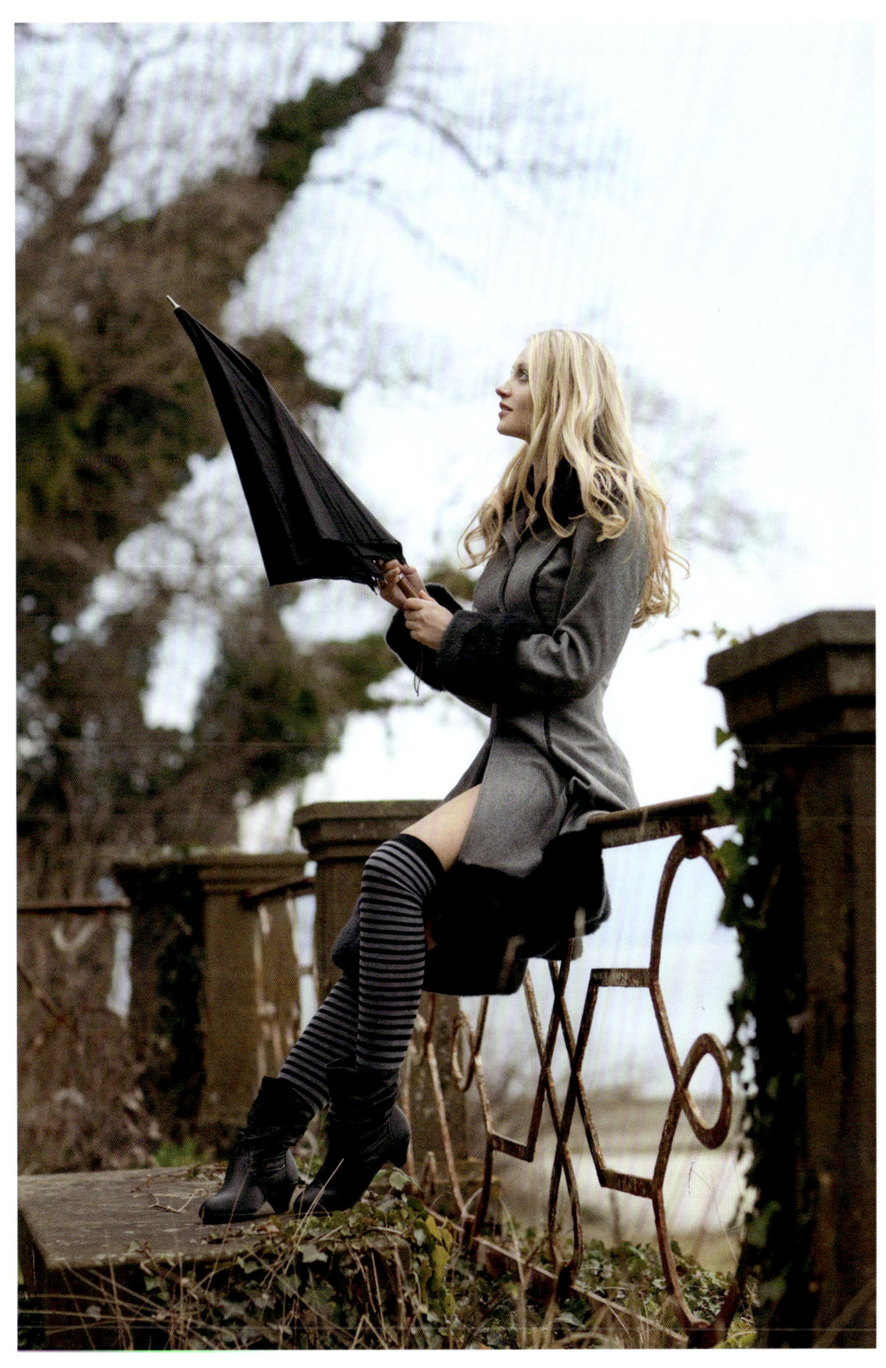

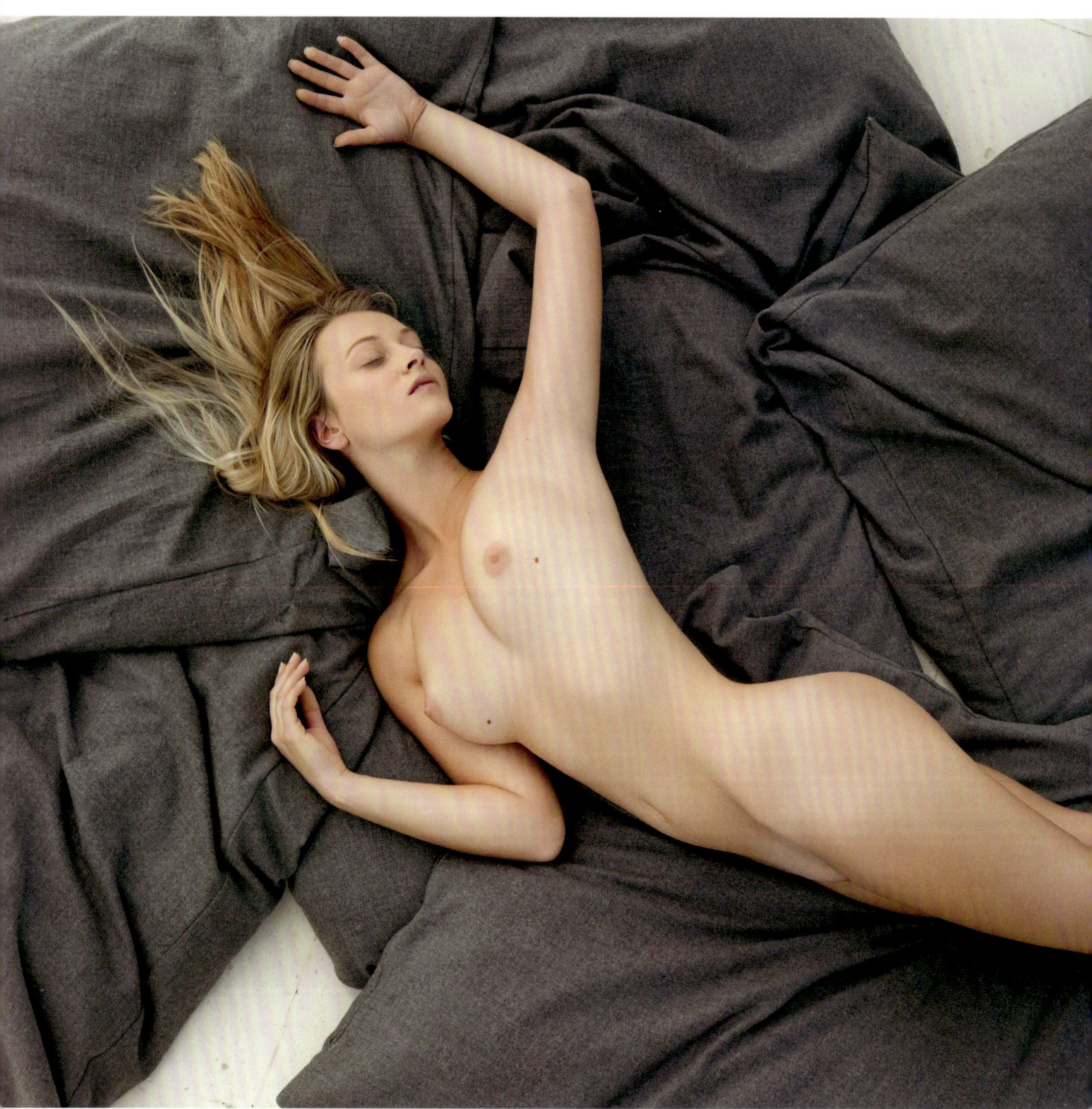

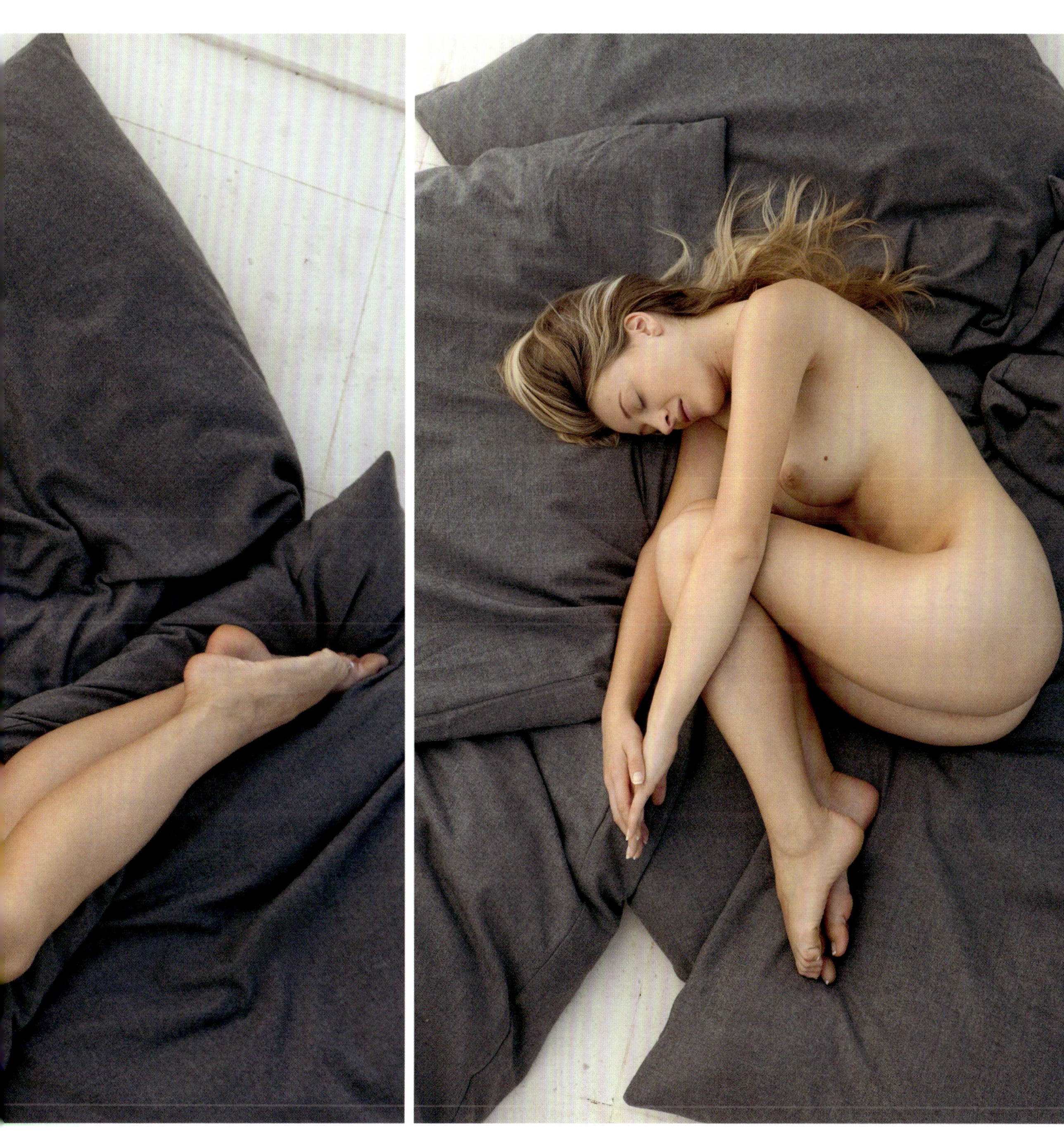

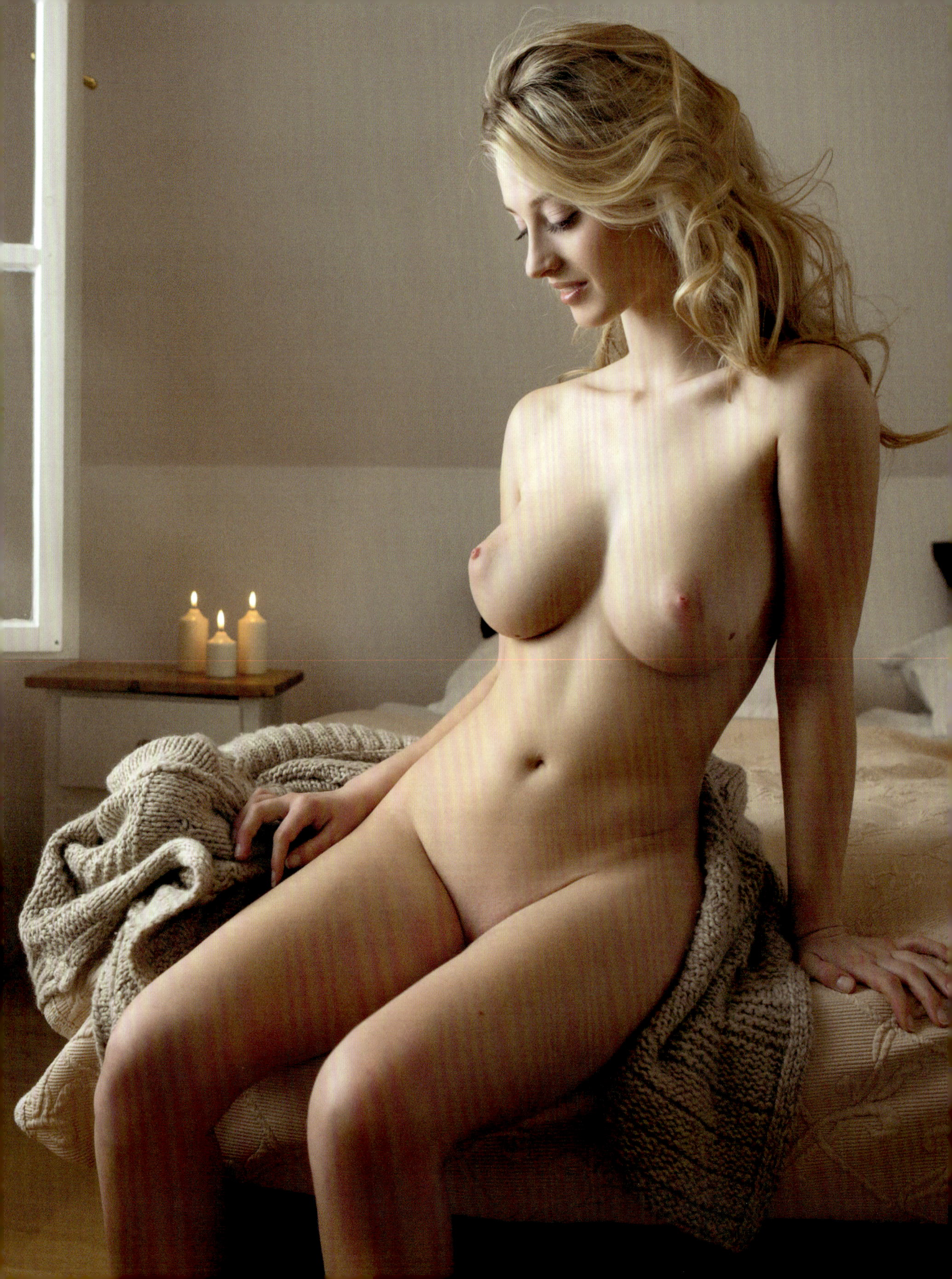

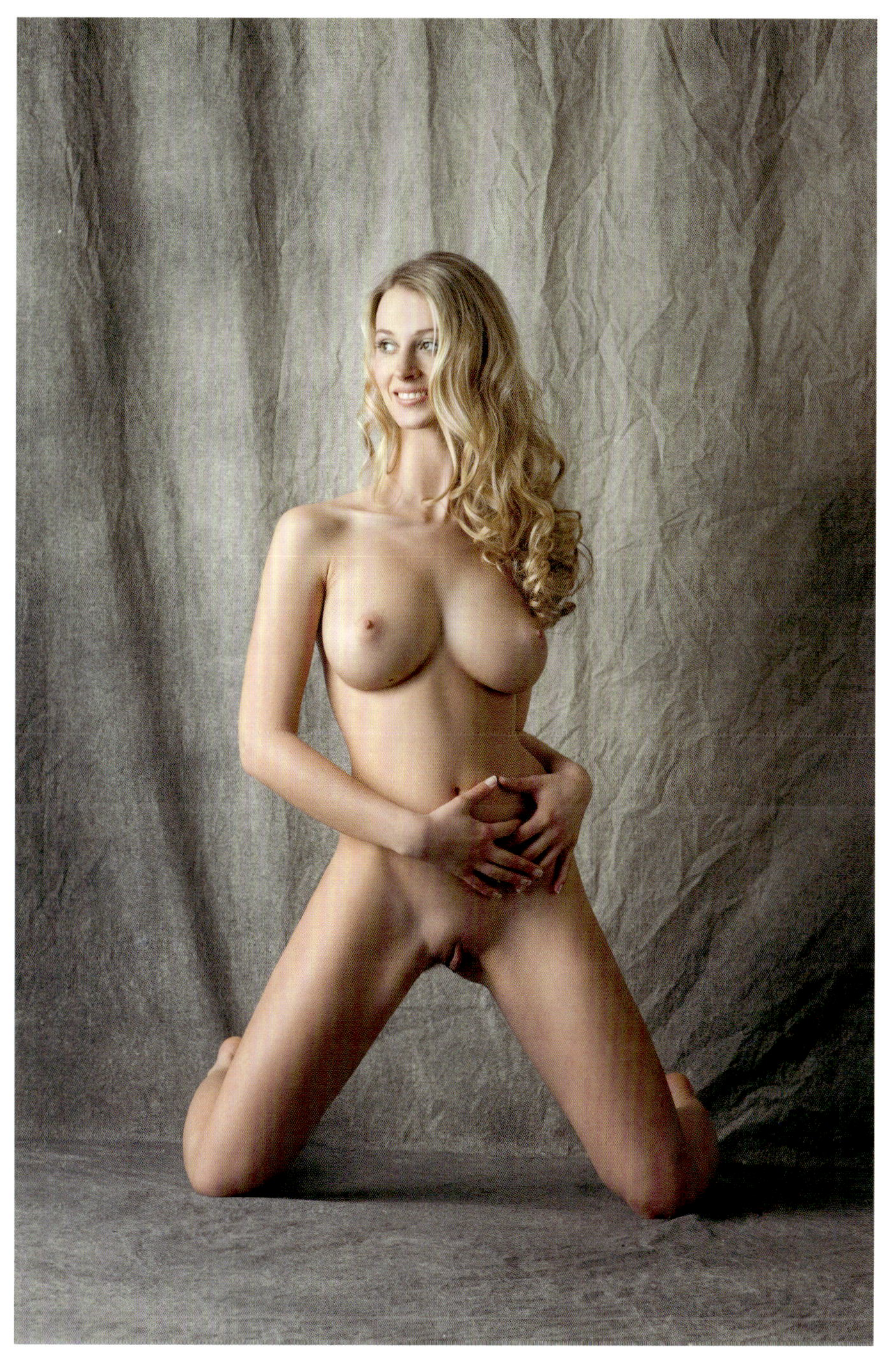

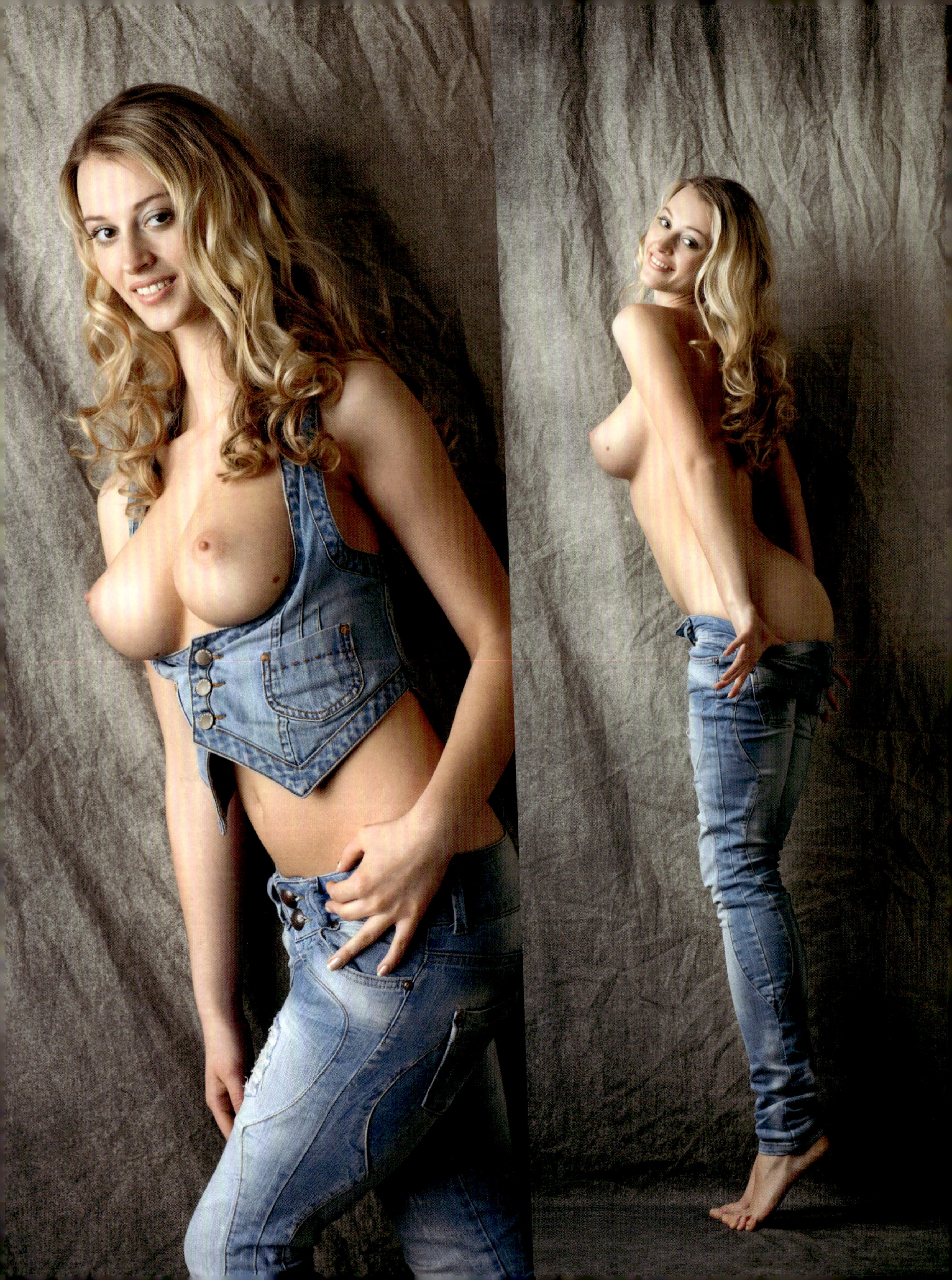

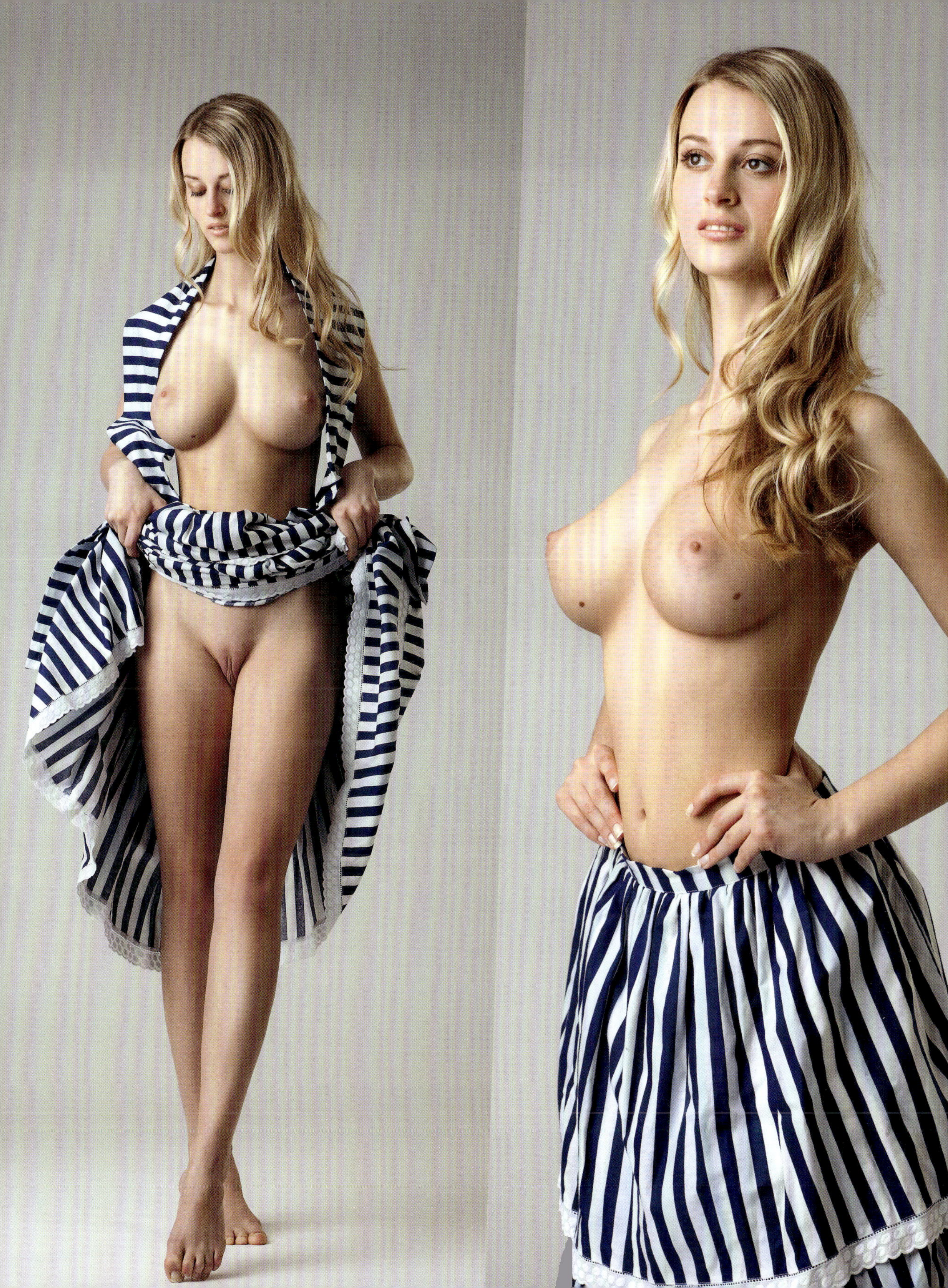

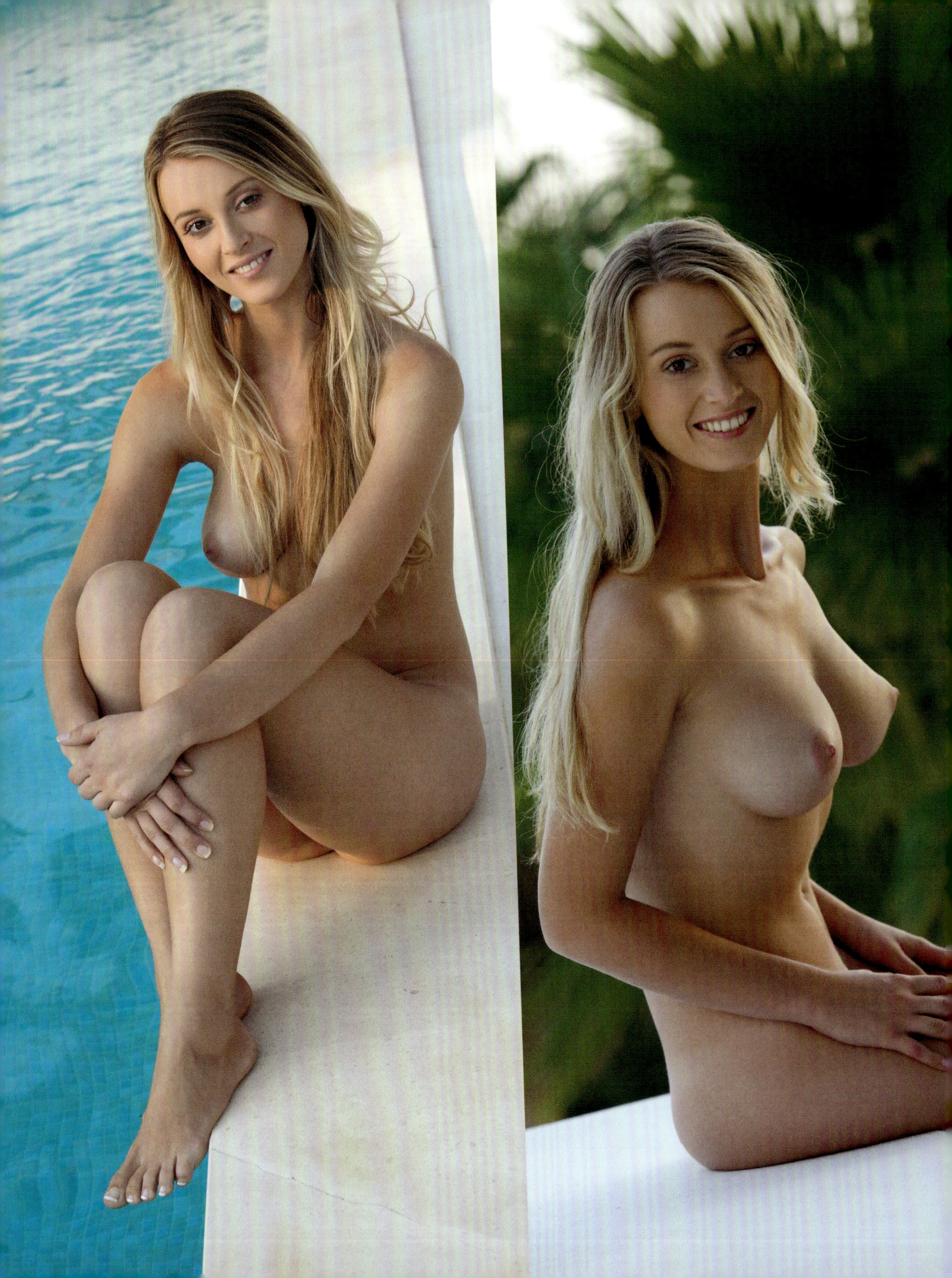

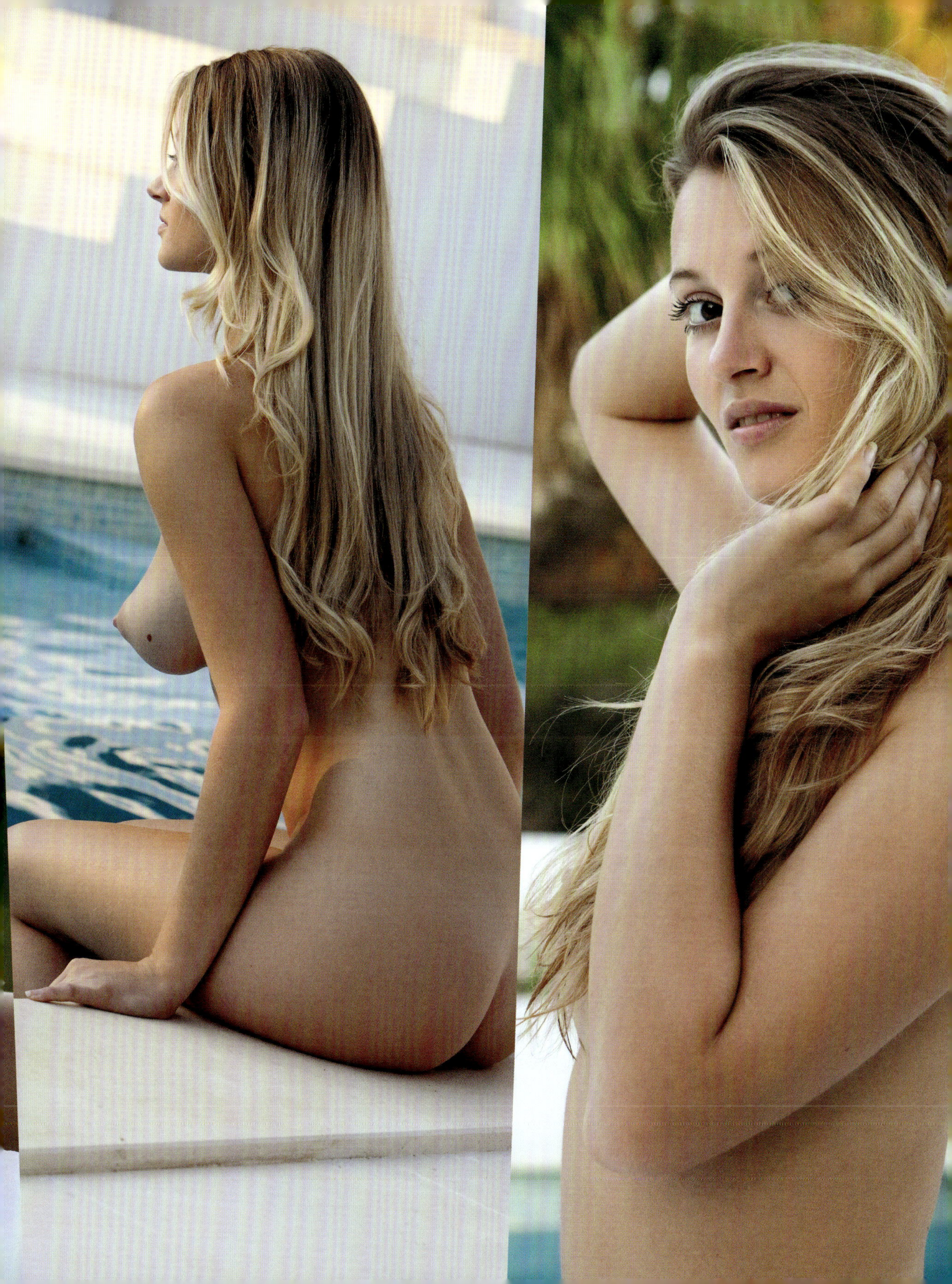

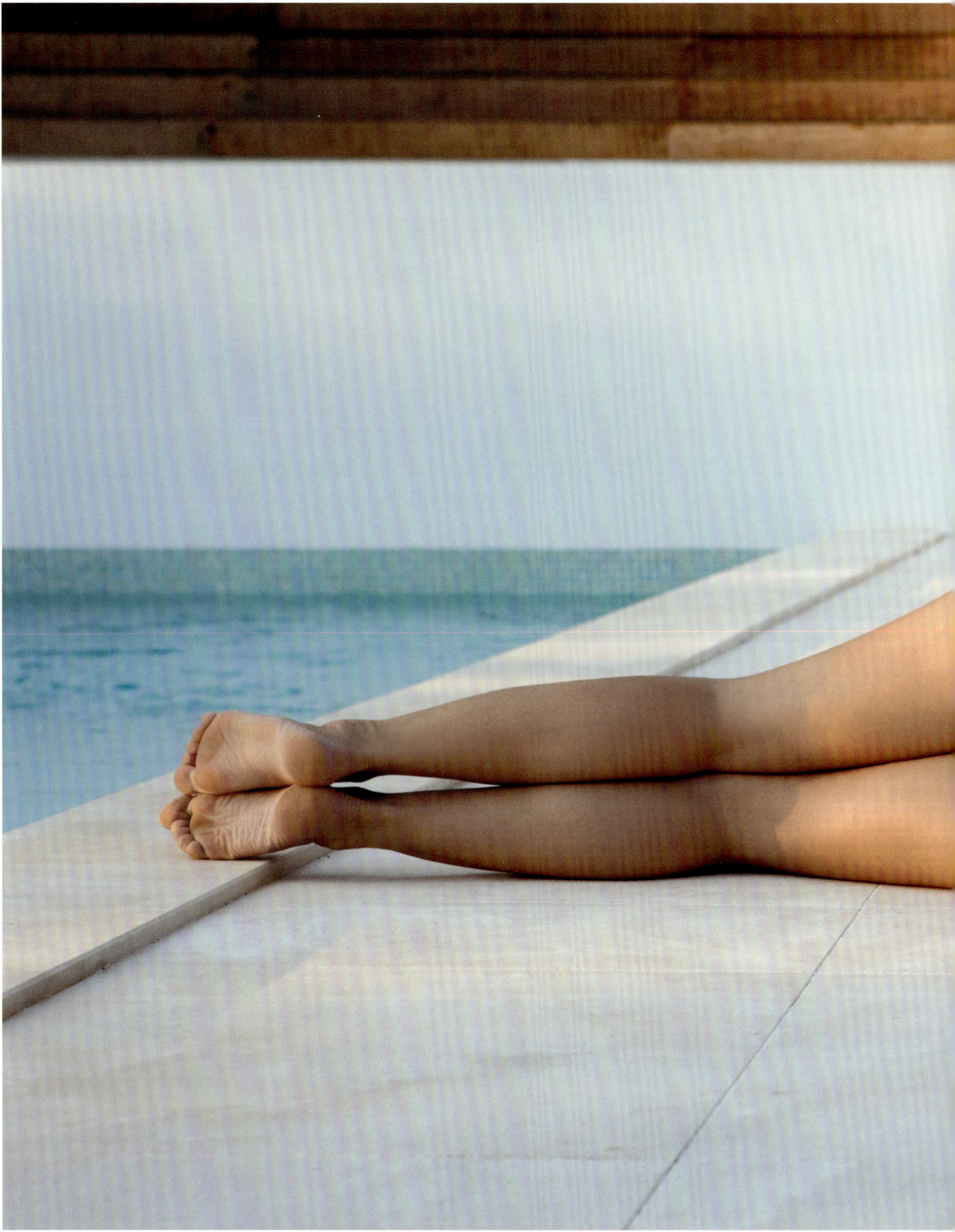

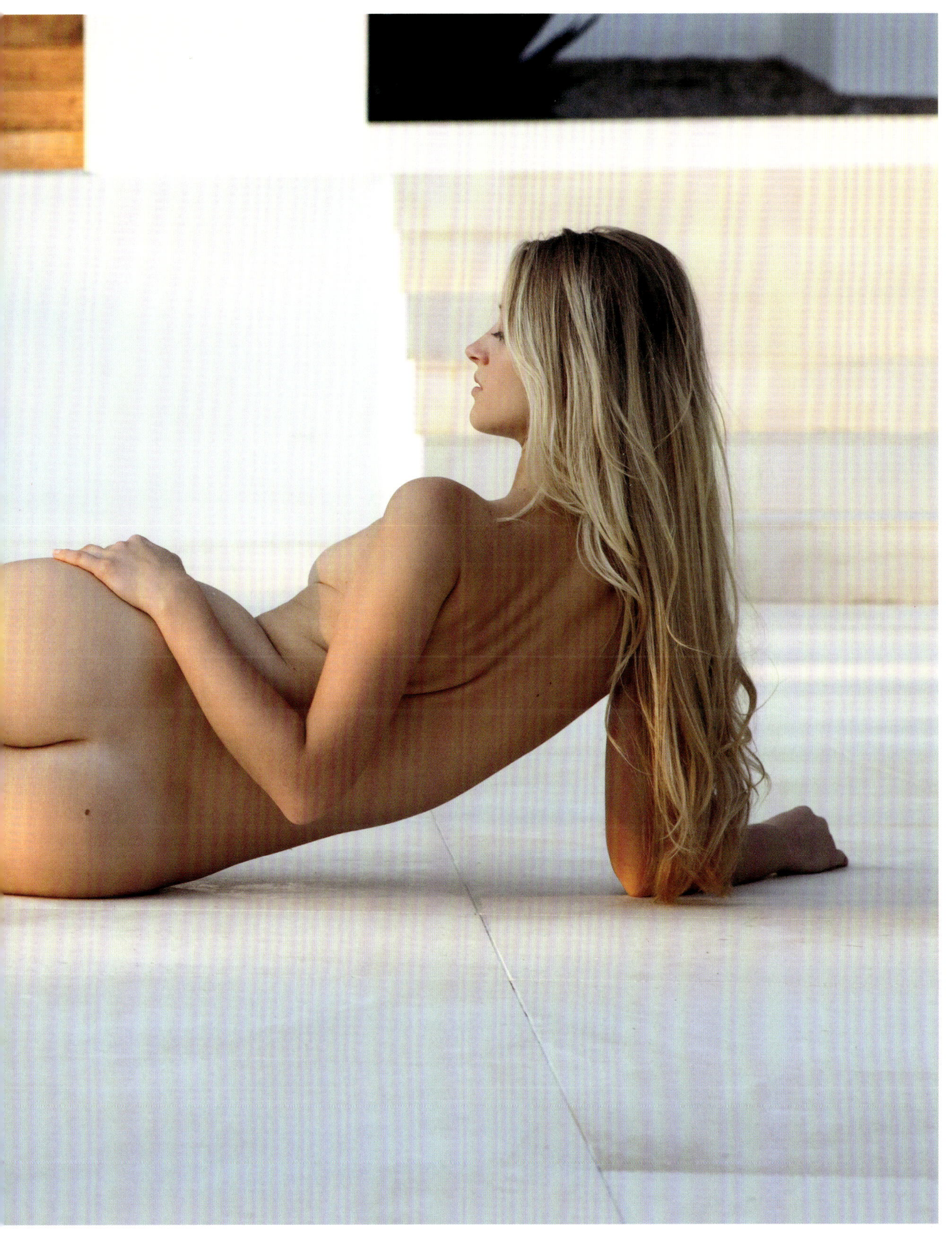

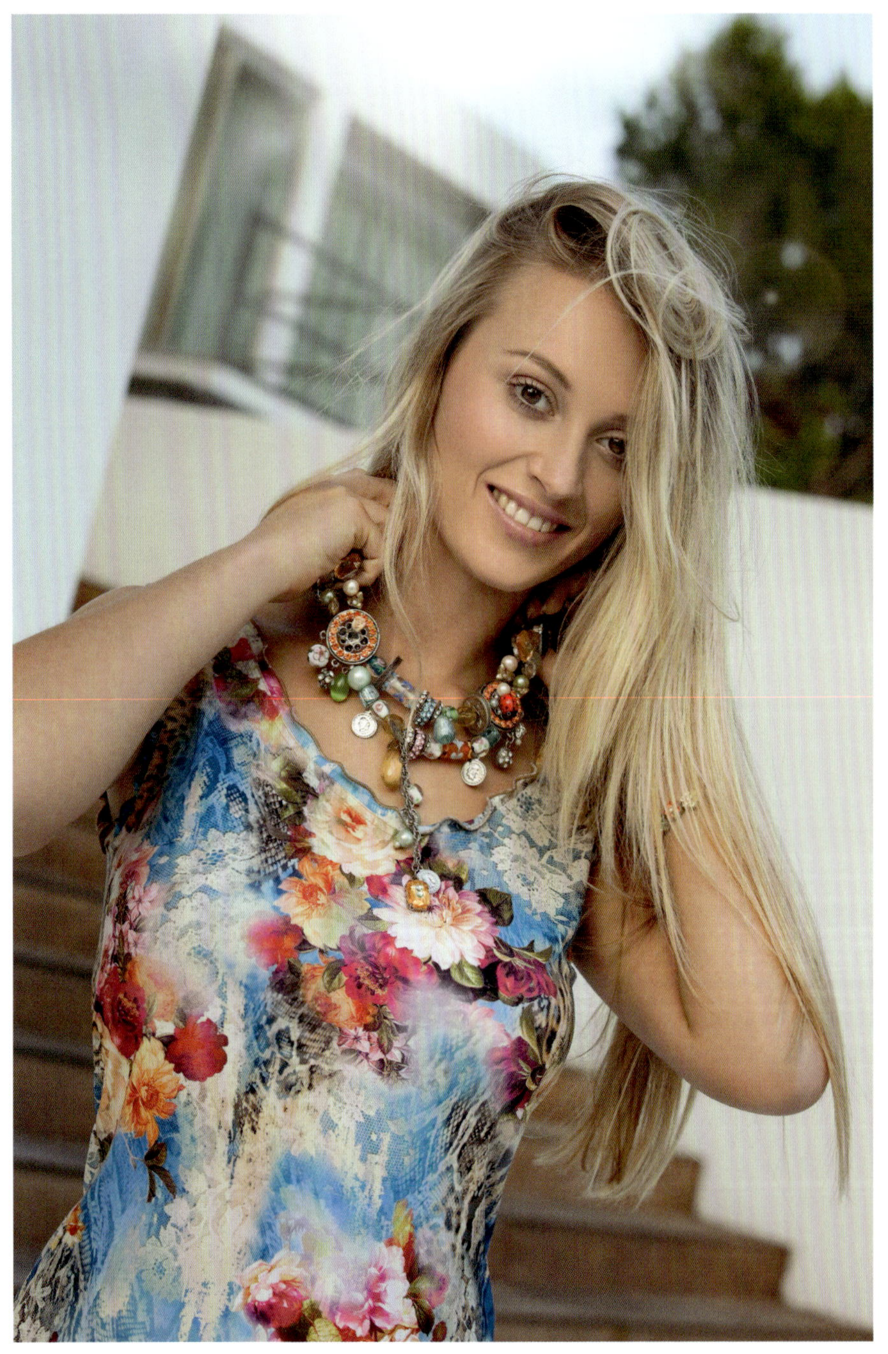

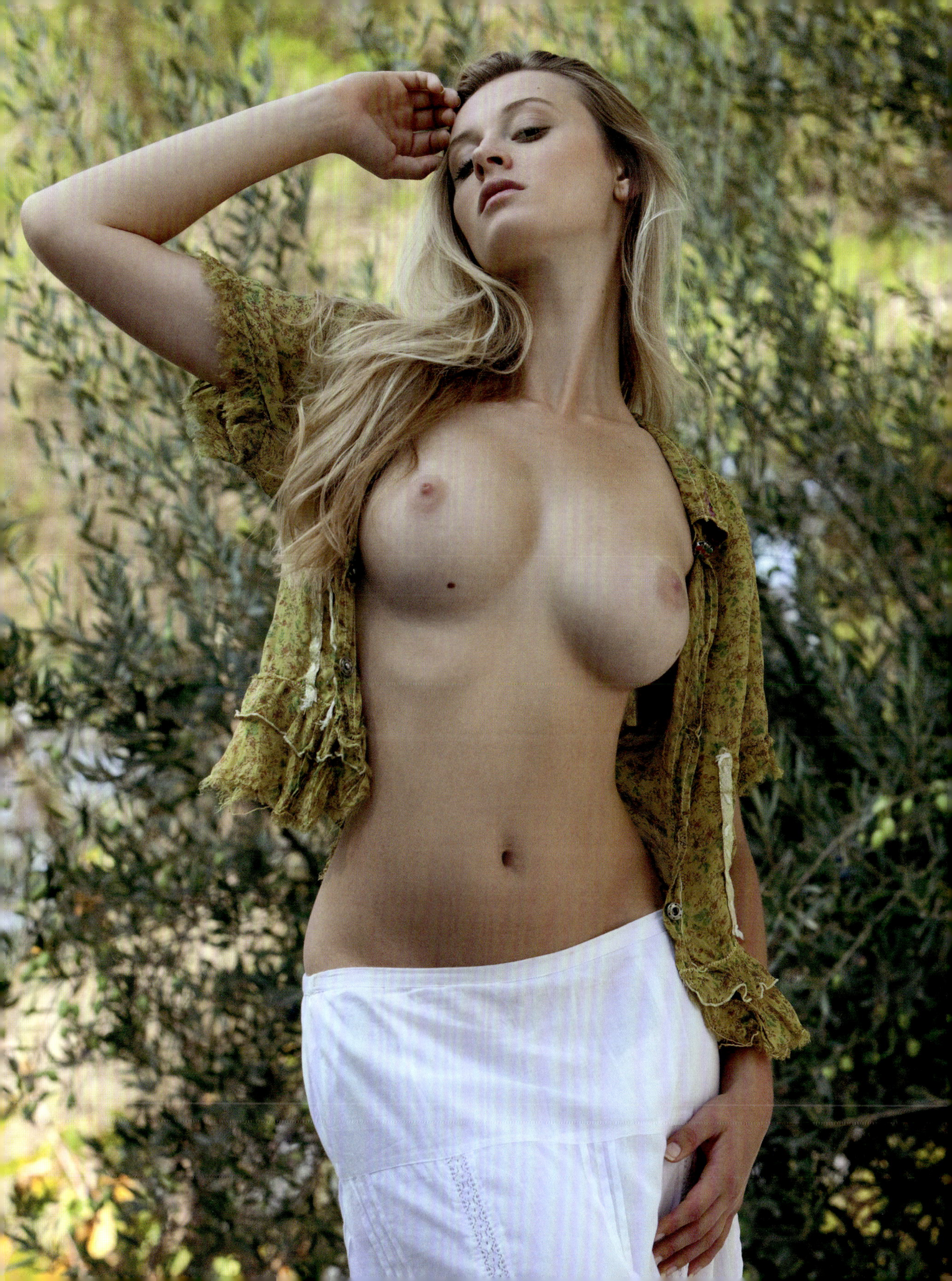

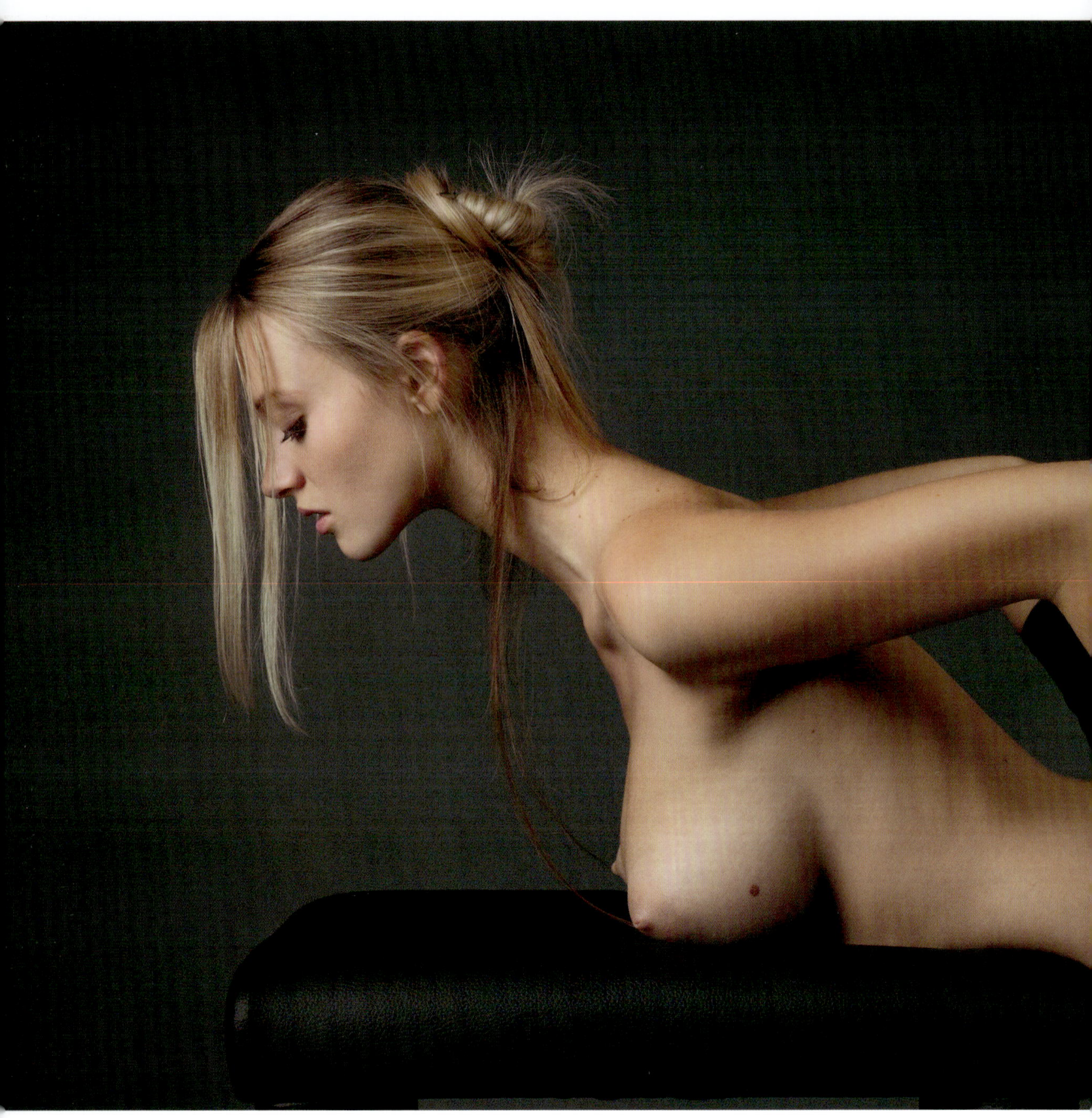

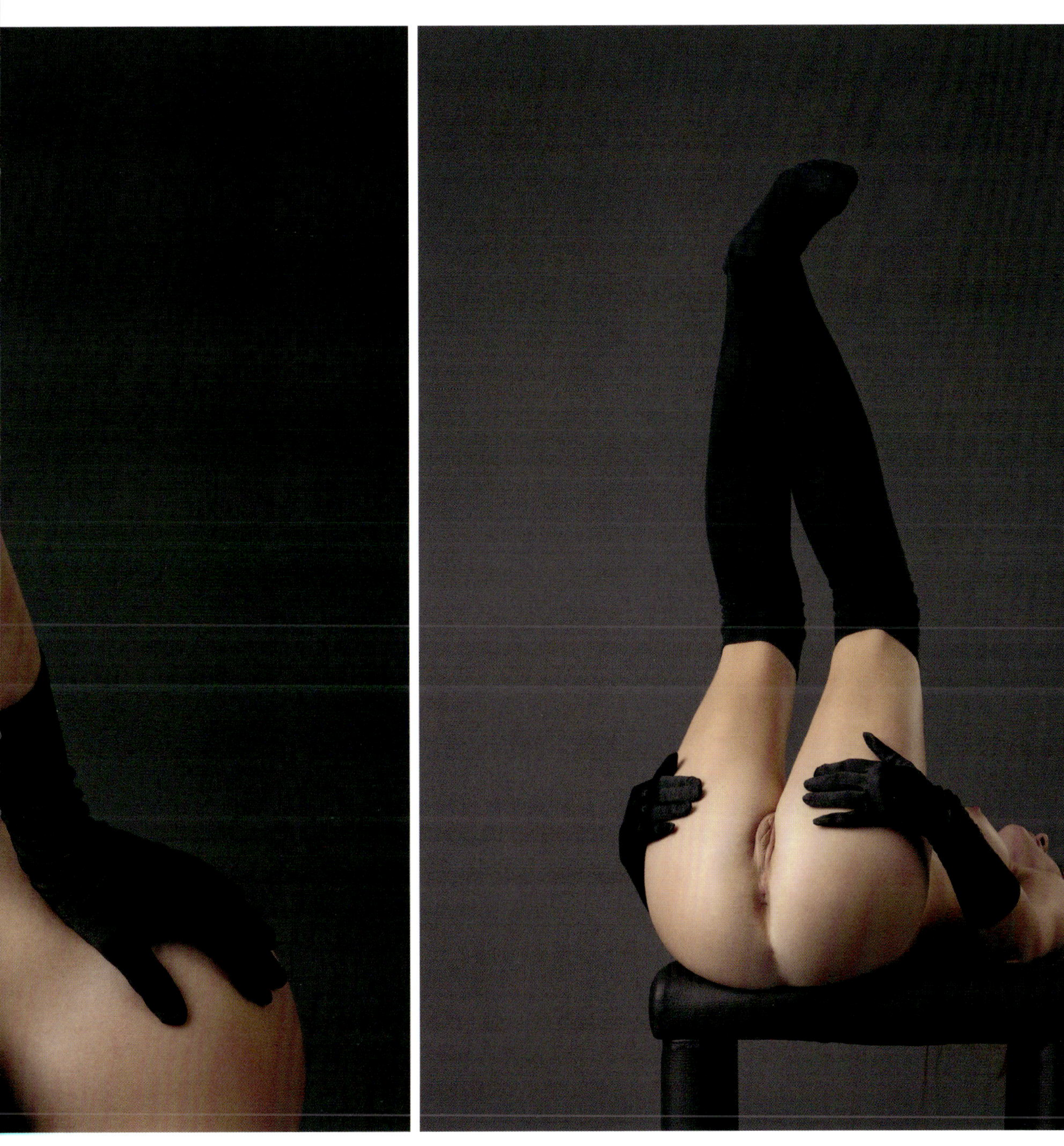

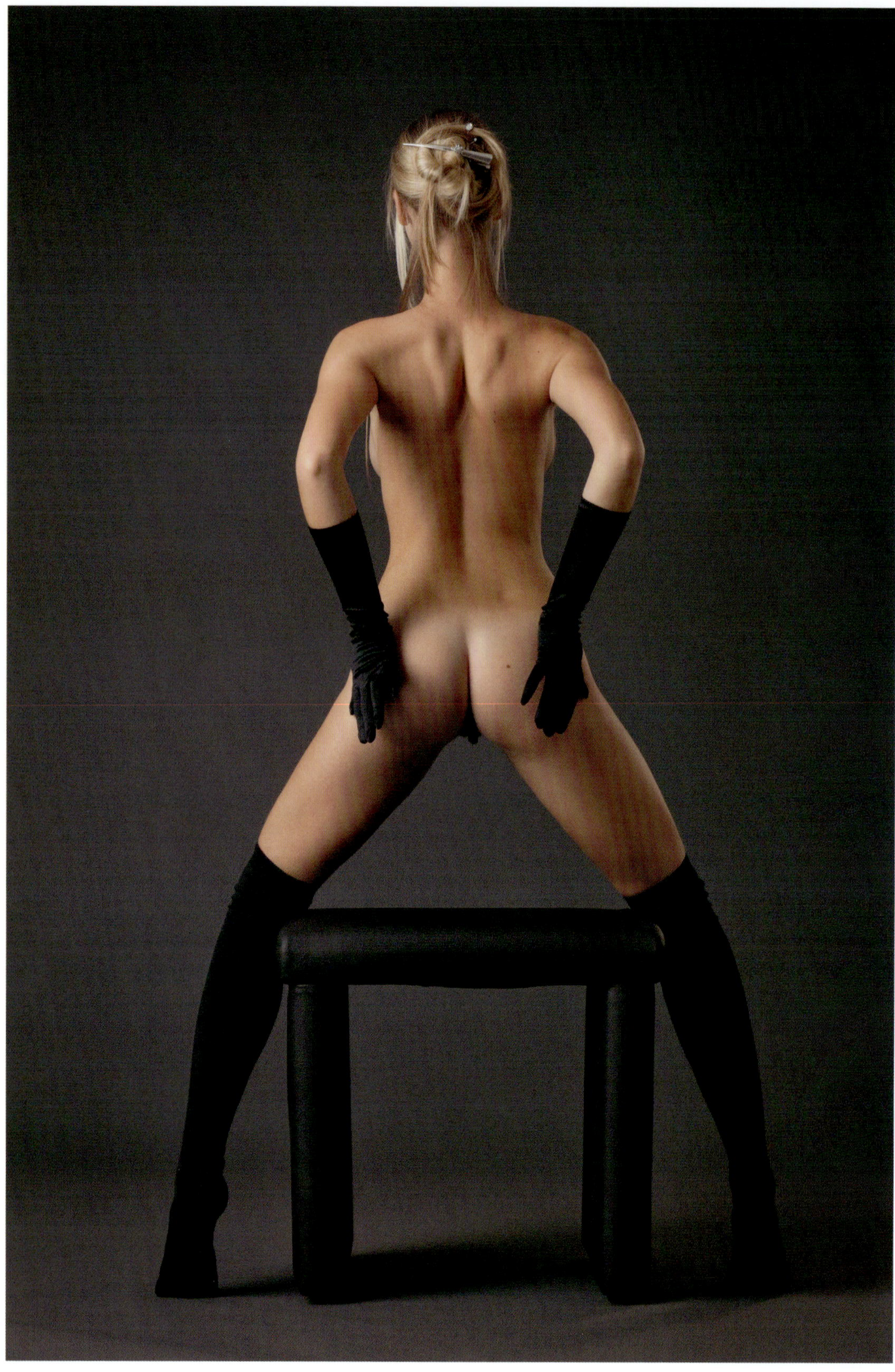

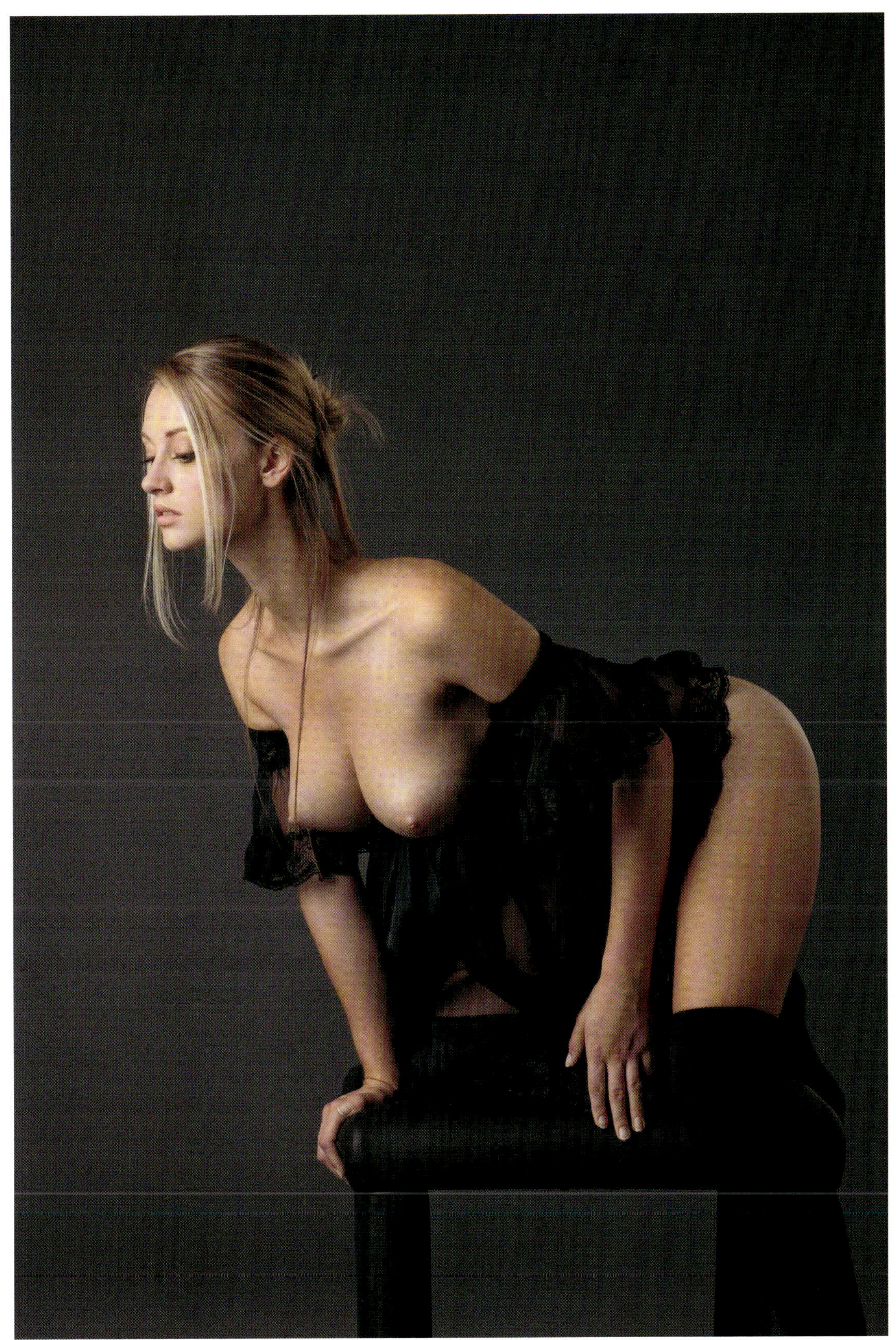

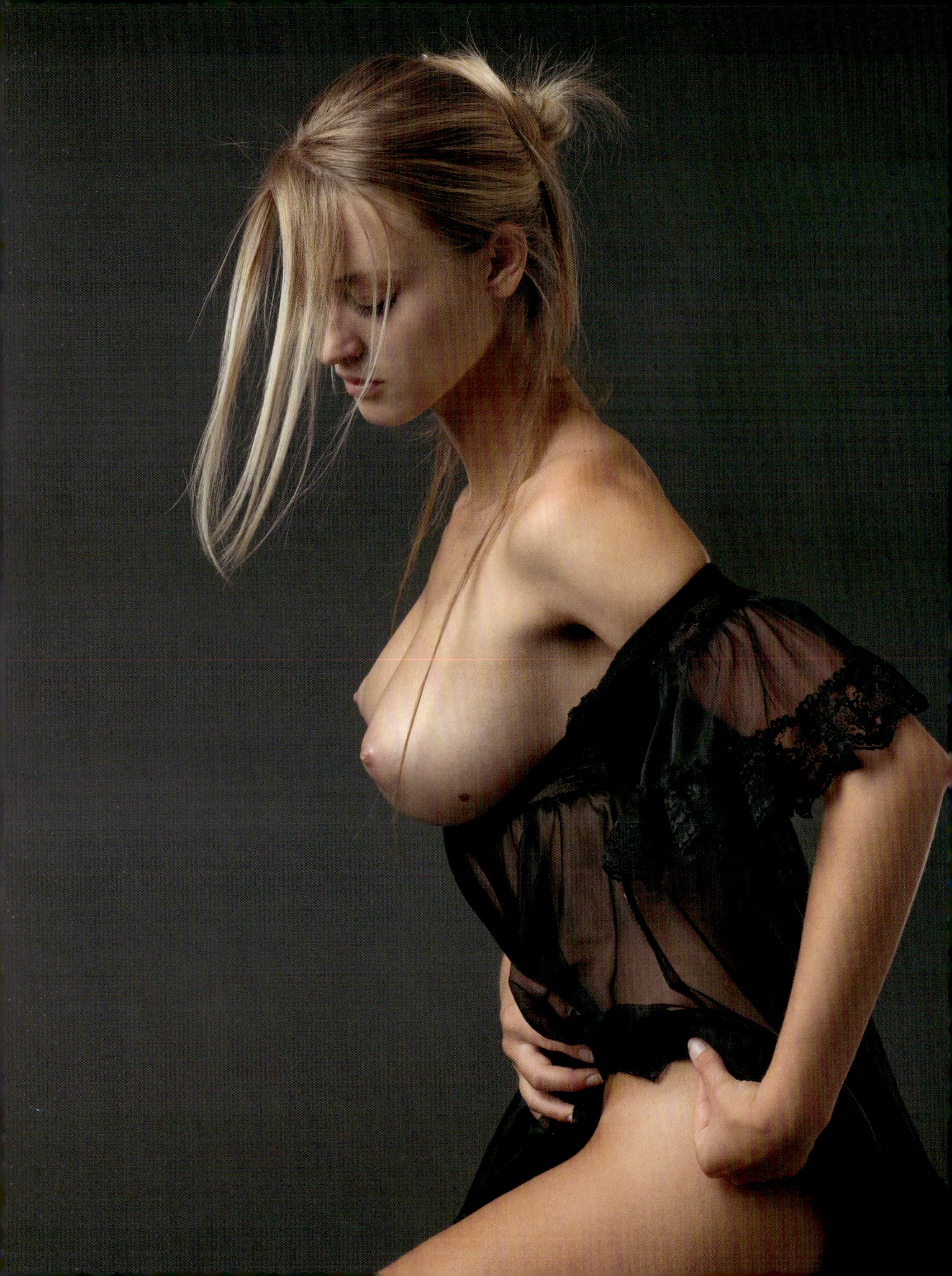

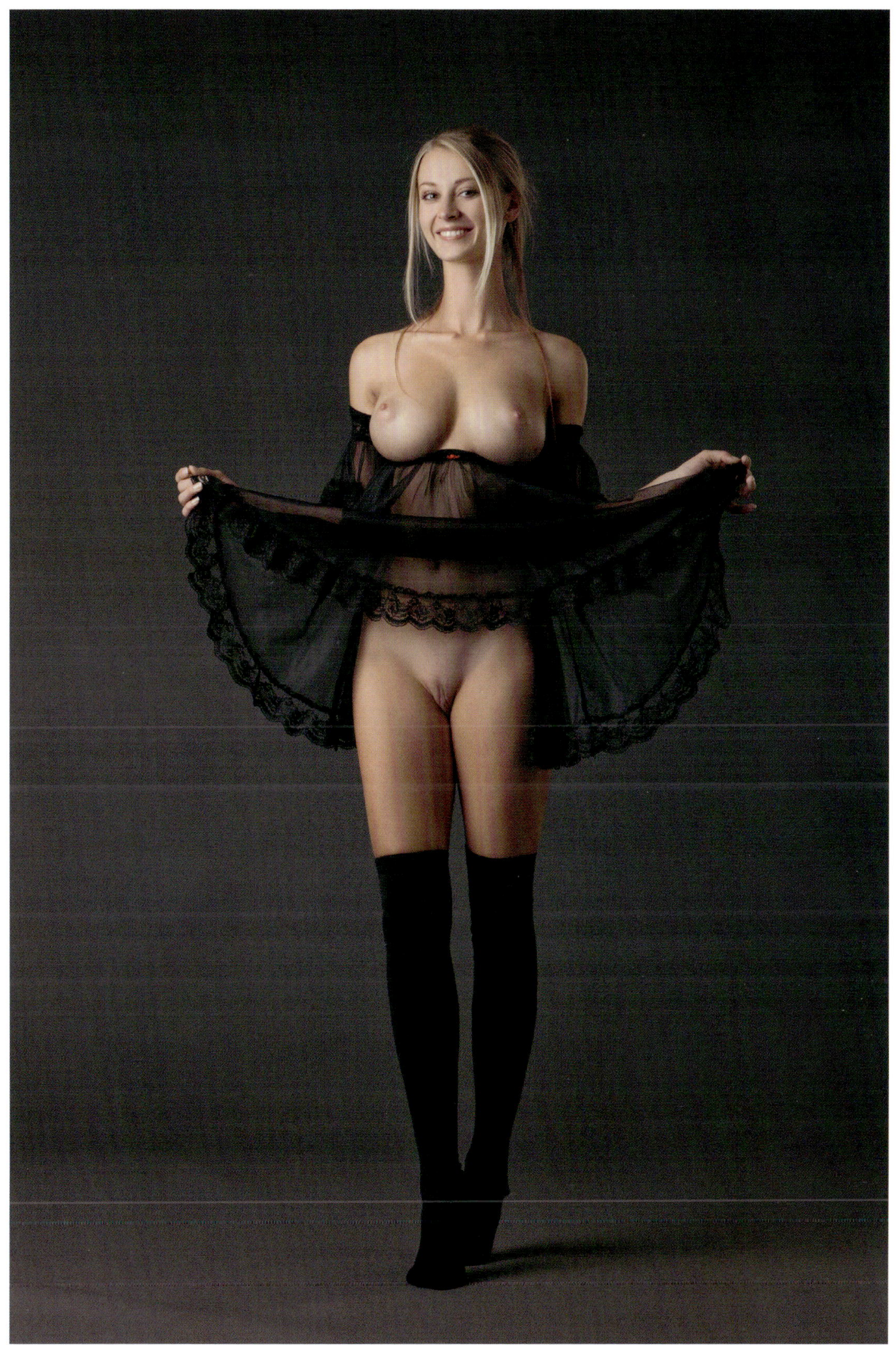

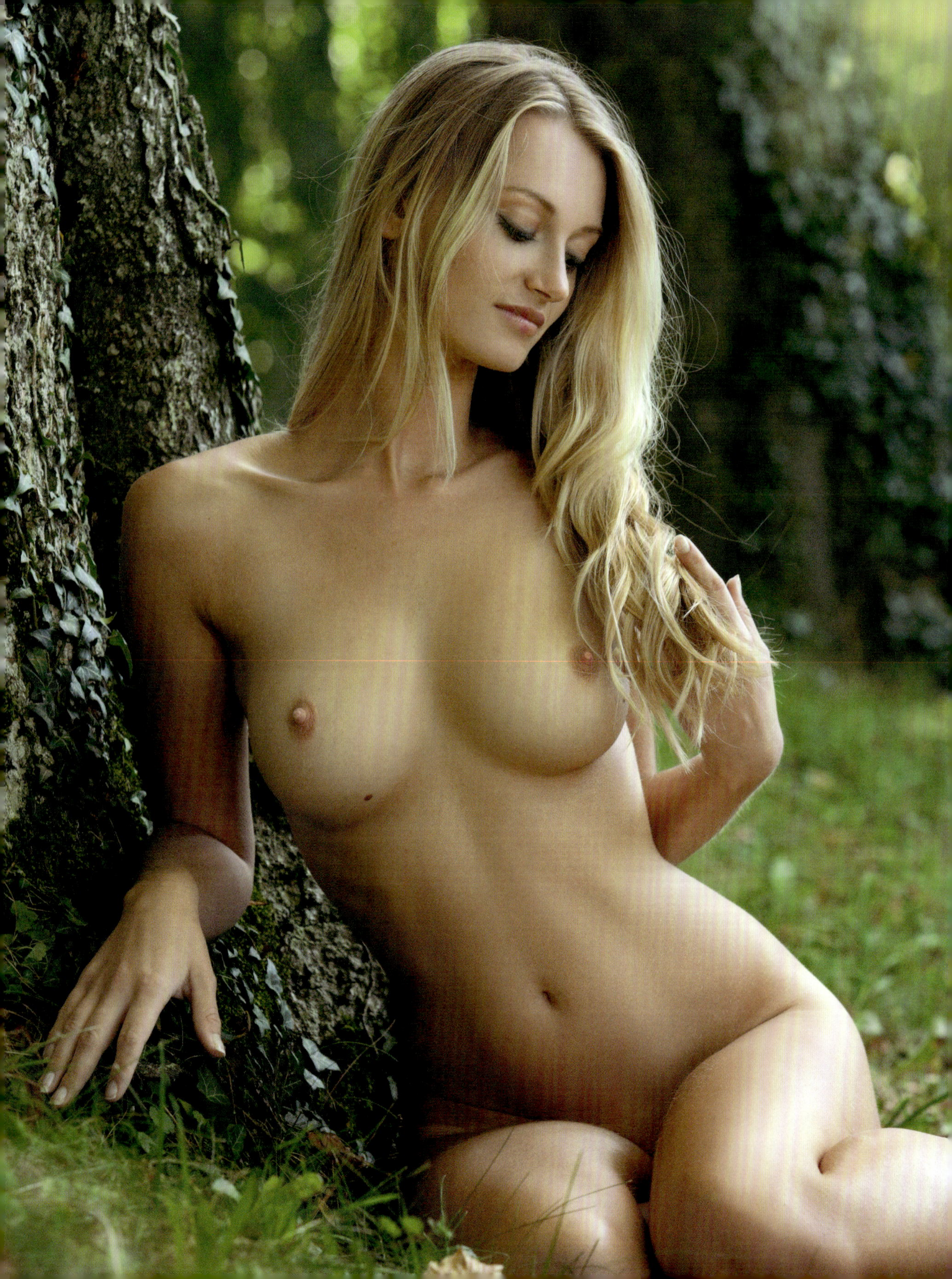

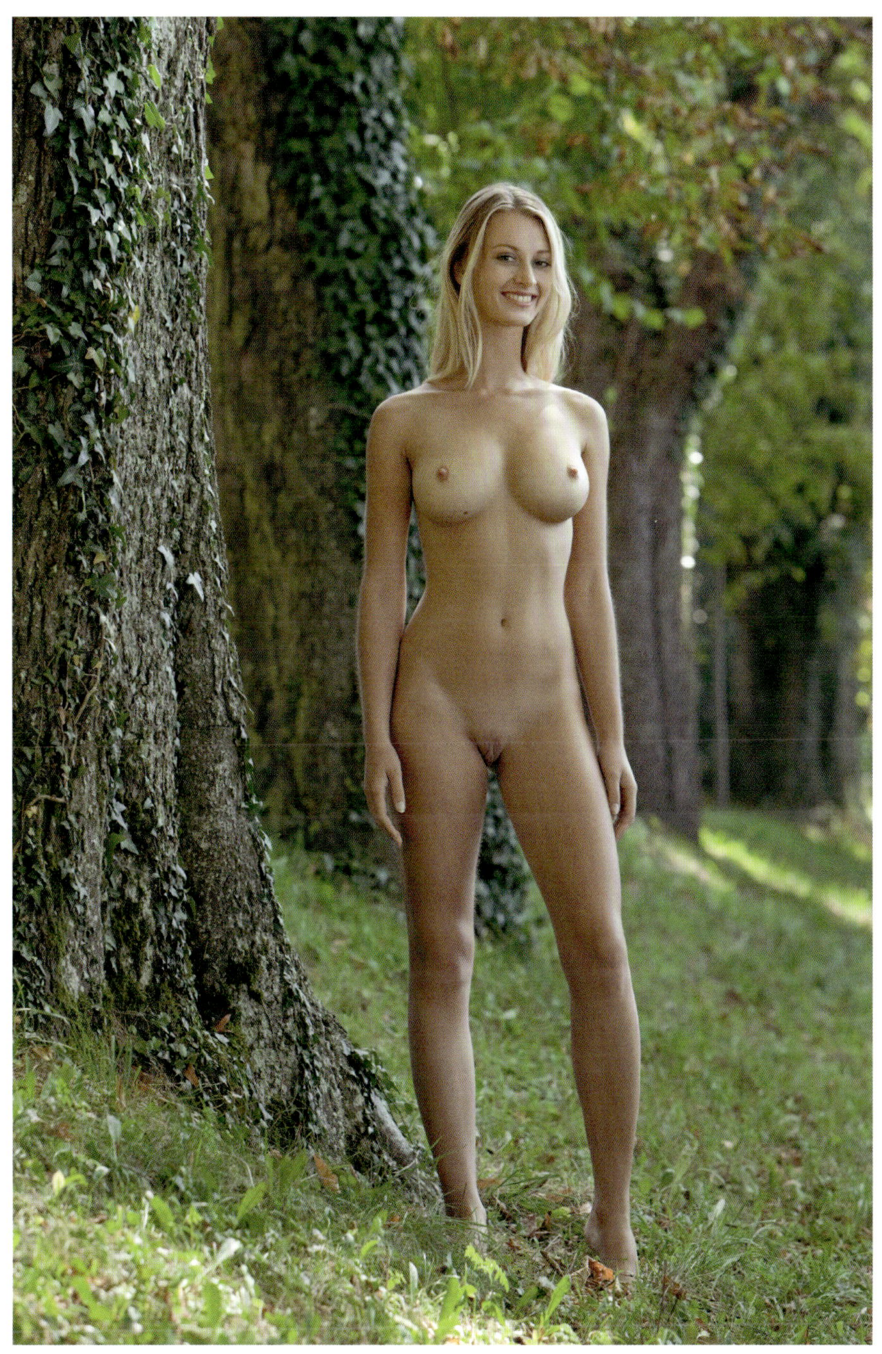

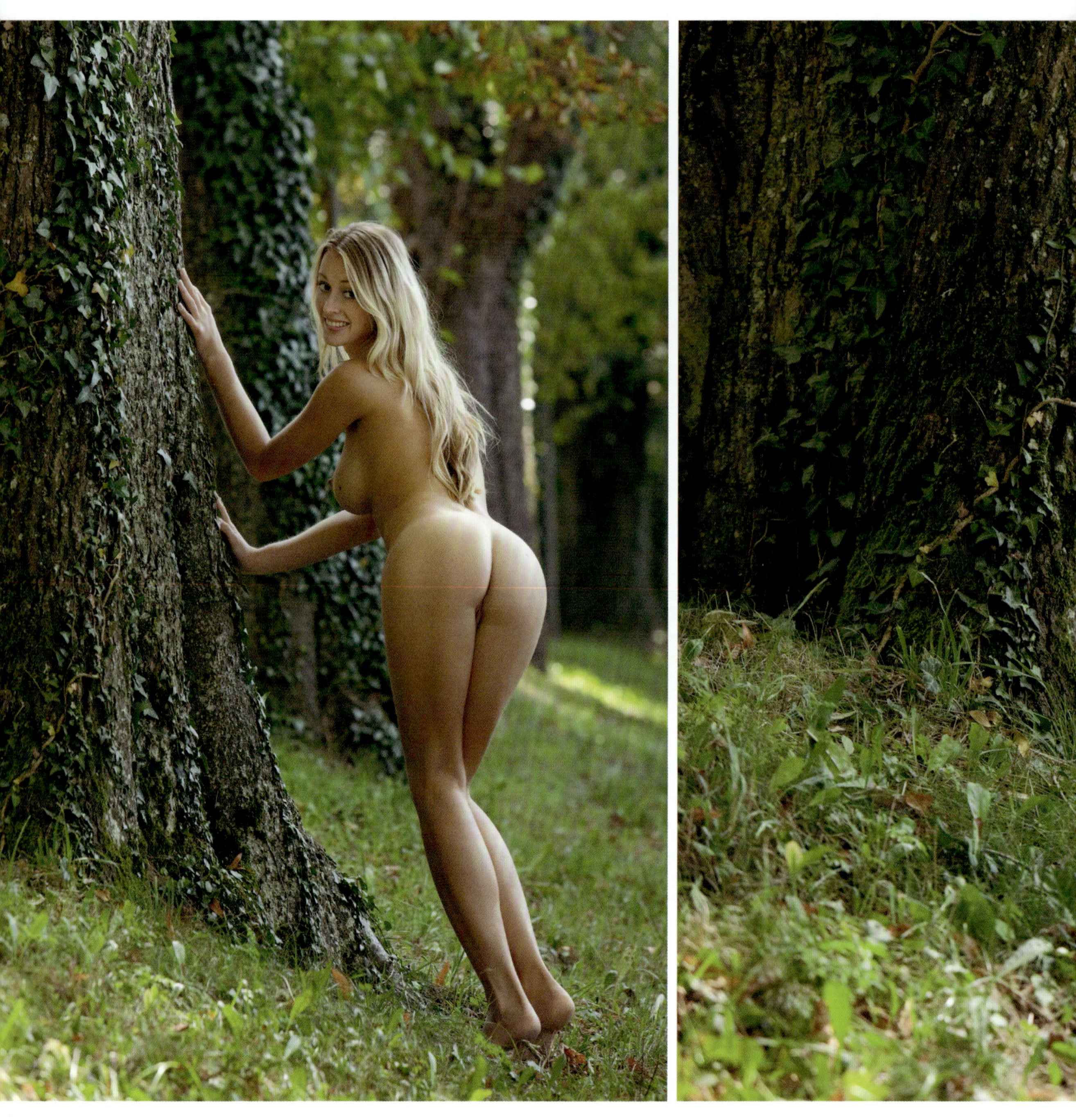

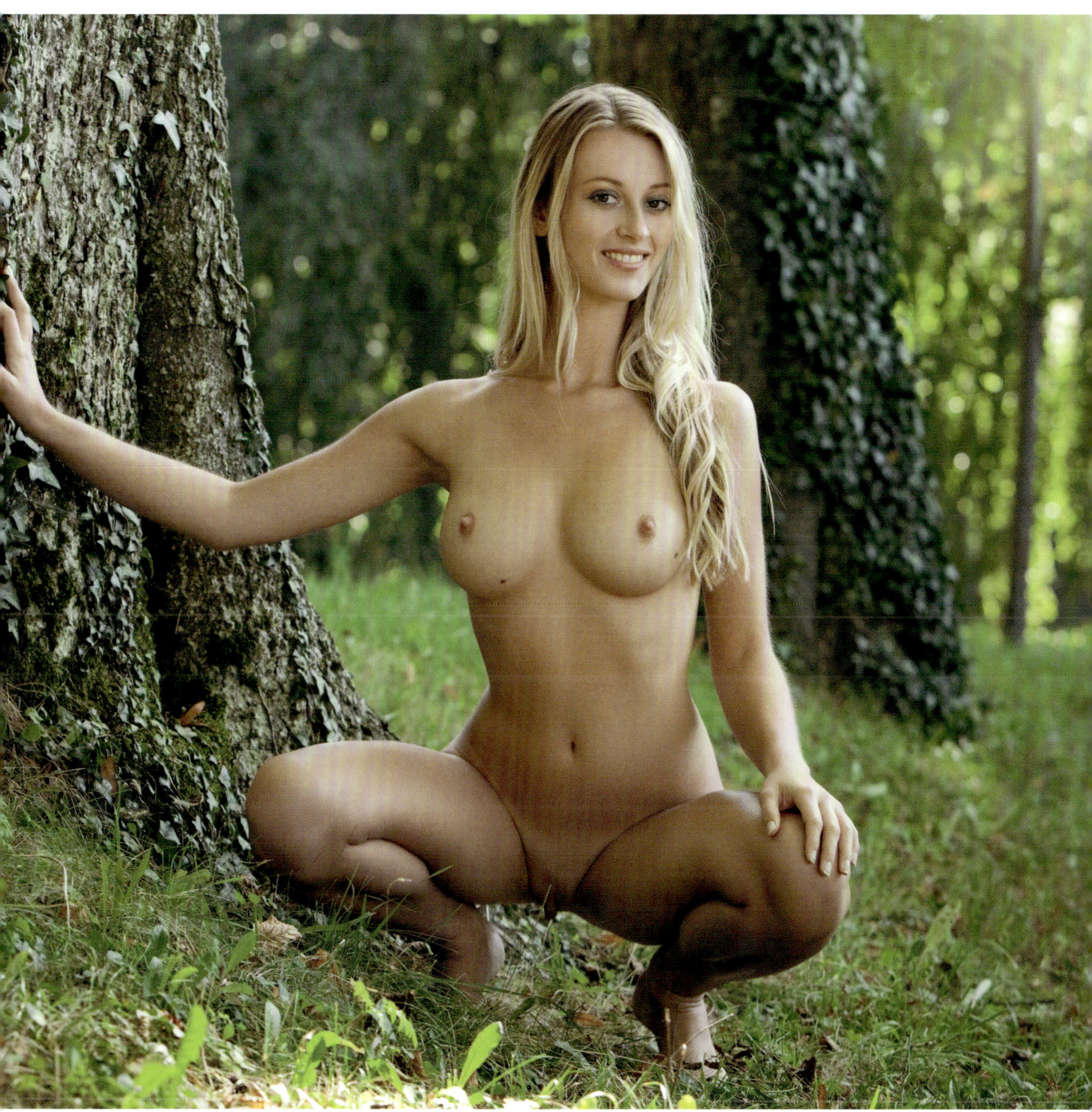

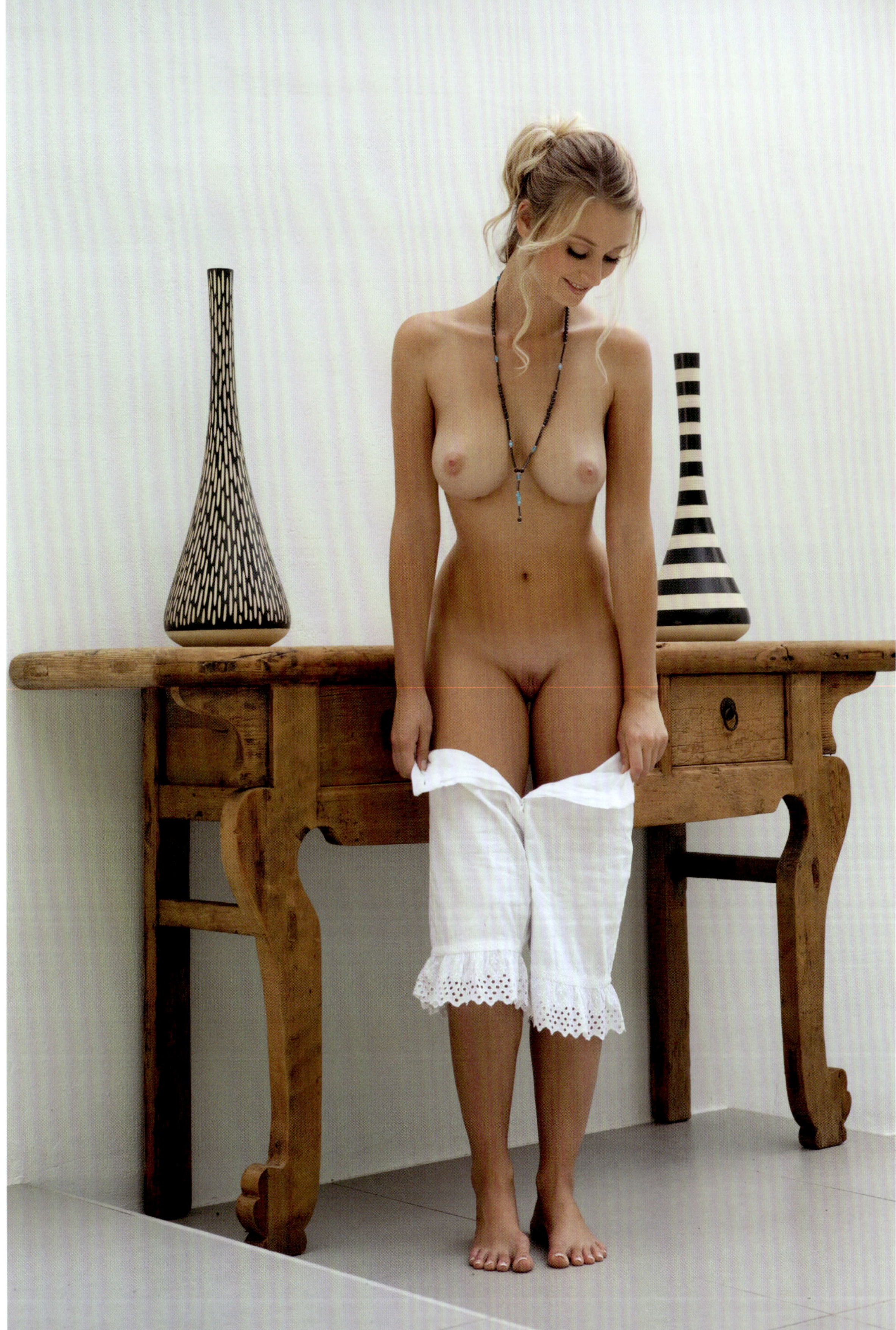

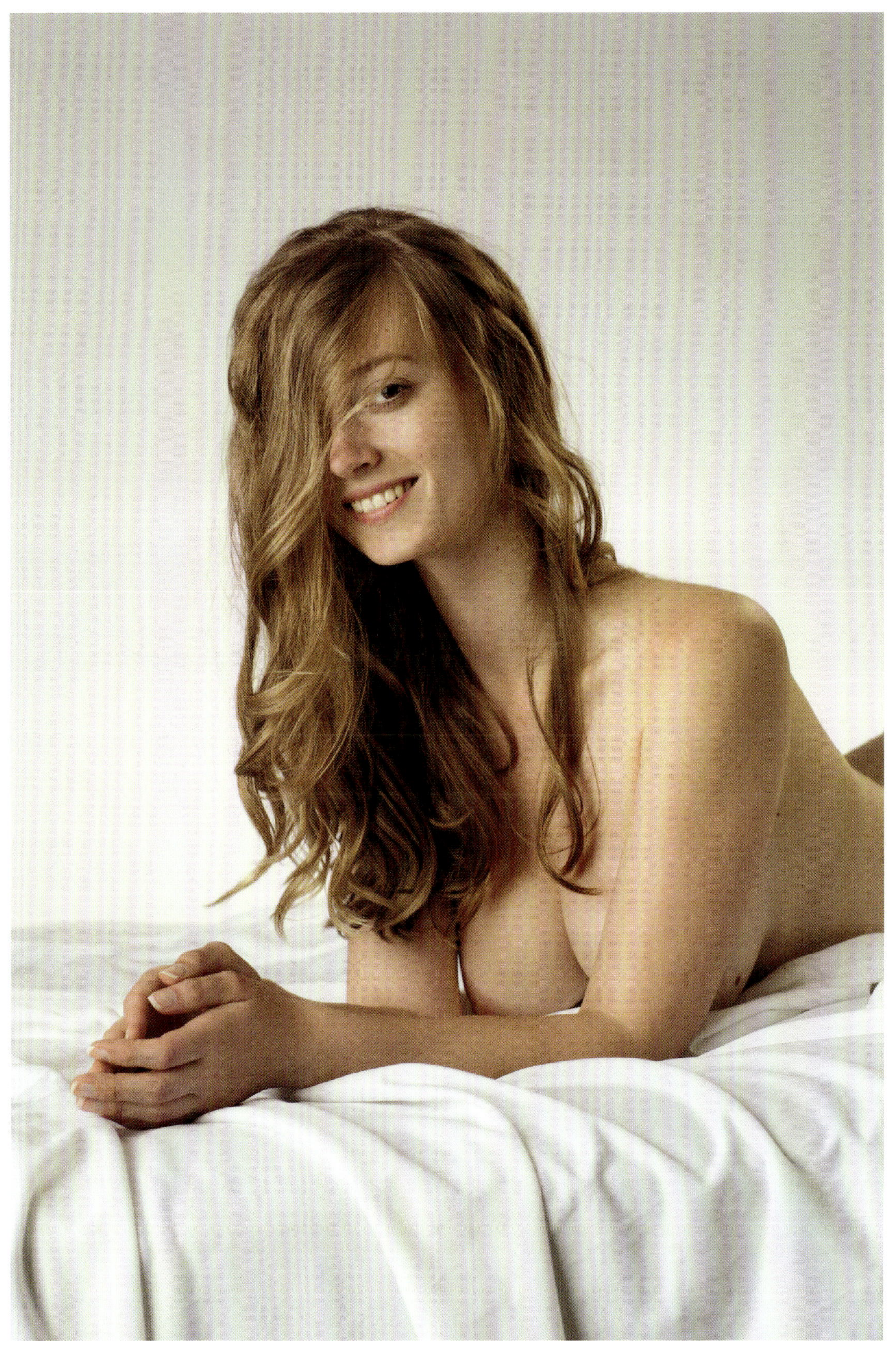

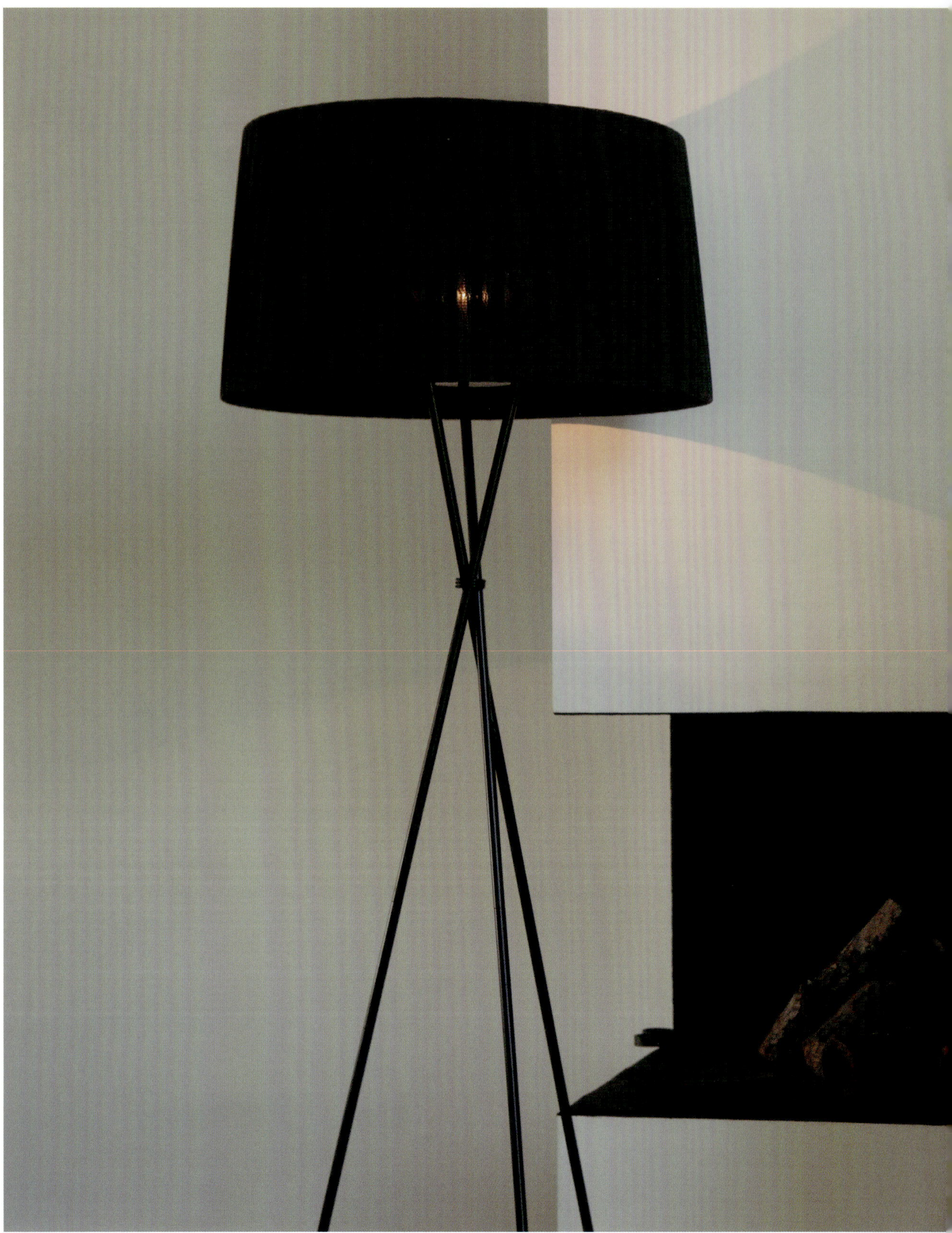

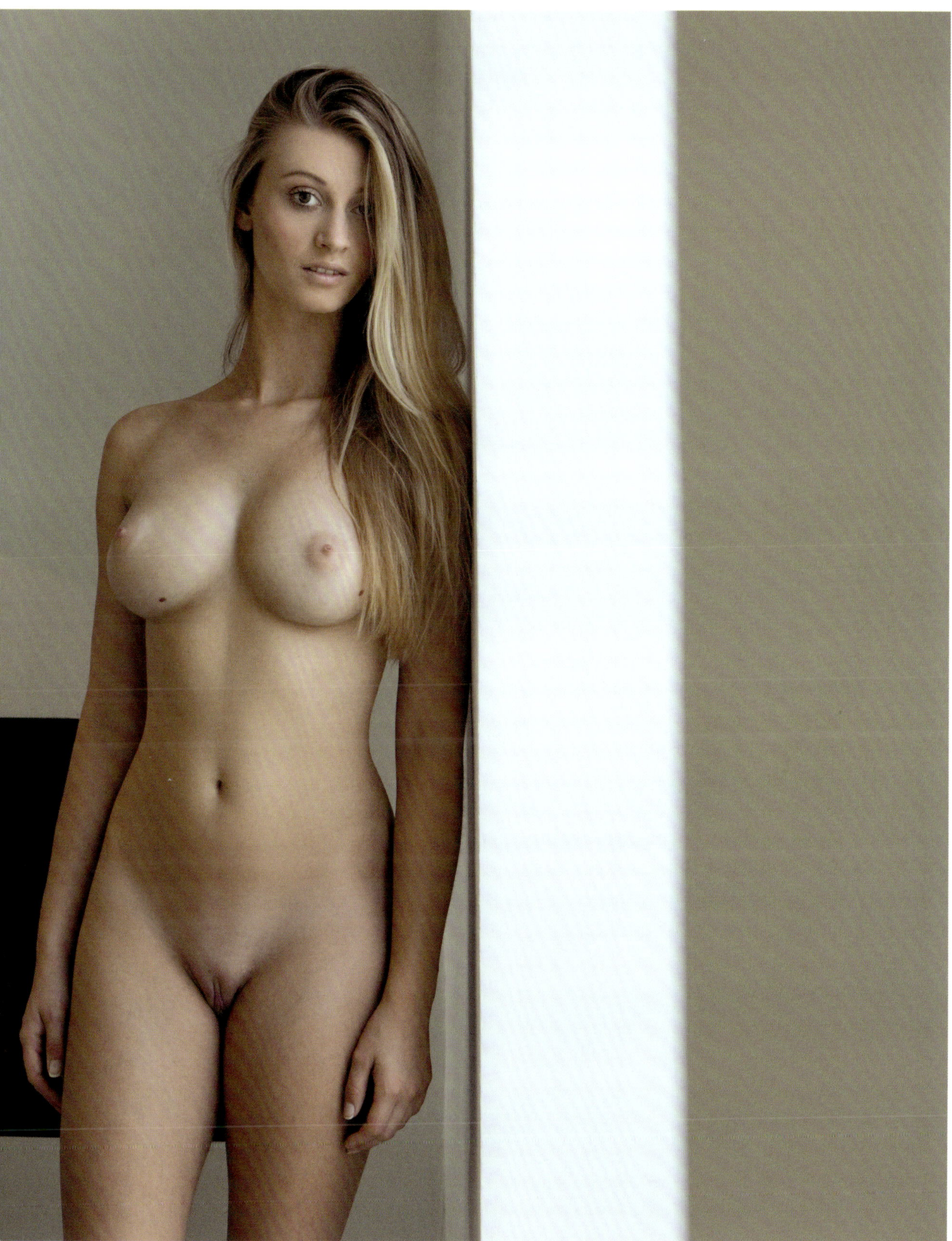

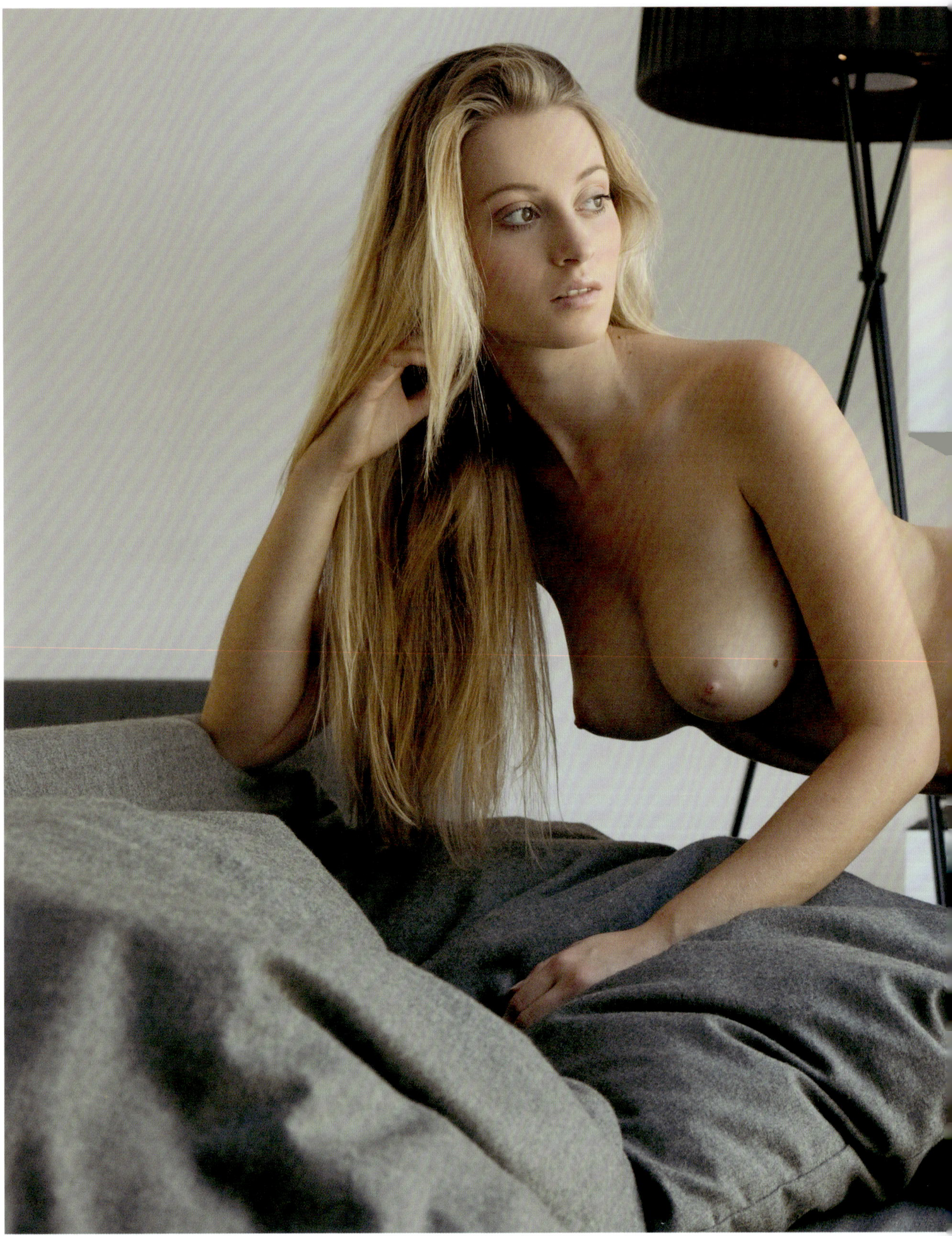

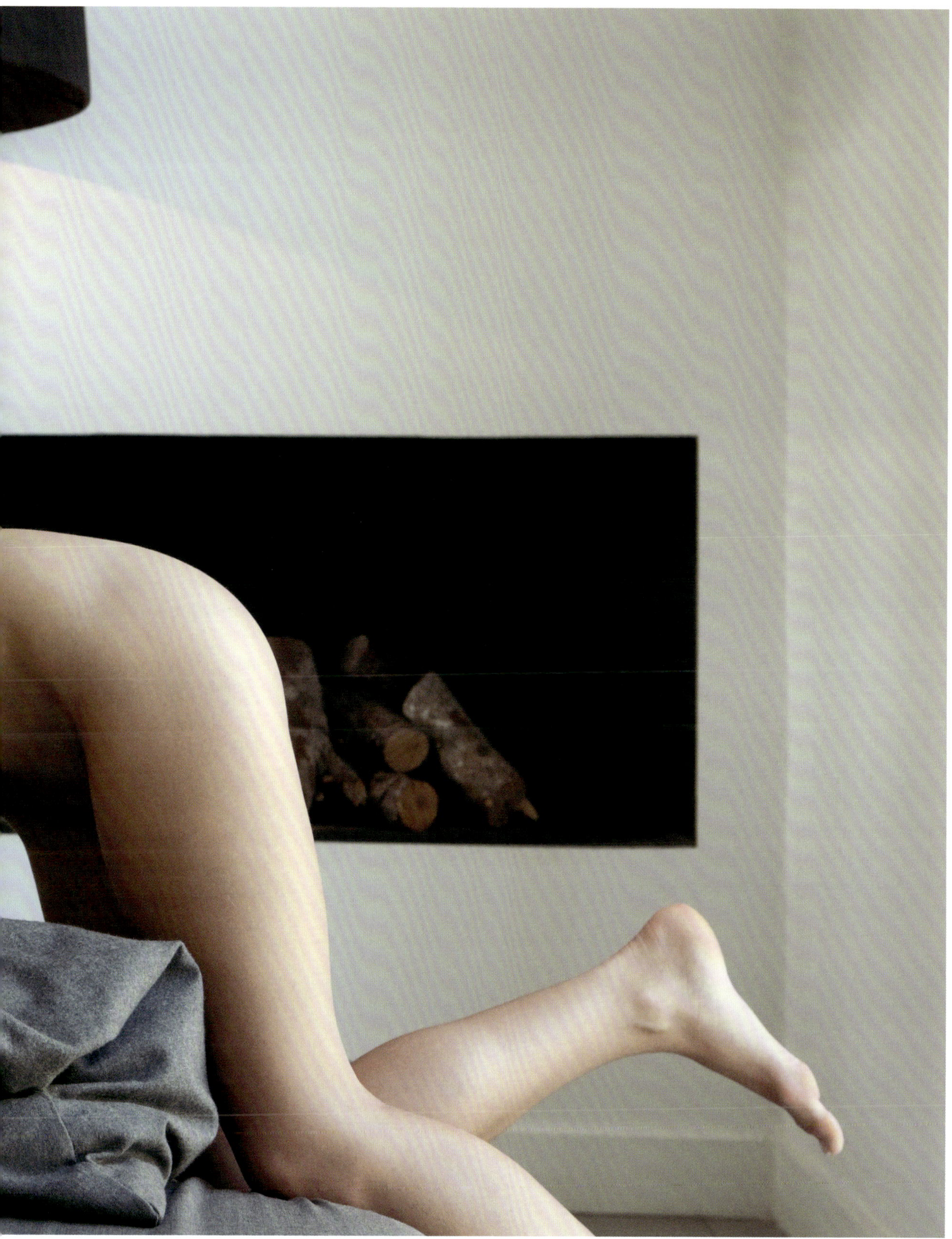

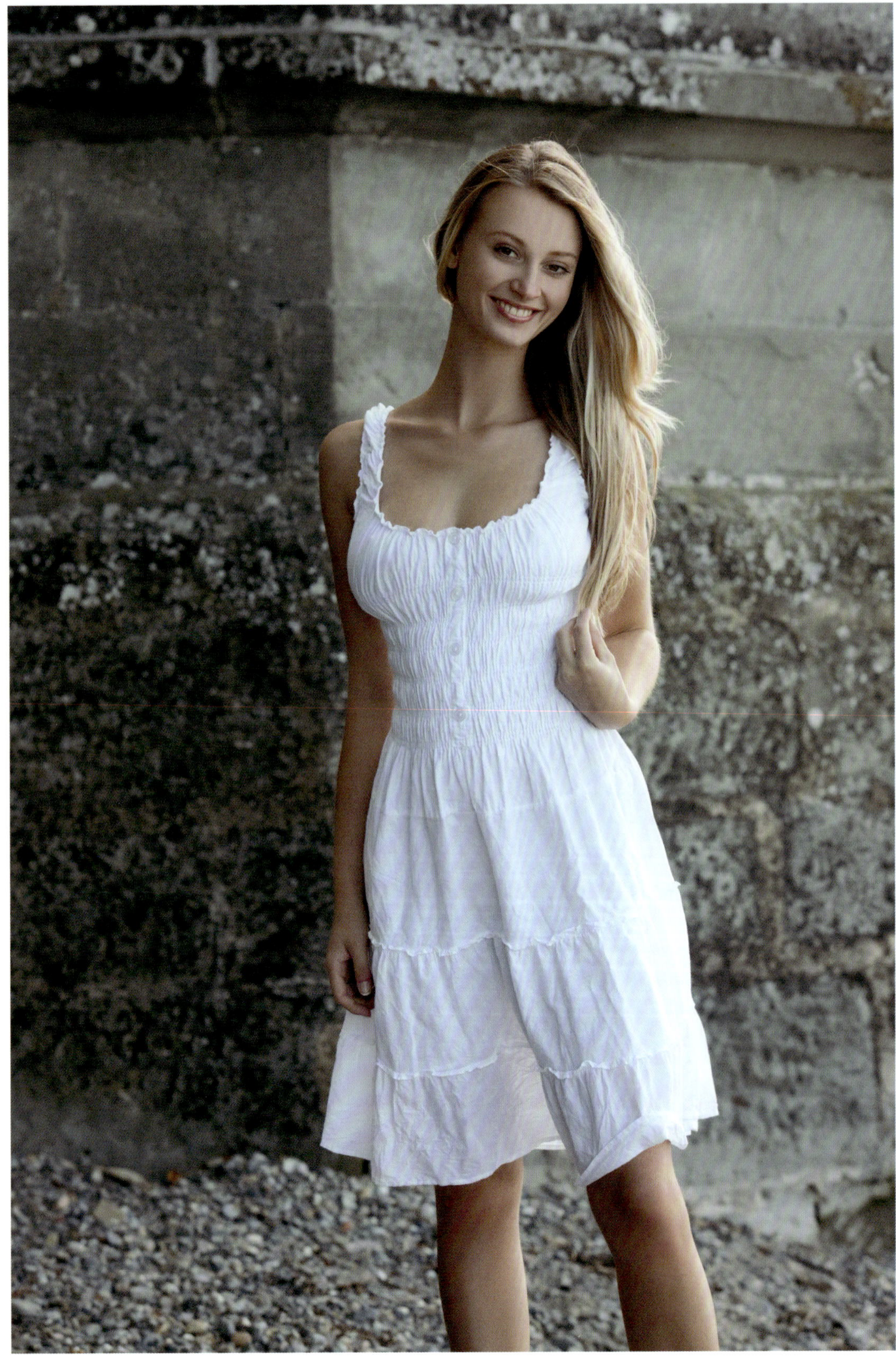

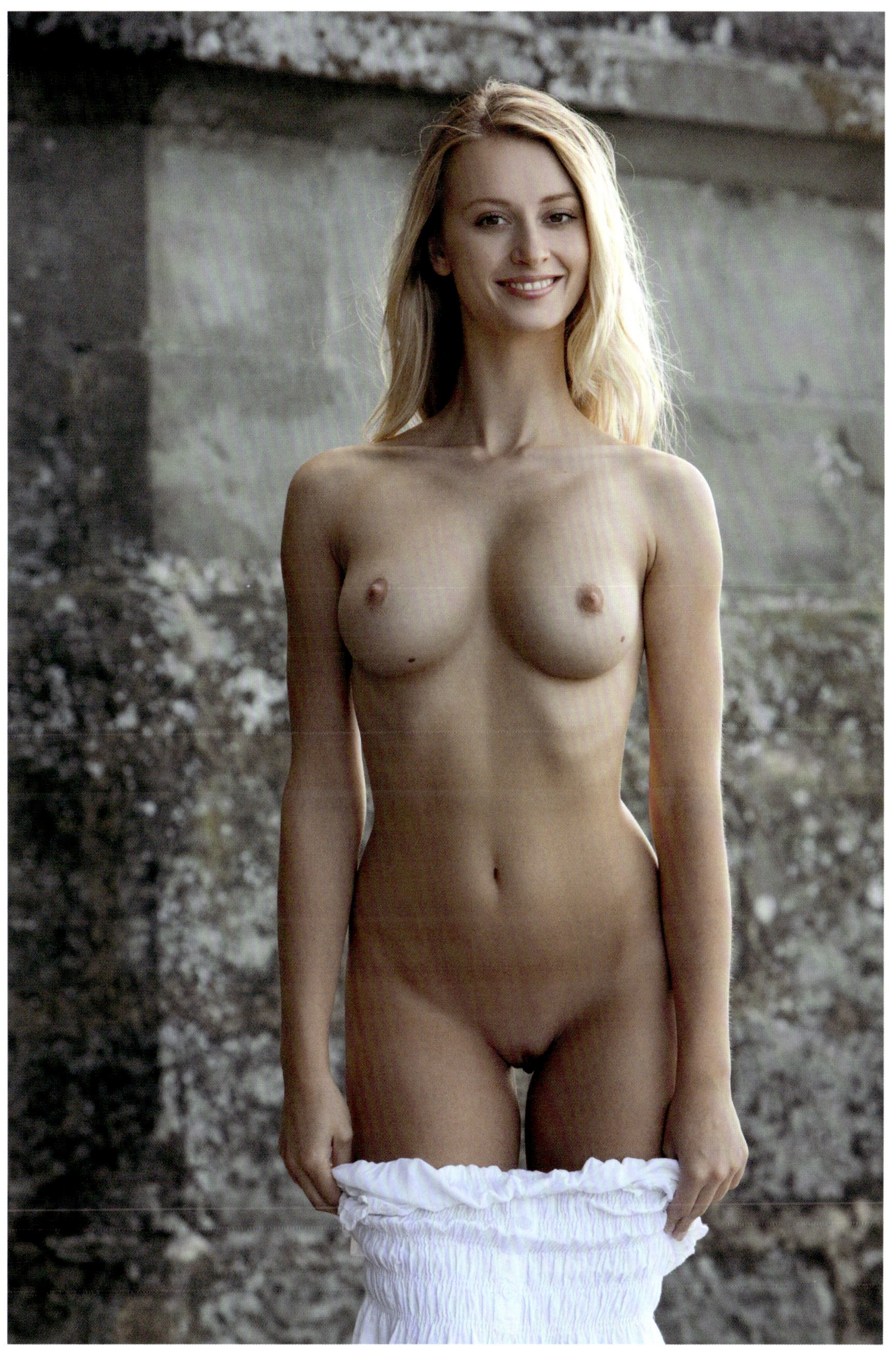

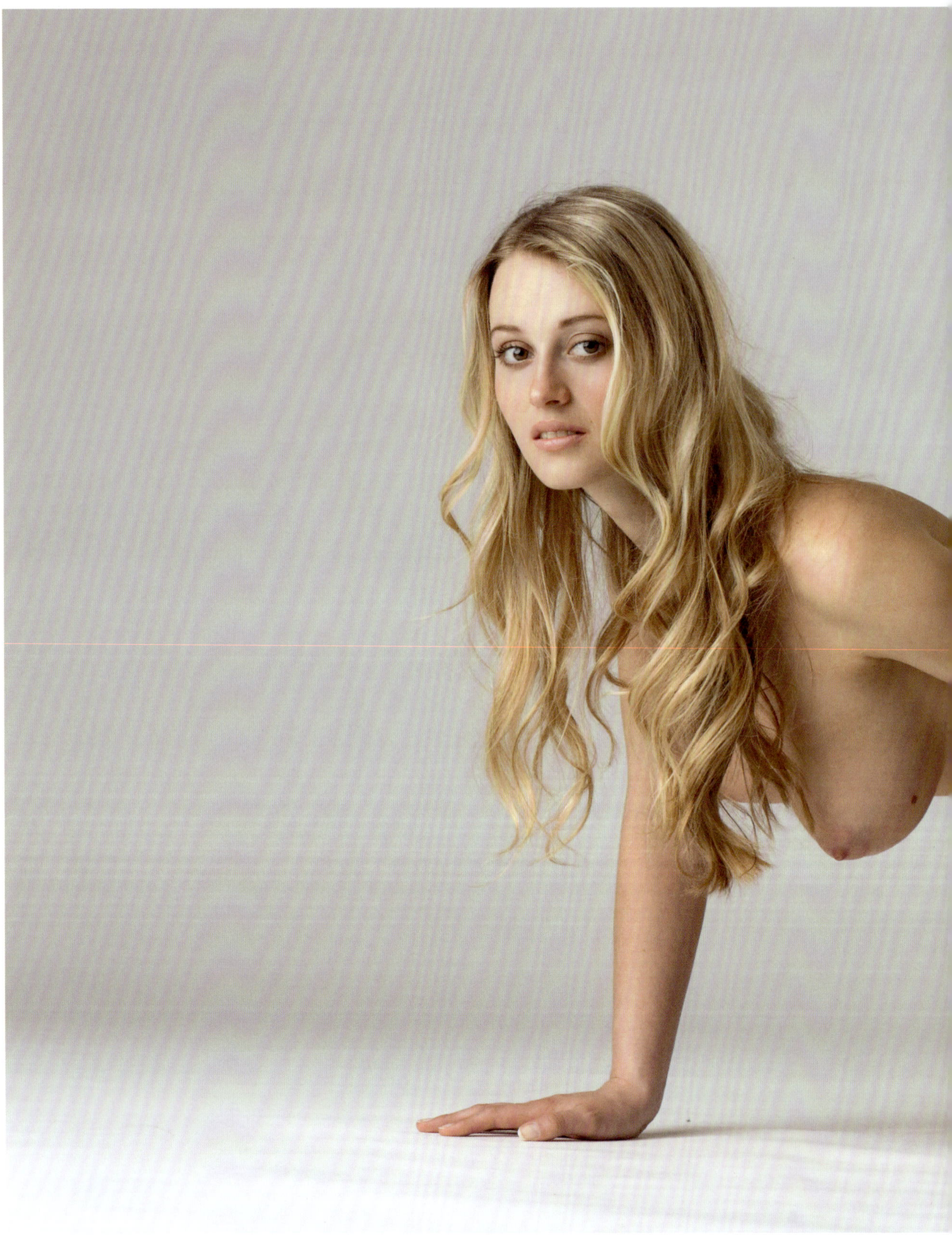

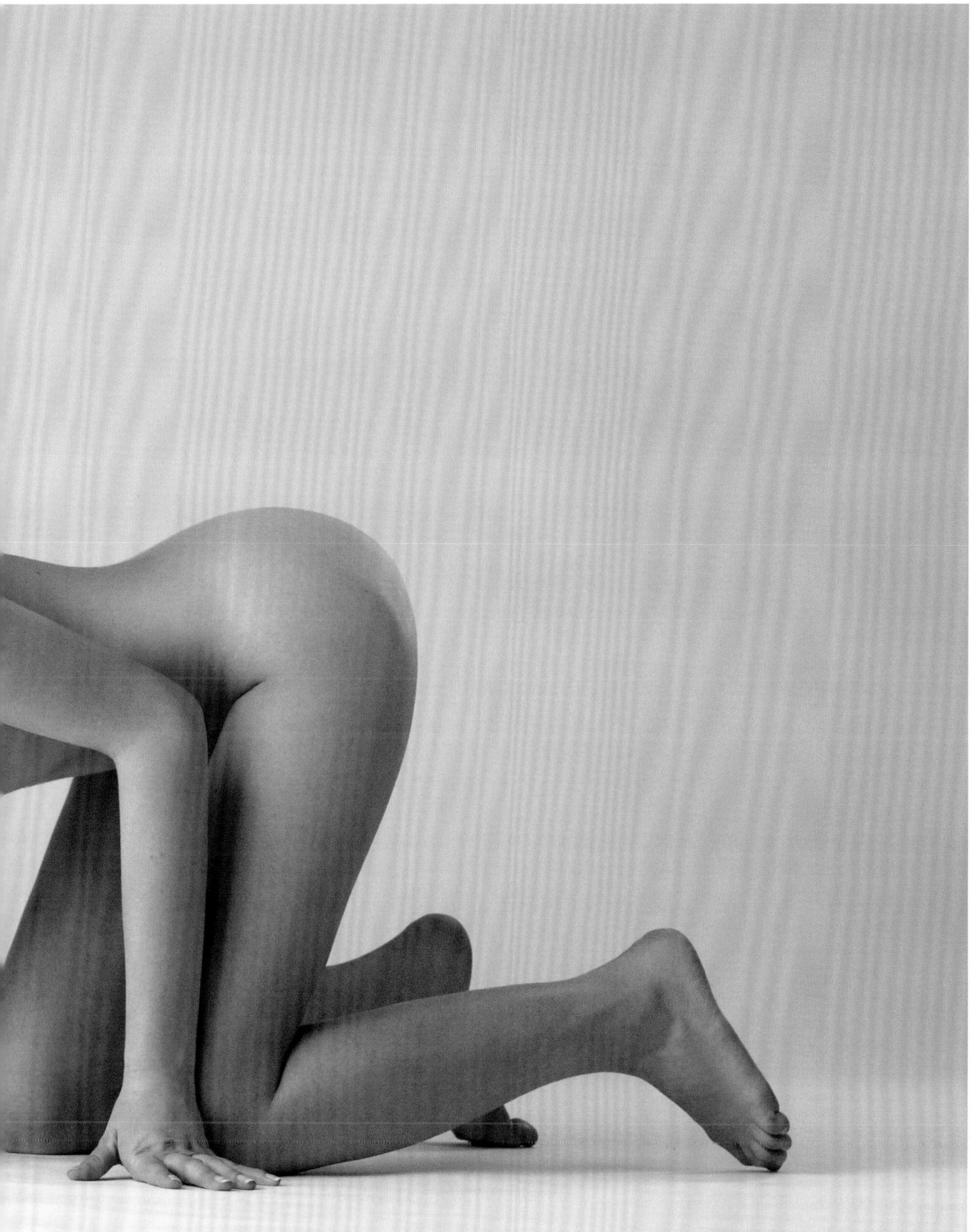

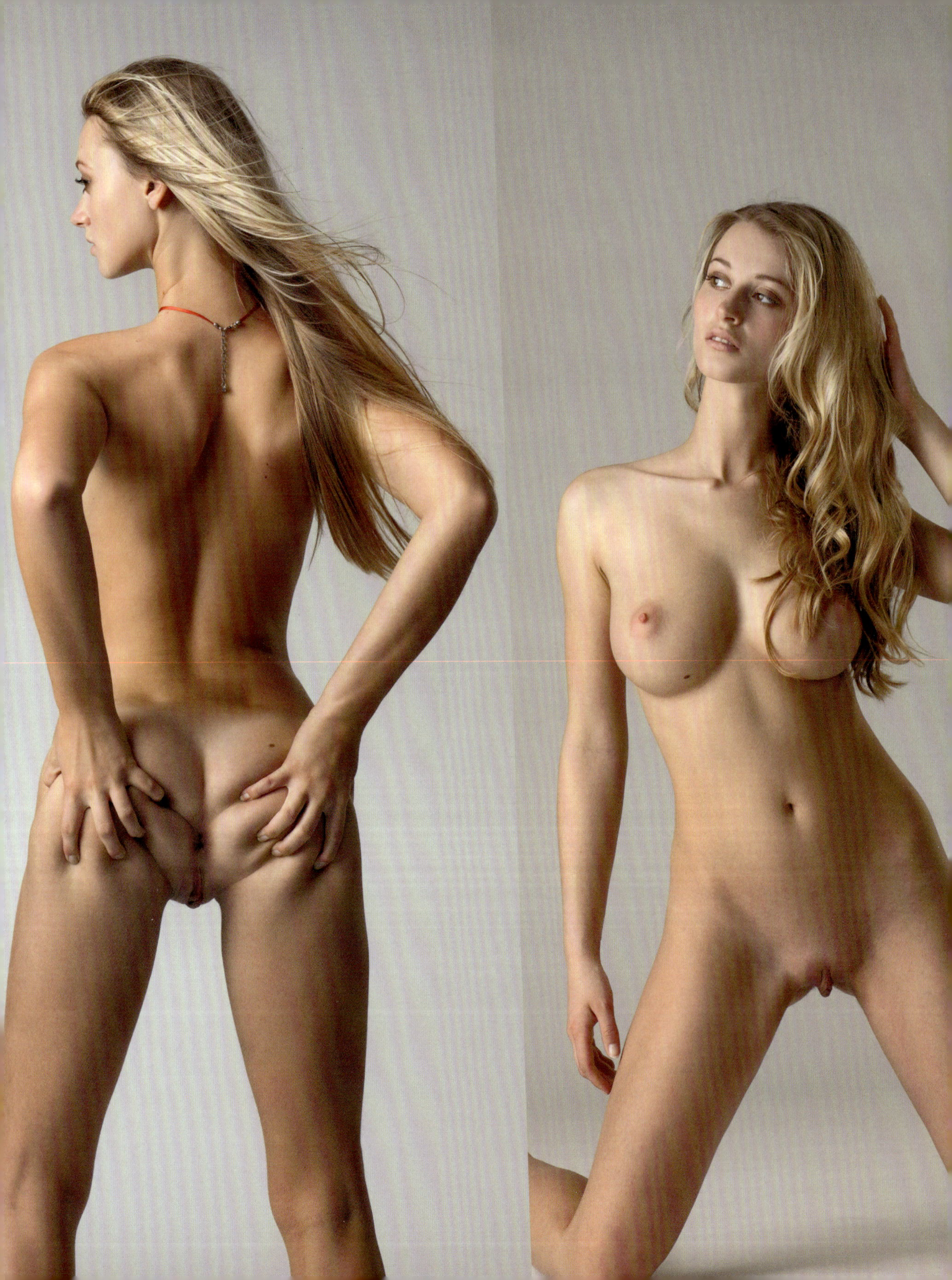

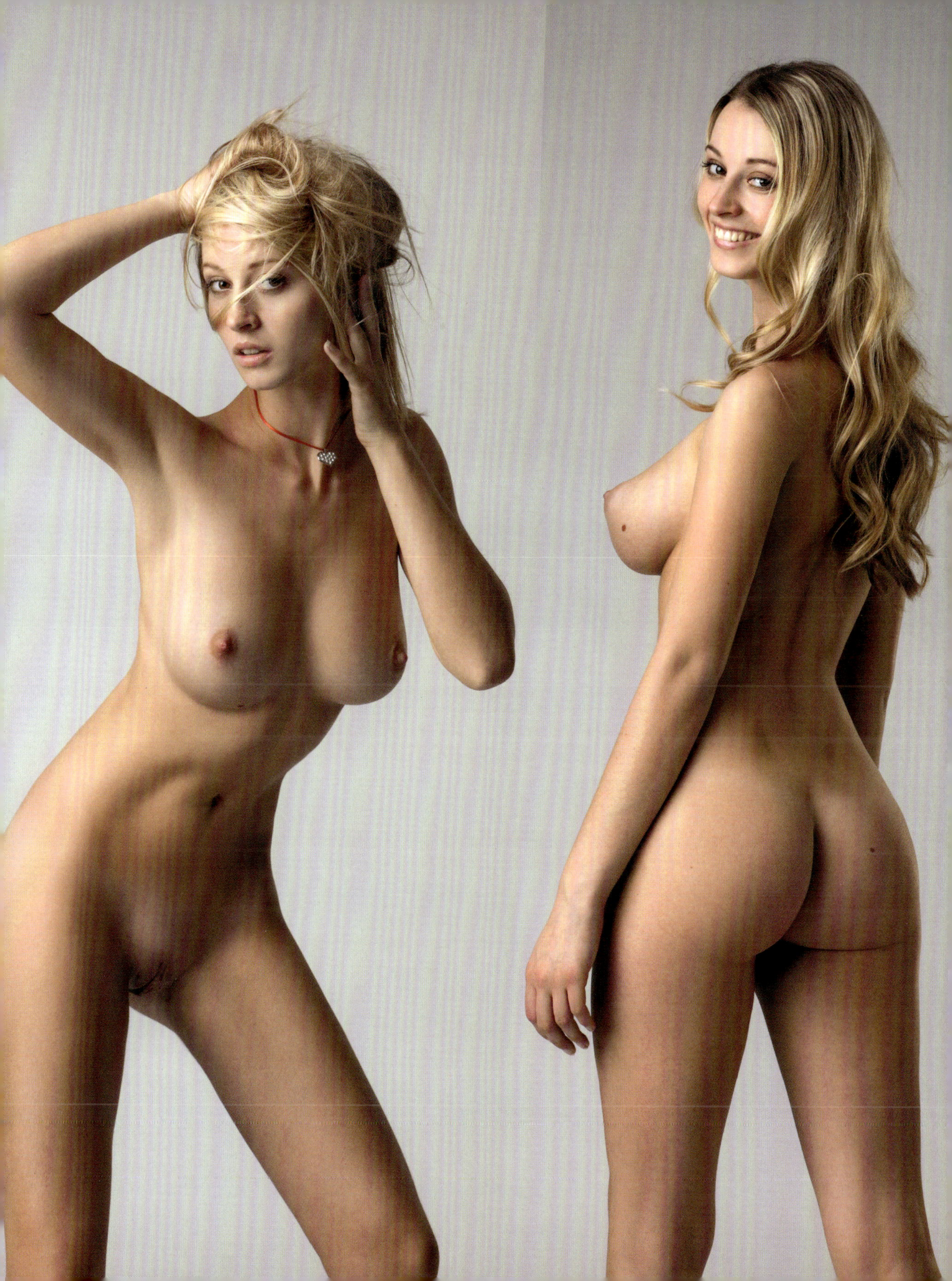

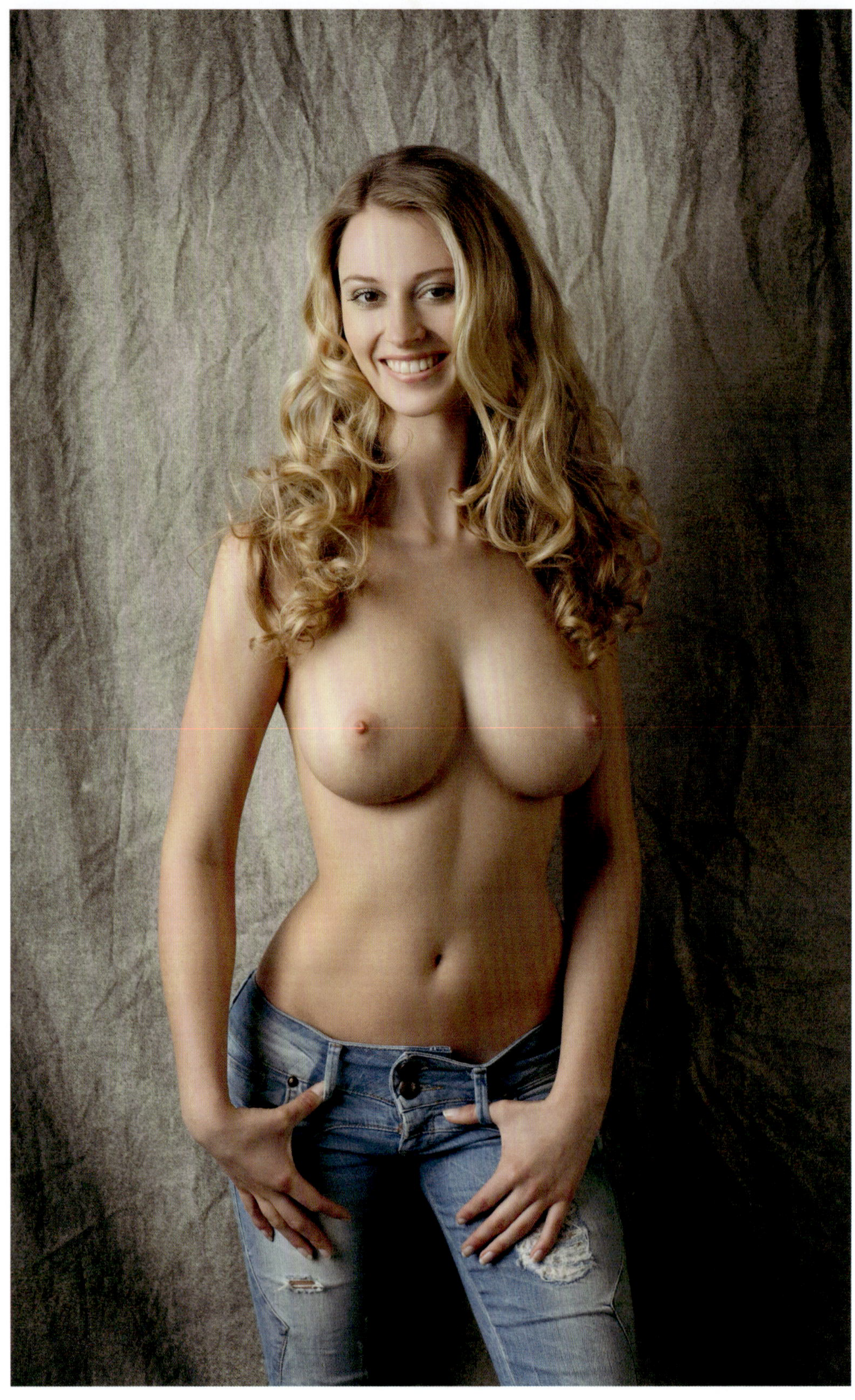

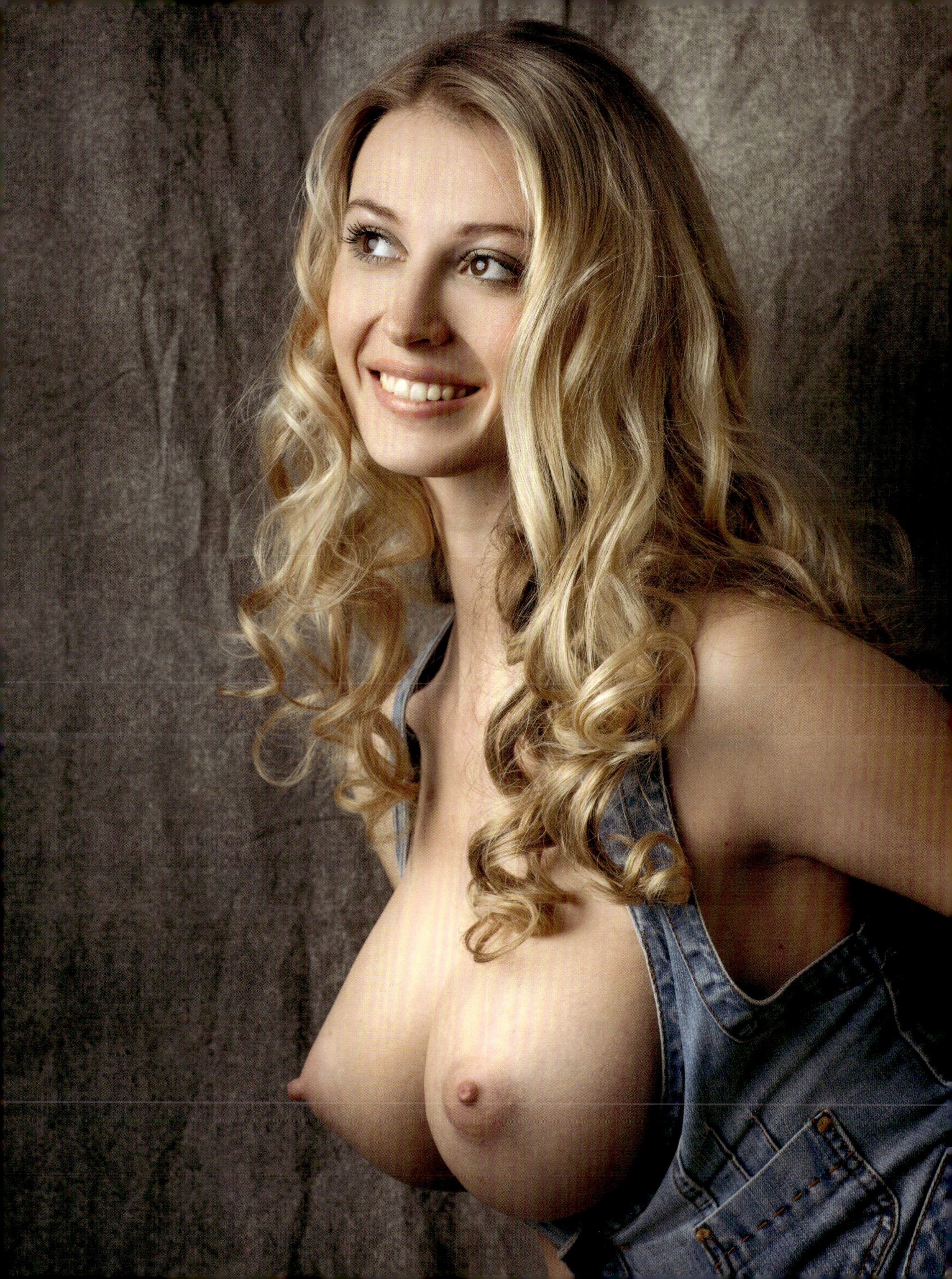

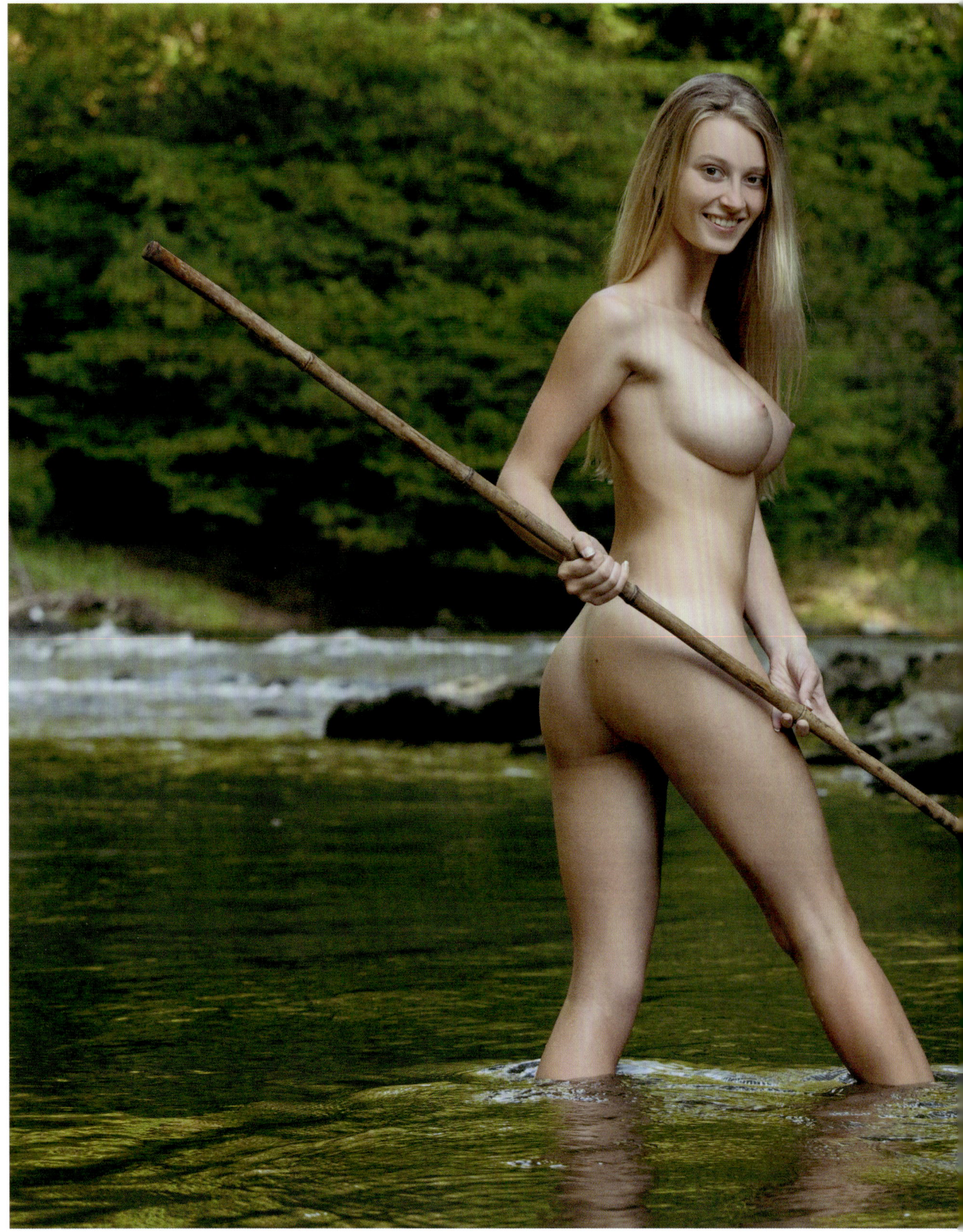

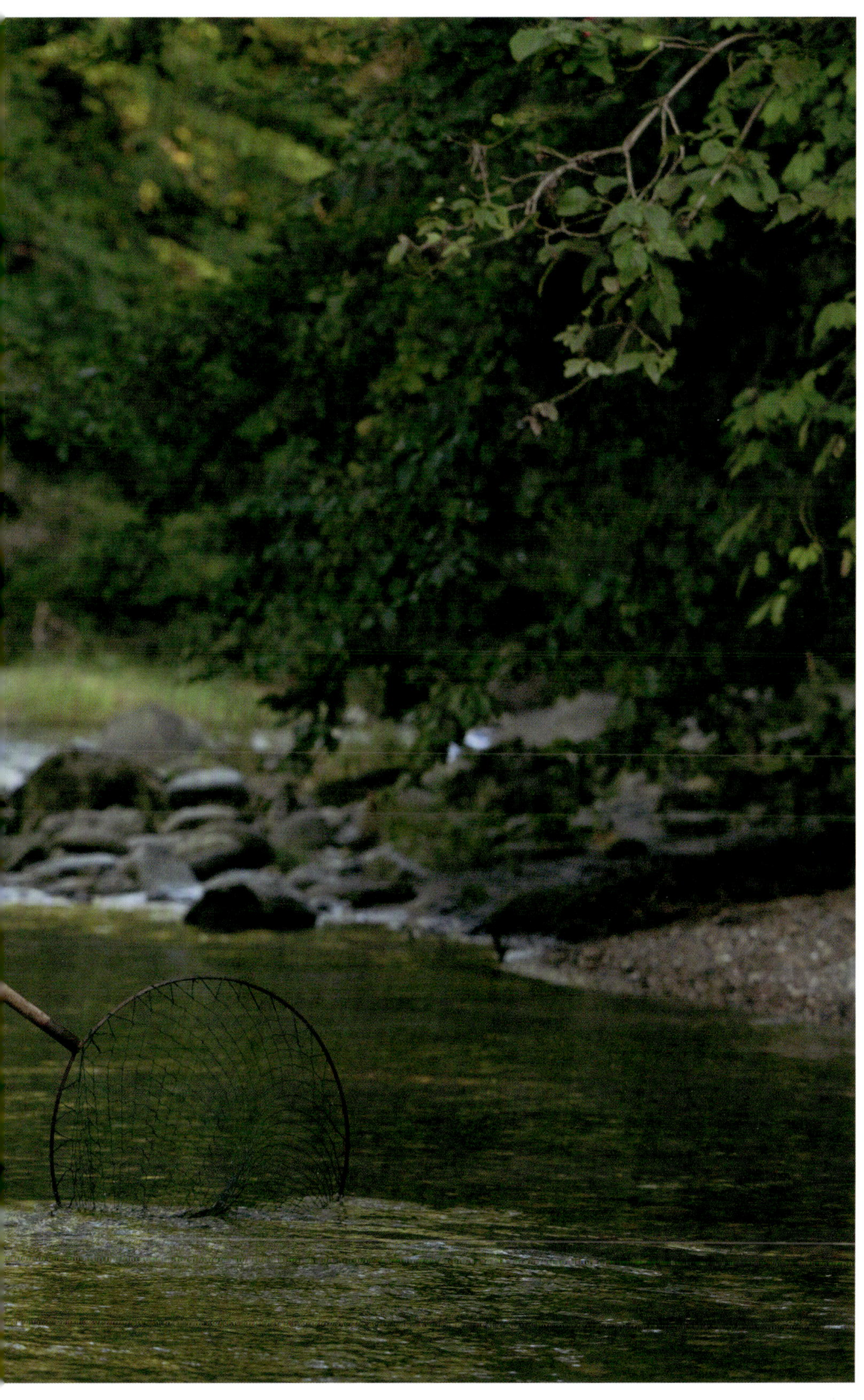

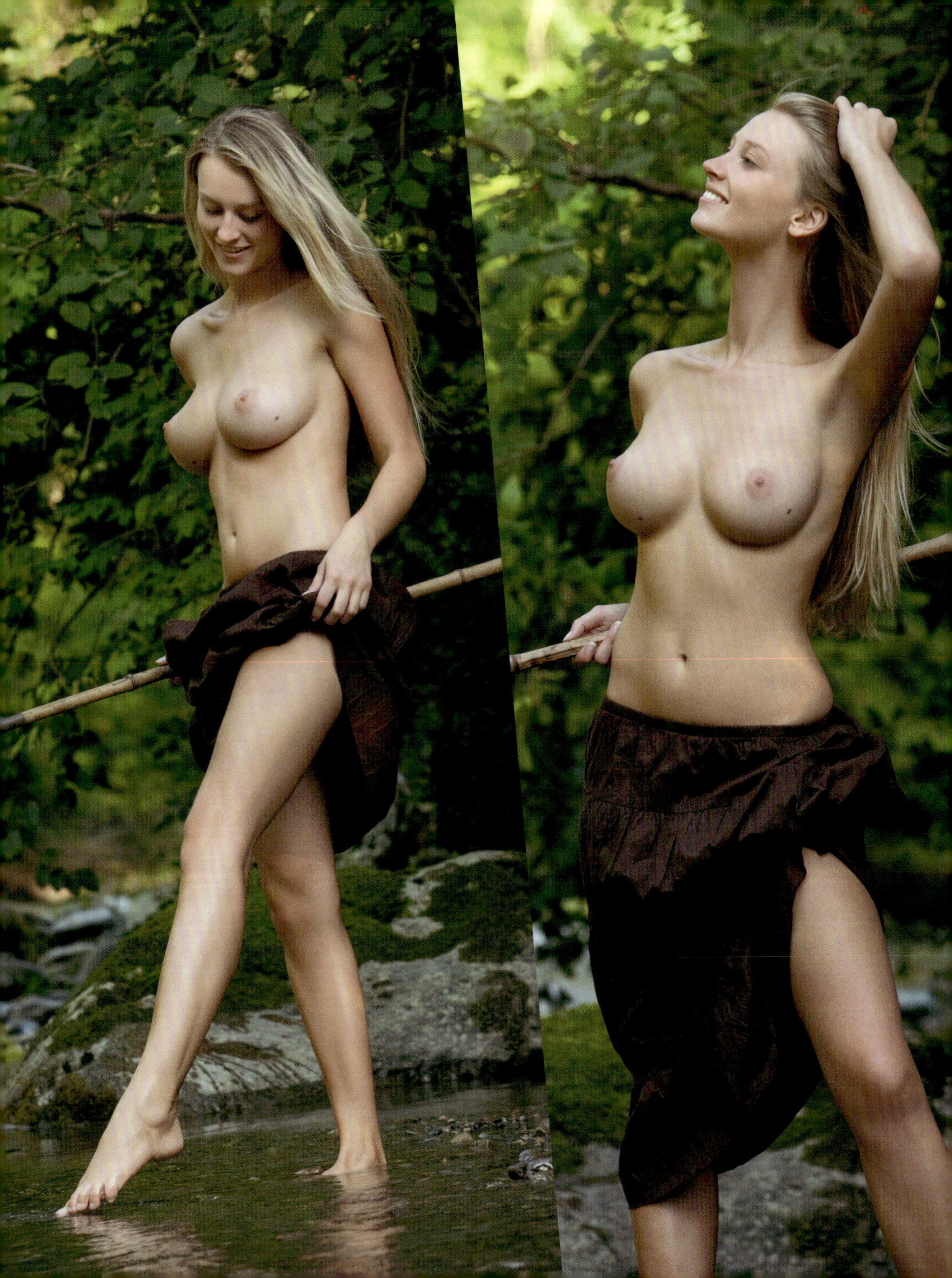

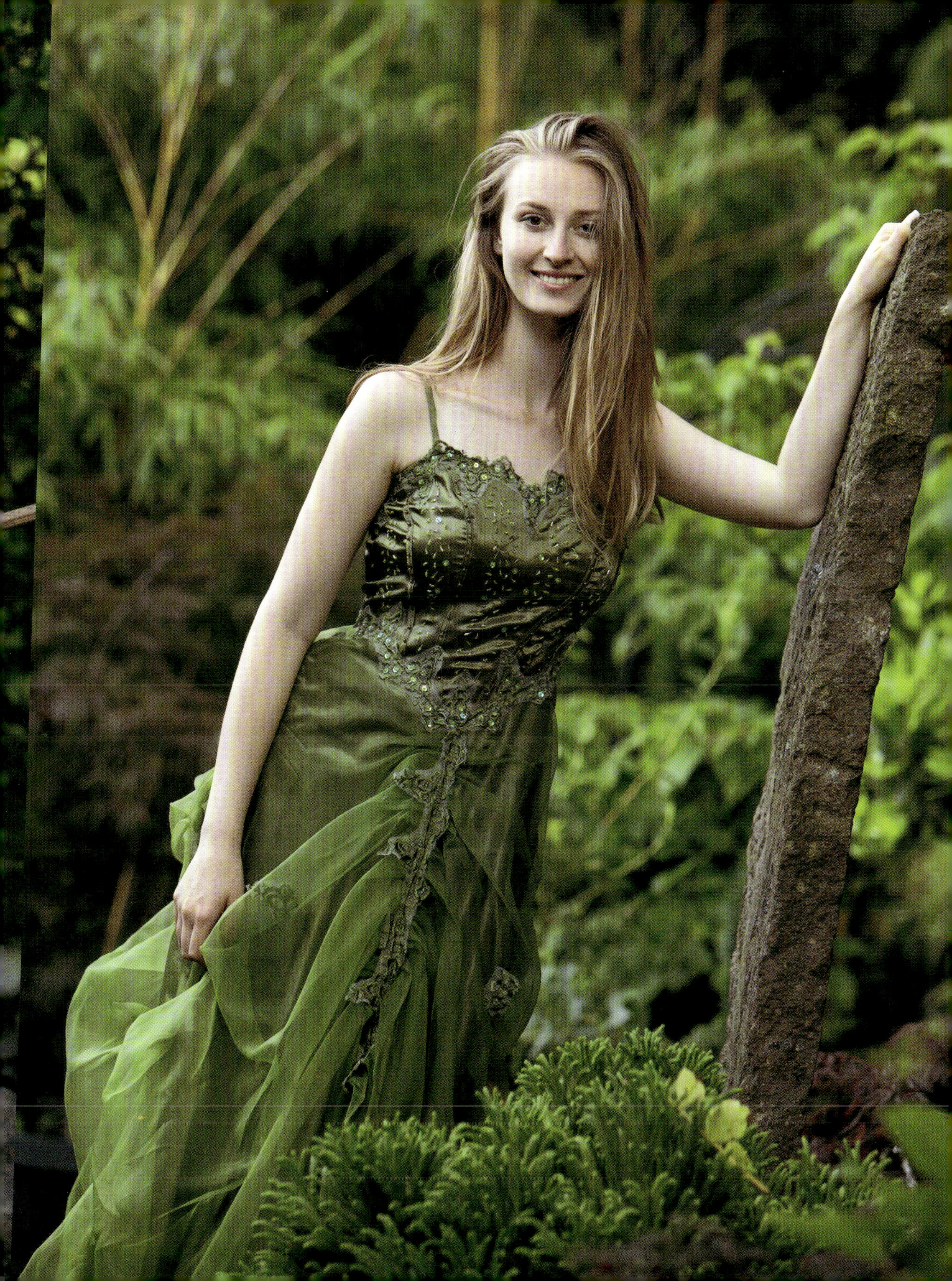

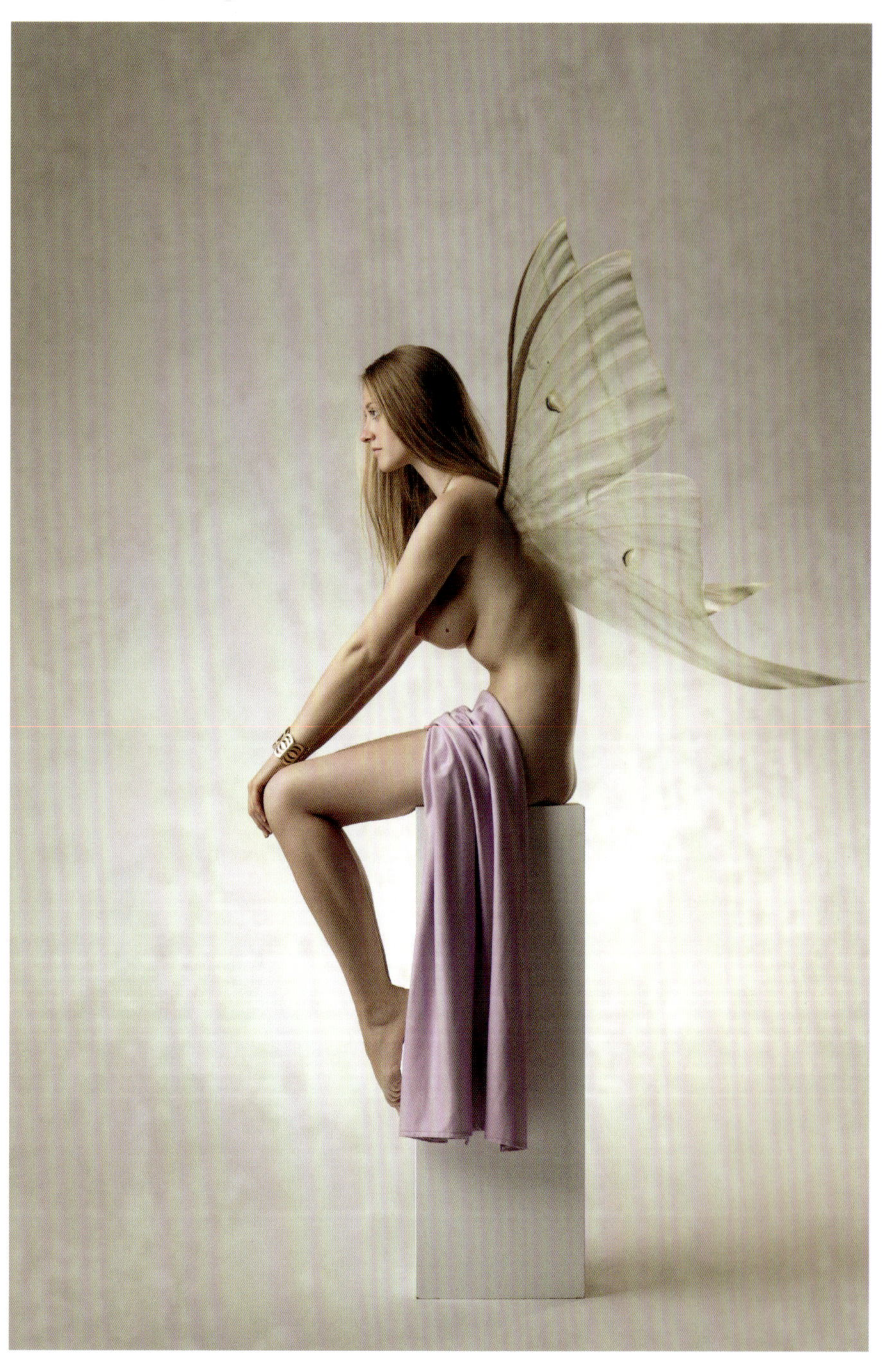

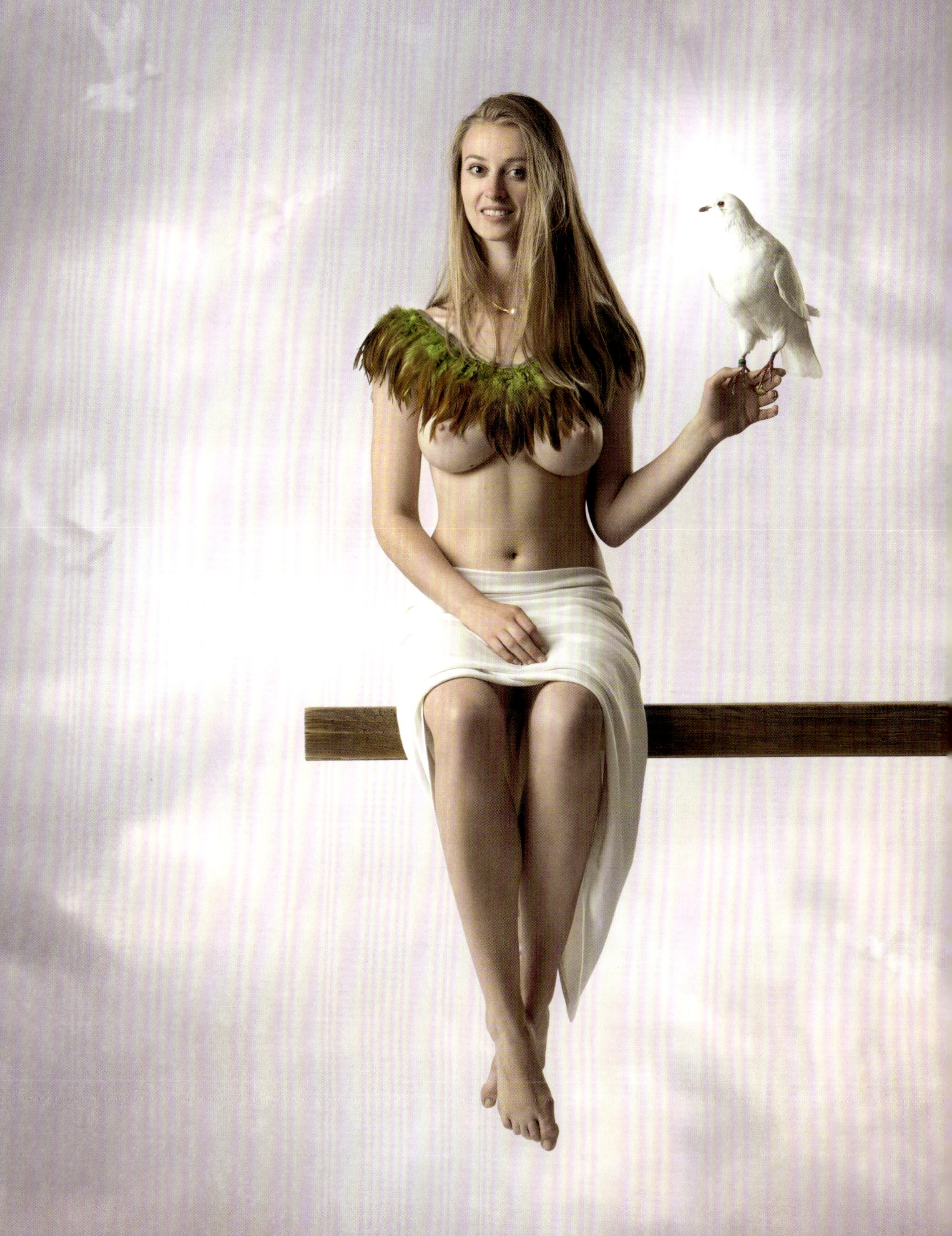

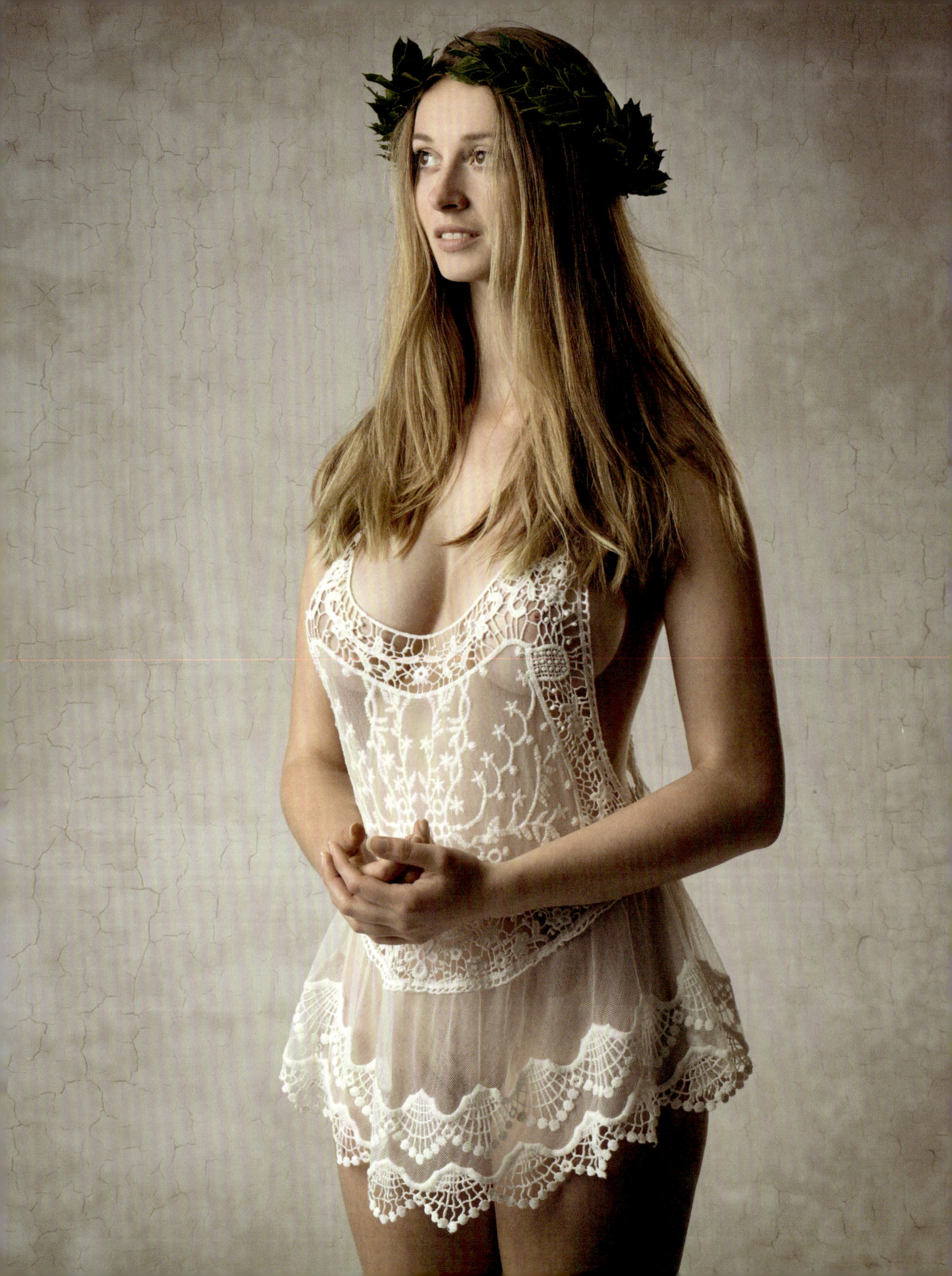

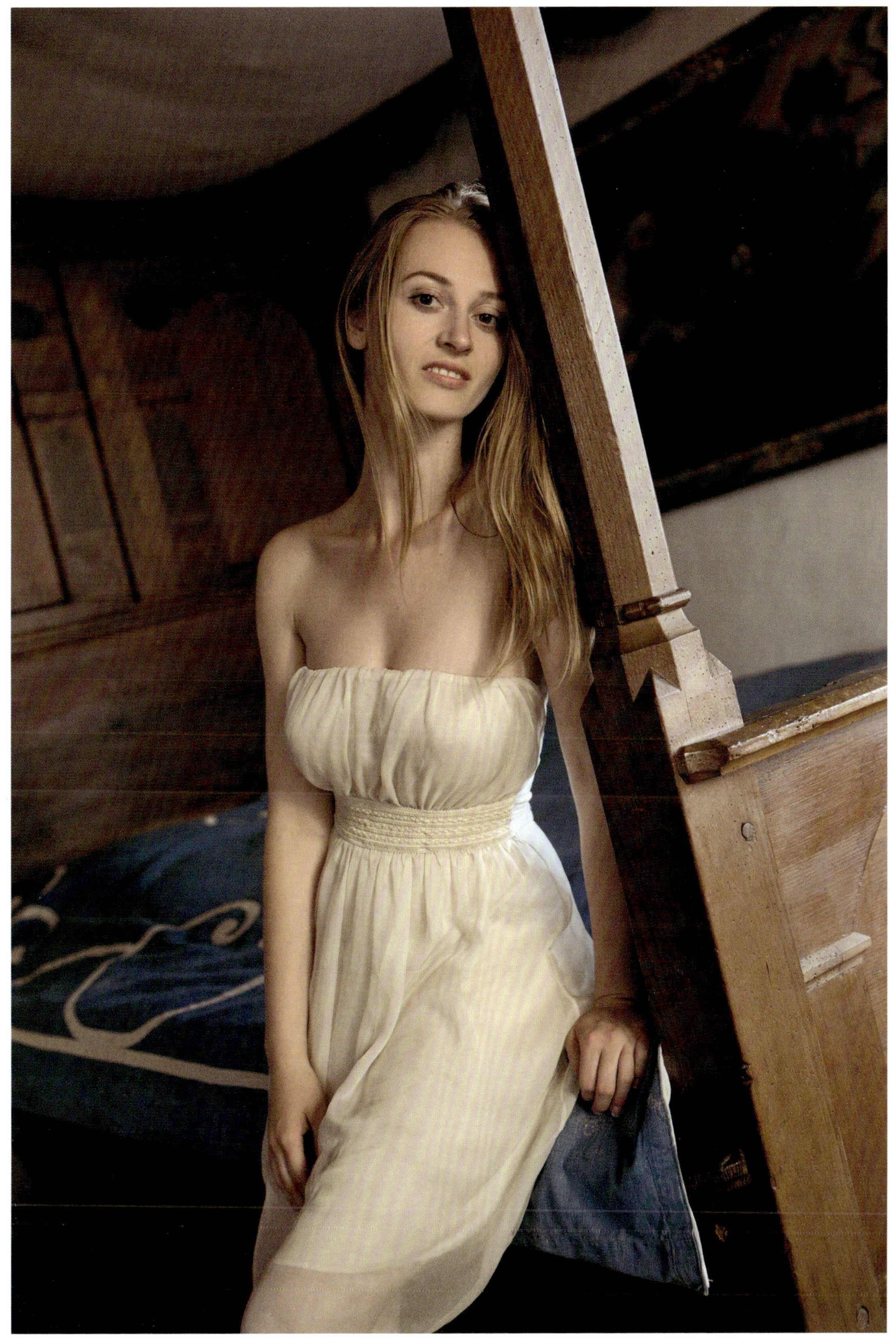

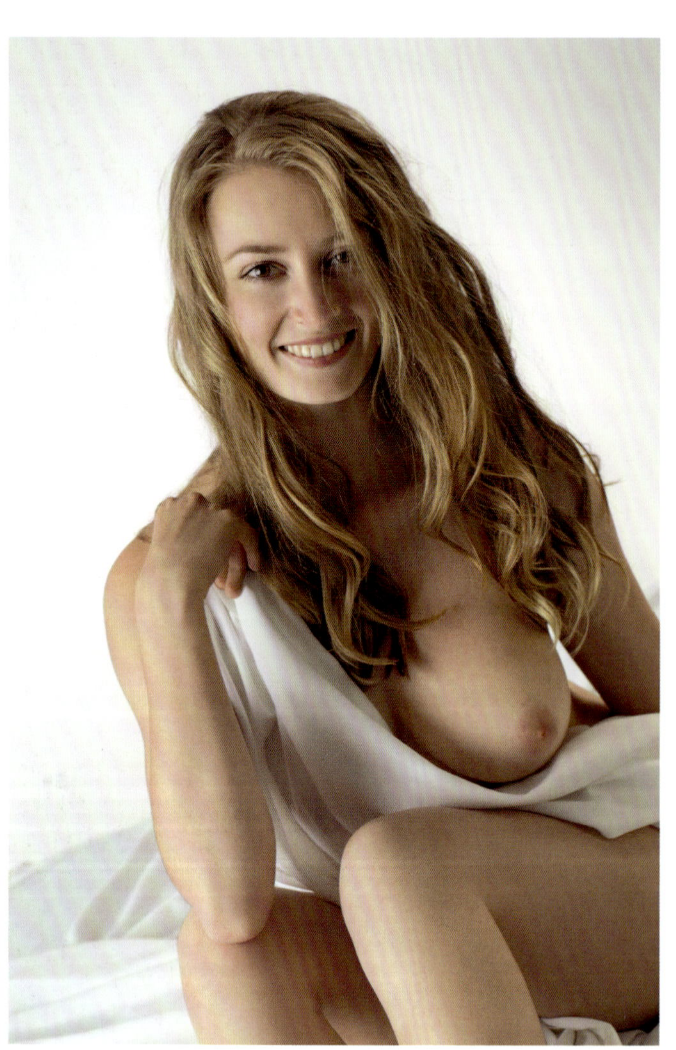